Employment Law Solutions

Malcolm MacKillop
Hendrik Nieuwland
Meighan Ferris-Miles

LexisNexis

Employment Law Solutions
© LexisNexis Canada Inc. 2010
August 2010

All rights reserved. No part of this publication may be reproduced, stored in any material form (including photocopying or storing it in any medium by electronic means and whether or not transiently or incidentally to some other use of this publication) without the written permission of the copyright holder except in accordance with the provisions of the Copyright Act. Applications for the copyright holder's written permission to reproduce any part of this publication should be addressed to the publisher.

Warning: The doing of an unauthorized act in relation to a copyrighted work may result in both a civil claim for damages and criminal prosecution.

Members of the LexisNexis Group worldwide

Canada	LexisNexis Canada Inc, 123 Commerce Valley Dr. E. Suite 700, MARKHAM, Ontario
Australia	Butterworths, a Division of Reed International Books Australia Pty Ltd, CHATSWOOD, New South Wales
Austria	ARD Betriebsdienst and Verlag Orac, VIENNA
Czech Republic	Orac, sro, PRAGUE
France	Éditions du Juris-Classeur SA, PARIS
Hong Kong	Butterworths Asia (Hong Kong), HONG KONG
Hungary	Hvg Orac, BUDAPEST
India	Butterworths India, NEW DELHI
Ireland	Butterworths (Ireland) Ltd, DUBLIN
Italy	Giuffré, MILAN
Malaysia	Malayan Law Journal Sdn Bhd, KUALA LUMPUR
New Zealand	Butterworths of New Zealand, WELLINGTON
Poland	Wydawnictwa Prawnicze PWN, WARSAW
Singapore	Butterworths Asia, SINGAPORE
South Africa	Butterworth Publishers (Pty) Ltd, DURBAN
Switzerland	Stämpfli Verlag AG, BERNE
United Kingdom	Butterworths Tolley, a Division of Reed Elsevier (UK), LONDON, WC2A
USA	LexisNexis, DAYTON, Ohio

Library and Archives Canada Cataloguing in Publication

MacKillop, Malcolm
    Employment law solutions / Malcolm MacKillop, Hendrik Nieuwland and Meighan Ferris-Miles

Includes index.
ISBN 978-0-433-46538-6

    1. Labor laws and legislation—Canada. I. Nieuwland, Hendrik II. Ferris-Miles, Meighan III. Title.

KE3247.E47 2010   344.7101   C2010-903733-2
KF3457.E47 2010

Printed and bound in Canada

To my adorable wife, Judy, who always lends her support to these projects and to my son, Evan, who continuously reminds me of the simplicity of being young.

Malcolm MacKillop

For my wife, Olivia.

Hendrik Nieuwland

To my husband, Jonathan, for encouraging me to take time to "just be".

Meighan Ferris-Miles

Foreword

While the Canadian employment law field has given birth to numerous texts, there are few that cover the landscape and provide practical tips to employers and employees alike in the fashion achieved by *Employment Law Solutions*.

Malcolm MacKillop, Hendrik Nieuwland and Meighan Ferris-Miles are to be congratulated for the considerable time and effort they have dedicated to the preparation of this outstanding book. The Shields O'Donnell MacKillop LLP law firm prepares a newsletter entitled "Snapshot". It contains timely and practical advice on leading-edge issues. This book contains many of those articles and will provide a lasting reference source for the reader.

In the spring of 1989, three significant events occurred in my life. In April, my son, Rob, was born; in June, my beloved Blue Jays played their first game in SkyDome; and in May, I first met and began practising law with Malcolm J. MacKillop at the Borden & Elliot law firm.

As soon as I met him, I was struck with his intellect, drive, ambition, creativity and love of employment law. Over the next two decades, I had the privilege of watching him grow into one of Canada's leading employment law lawyers, duly certified by the Law Society of Upper Canada as a Specialist in Civil Litigation and regularly referred to as one of Canada's Top 500 Lawyers and amongst the Best Lawyers in Canada. I have been proud to work with him and consider him my dear friend over these many, many years. He is truly an exceptional individual! In addition to litigating extensively, Malcolm has taught law, written, spoken and made numerous media appearances. However, most importantly, he has dedicated himself to mentoring a number of younger employment lawyers. *Employment Law Solutions* exemplifies his dedication to two of his protégés, Hendrik Nieuwland and Meighan Ferris-Miles.

I first met Hendrik when he clerked at our Court in 2006-2007 before joining Shields O'Donnell MacKillop LLP in 2007. His work at the Court was outstanding! It was clear from the outset that an exceptional career lay ahead for him. To have participated in the publication of a book such as this at this early stage in his professional development is a significant accomplishment. The high quality of its contents reflect favourably upon the authors.

Meighan Ferris-Miles joined Shields O'Donnell MacKillop LLP shortly after Mr. Nieuwland in 2008 and has dedicated herself to employment law. She is a highly-regarded member of the Ontario Bar at this very early stage in her career. Her efforts in bringing about the publication of this well-organized and well-written book are exceptional and are to be commended. Clearly Meighan has a bright career path ahead of her.

Employment Law Solutions is the product of the efforts of three very talented Canadian employment law lawyers. This book contains a thorough examination of the law and practical analysis of an extremely high quality. I am convinced that readers will find this book instructive and useful.

It is my privilege to congratulate the authors and to acknowledge a debt of gratitude for their efforts.

The Honourable Mr. Justice Randall Scott Echlin
Superior Court of Justice (Ontario)

Toronto, Ontario
May 2010

About the Authors

Malcolm MacKillop has practised exclusively employment law for more than 25 years. He now practises at Shields O'Donnell MacKillop LLP, an employment and labour law boutique. Malcolm represents employers and senior executives in all aspects of employment law, including issues involving just cause, fiduciary obligations and human rights.

Over the last 25 years, Malcolm has been a successful trial lawyer, professional speaker, professor of law, an author of several highly-acclaimed legal texts and a columnist for the *Globe and Mail* and *The Toronto Star*. He has appeared on both local and national television and radio, including The Fifth Estate, W5, CBC – The National, CBC – The Journal, Pamela Wallin Live, CBC Radio and 680 News, among others. Malcolm is a past board member of The National Ballet of Canada, the Toronto Human Resources Professionals Association and the National Club.

Malcolm is certified by the Law Society of Upper Canada as a specialist in Civil Litigation and he has been recognized by both *The Lexpert®/American Lawyer Guide to the Leading 500 Lawyers in Canada* and *The Best Lawyers in Canada* as a leading employment law practitioner.

Hendrik Nieuwland represents employers in all areas of employment and labour law, including wrongful dismissal litigation, employee discipline and termination, employment standards complaints, human rights complaints, labour arbitration, fiduciary litigation, and drafting employment policies and contracts. He has acted or assisted in matters before labour arbitrators, the Ontario Labour Relations Board, the Ontario Human Rights Commission and Tribunal, the Ontario Superior Court of Justice and the Ontario Court of Appeal.

Hendrik received his LL.B. from Queen's University and was called to the Ontario Bar in 2006. He clerked with the judges of the Divisional Court of the Superior Court of Justice

(Ontario) in 2006-2007 and joined Shields O'Donnell MacKillop LLP in 2007.

Hendrik is a member of the Law Society of Upper Canada, the Canadian Bar Association, the Ontario Bar Association, the Toronto Lawyers Association and The Advocates' Society.

Meighan Ferris-Miles represents employers in all areas of labour and employment law, including wrongful dismissal litigation, human rights complaints, employee discipline and termination, labour arbitration, fiduciary litigation, employment standards, and drafting employment policies and contracts.

Meighan has conducted workplace investigations. She has acted and assisted in matters before the Ontario Superior Court of Justice, labour arbitrators, the Ontario Labour Relations Board and the Human Rights Tribunal of Ontario. She has also appeared before the Workplace Safety and Insurance Appeals Tribunal and has conducted hearings before the Workplace Safety and Insurance Board.

Meighan joined Shields O'Donnell MacKillop LLP in 2008 after articling with a national law firm and practising for two years at a boutique litigation firm.

Meighan received her LL.B. from the University of Windsor, earning an award for the highest mark in Labour Arbitration. She holds a Bachelor of Science in Kinesiology from Dalhousie University.

Preface

After 26 years of practising employment law, I find myself practising law with some of the best lawyers in the business. Dan Shields and Julie O'Donnell both have decades of experience in providing their corporate clients with practical and effective labour and employment law advice. Creating the firm Shields O'Donnell MacKillop LLP was an opportunity of a lifetime for me, one that I could not pass on.

I have long come to realize that without the support from a strong and talented team of associates I could not service my clients effectively. Meighan Ferris-Miles and Hendrik Nieuwland, my co-authors, are extremely talented young lawyers with bright futures. They work hard, they are dependable and they care about our clients. It just does not get better than that for a senior lawyer.

I also want to express my gratitude to Heather Wood-London and Alison Adam, who also work long hours and are dedicated to their respective practices. They also have our gratitude for their assistance and contribution to this book.

As most of you who read this book should know, my day-to-day practice is managed and organized by my very dedicated law clerk, Adela Zawadzki, to whom I also wish to express my sincere gratitude because without her hard work things would likely come to a grinding halt.

Your family, your friends, your clients all help to weave the fabric of your professional life. I have been fortunate over the last 26 years to have worked with so many talented and wonderful people.

Many of my clients are close friends and their loyalty and support over many years is the reason that I have enjoyed such a vibrant and rewarding professional life. To all of you, a sincere and heartfelt thank you.

Good mentors are hard to find. In the legal profession, a mentor can make or break your professional career. As for me, I was very fortunate in finding an experienced and caring mentor in Randy Echlin. Now Mr. Justice Echlin, Randy has successfully mentored several people, but in many respects, Randy has been more than a mentor to me. He has been a close friend, a confidant and in many ways like an older brother, in addition to all the professional endeavours that we took on together. In many ways, my life would have been very different without Randy. It is difficult to be very specific on such a hypothtetical musing but I appreciate and deeply value the significant and ongoing contributions and support that he has provided to me during the last 20 years or more.

This book is dedicated to my good friend "Randy", now Mr. Justice Echlin, as only a token of my sincere appreciation for his lifelong friendship and professional mentorship.

If you have any questions about how the decisions discussed in this book may affect your workplace or how to prepare appropriate contracts for dependent contractors, a Shields O'Donnell MacKillop lawyer will be pleased to assist you.

Last, but by no means least, I also want to recognize the love and support from my wife, Judy Cotte, LL.M., a successful and well-recognized securities lawyer in her own right, and to my very special and adorable stepson, Evan, who reminds me daily of what really matters in this world.

Malcolm MacKillop
Toronto, Ontario
June 2010

Testimonials

"A real, practical guide to workplace issues that I can have at my fingertips."

Donald Webster
Senior Corporate Counsel
Mercer HR Consulting Limited

"Nice to know that some lawyers still find practical solutions to some challenging human resources issues."

Mark Cooper
General Counsel
Marsh Canada Limited

"*Employment Law Solutions* is a valuable resource tool when you are facing a complicated employment law issue. The book covers numerous topics from hiring issues to dealing with the difficult topic of disability. The authors have done a great job of providing practical advice to the reader."

Karen Trenton
Managing Director, Human Resources
Sherritt International Corporation

"*Employment Law Solutions* has succeeded in providing the reader with easy-to-read and practical advice on how to approach difficult workplace issues. I highly recommend the text to any human resources professional."

Roxanne Rose
Director, Human Resources
Linamar Corporation

"Well researched and practical with great sensitivity to unique solutions, Malcolm and his team are our 'go to' reference for employment law."

Nickey Alexiou
Vice President, Human Resources
Heart & Stroke Foundation of Ontario

"The authors have done a great job in simplifying the correct approach to difficult employment law issues in their most recent text. I highly recommend the book to anyone working in human resources."

Shelly Rae
VP, Human Resources
The Dominion of Canada General Insurance Company

TABLE OF CONTENTS

Dedication iii
Foreword v
About the Authors vii
Preface ix
Testimonials xii

PART ONE
BEGINNING THE EMPLOYMENT RELATIONSHIP

1. Ten Questions to Ask Yourself When Hiring 3
1. How Much do I Need to Know About the Applicant Before I Make an Offer? 4
2. How Long do I Need to Properly Assess this Candidate's Skills? 4
3. What Promises Have I Made? 4
4. What Kind of Changes Can I Expect? 5
5. What Do I Consider to be Unforgivable? 5
6. How Much am I Willing to Pay to End the Relationship? .. 6
7. Do I Have Any Secrets That Must be Kept? 6
8. Do I Have Any Client Relationships That Need to be Protected? 6
9. Have I Communicated My Performance Expectations? 7
10. Have I Put This All in Writing? 7

2. "Let me be clear!" — The Failure of Non-Competition and Non-Solicitation Agreements in an Age of the Overly-cautious Employer 9

3. Restrictive Covenants: Protecting Your Company 11
1. Get it in Writing 12
2. Ensure the Employee Gets Something in Return 12
3. Make it Reasonable 13
4. Control and Clearly Define the Scope 13
5. Independent Legal Advice 13

4. Restrictive Covenants Difficult to Enforce 15
   What to Take Away 17

5. Broader is not Better: Court of Appeal Restricts Use
   of Non-Competition Clauses to Protect "Trade
   Connections" with Clients...19

6. Substance Over Form: Establishing Independent
   Contractor Status is Easier Said Than Done................23

7. Tips for Creating a Proper Independent Contractor
   Relationship...29
   1. The Fourfold Test 30
   2. The Control Test 30
   3. The Permanency Test..30
   4. The Organization Test 31

8. Employees v. Dependent Contractors v. Independent
   Contractors..33
   1. The Facts..33
   2. Dependent Contractors 34
   3. Findings 35
   4. What Employers Should Know 36

9. The Employee Signed The Contract, BUT... Are
   You Sure It's Binding? 37

10. The Case of the Enforceable Termination Clause –
    Clarke v. Insight Components (Canada) Inc..................41

Part Two
The Employment Relationship

11. Why Your Plant Needs a Performance
    Management Program..47
    1. Irregular or Tardy Reviews...49
    2. Leaving No Room for the Exercise of Discretion 49
    3. Dishonest or Misleading Reviews 49
    4. Insufficient Guidance or Instruction 50
    5. Reviewing Performance and Salary Simultaneously..........50
    6. Poor or Non-Existent Documentation.......................50
    7. No Employee Acknowledgement 50

12. The Dos and Don'ts of Performance Management 53

13. Why Workplace Harassment Investigations Fail 57
1. The Investigators 58
2. Lawyers 58
3. Not Protecting the Participants 59
4. The Scope of the Investigation 59
5. Zero Tolerance 60
6. Lack of Flexibility 60
7. Remedial Action 60

14. Experience Counts When Conducting a Workplace Investigation 63

15. Investigating Harassment in the Workplace Must be Prompt 67
1. Conducting a Proper Investigation 68
2. Prepare the Complainant for Possible Future Litigation ... 69

16. When Your Boss is a Bully 71
1. Communicate With Your Manager 72
2. Document the Behaviour 72
3. File an Internal Complaint 72
4. File an External Complaint 72
5. Commence a Civil Action 73
6. Consider Resigning 73

17. How to Cope with the Hostile Employee 75
1. Look Beyond Technical Skills 76
2. Conduct More Than One Interview Before Hiring 76
3. Conduct Proper Reference Checks 76
4. Implement a Probation Term 77
5. Document Performance or Attitude Problems as They Occur 77
6. Conduct All Meetings with Hostile Employees with a Company Witness Present 77
7. Consider Whether There are any Extenuating Circumstances Causing the Employee's Behaviour 78
8. Terminate Early if Circumstances Warrant Dismissal 78

18. Workplace Disputes Fuel Retention Problems 79
1. Workplace Harassment 80
2. Failure to Comply with Statutory Obligations 80

3. Poor Hiring Practices 81
4. Harsh Treatment at the Time of Departure 82
5. The Duty to Accommodate 82
6. Constructive Dismissal 83
7. Create Workplace Policies 83

19. Employees in Crisis: How to Deal with a Suicidal or Unstable Employee 85
1. Take It Seriously 86
2. Remove the Individual from the Workplace 86
3. Secure the Workplace 87
4. Provide Assistance 87

20. Business, Pleasure or Both? Company Retreats and Compensation Issues 89

21. Overtime Issues in Your Workplace: How to Prevent Unforeseen Claims for Overtime Pay 93

22. Requests for Medical Information Must Respect Privacy 97

23. Identifying and Managing Disability Fraud 101
1. Seek Legal Advice 102
2. Conduct a Proper Investigation 102
3. Review Company Policies 102
4. Keep Communicating 103
5. Use Surveillance Very Cautiously 103

24. Video Surveillance and Biometrics in the Workplace: Balancing Security with Privacy and Religious Interests 105
1. Provide Employees with Notice 107
2. Prove There is a Legitimate Objective 107
3. Restrict the Scope of Surveillance 107
4. Limit the Use of Surveillance Records 107
5. Limit Retention and Access 108
6. Accommodate Religious Beliefs 108

25. Court Weighs Periodic Criminal Record Checks 109

PART THREE
ENDING THE EMPLOYMENT RELATIONSHIP

26. A New Meaning for "Just Cause" 113

27. When is Off-Duty Criminal Conduct Cause for Termination? 117

28. Disloyalty Can Result in Dismissal 121
   1. Employee Tips 122
   2. Employer Tips 123

29. When is a Workplace Romance Cause for Termination of Employment? 125

30. Rodrigues v. Powell (2007): An Examination of After-Acquired Cause 129
   How to Approach After-Acquired Cause 132

31. Update on Constructive Dismissal 135

32. Why Constructive Dismissal Claims Fail 139

33. Termination in Disguise: Legal Layoffs Require Both a Contractual Right and a Genuine Intention to Recall 145

34. Changing Employment Contracts 149

35. Video Surveillance of an Employee Can Constitute Constructive Dismissal 153

36. Long-Term Disability Benefits Must Continue After Dismissal 157

37. Turf Wars – Tips for the Departing Employee 163
   1. Review Your Employment Contract 164
   2. Provide Your Employer with Notice of Resignation 164
   3. Are You a Fiduciary? 164
   4. Disclose Your Prior Obligations to Your New Employer 165

5. Never Remove Customer Information 165
6. Protect Customer Interests 166
7. Plan Your Departure Carefully 166

38. Obligations of Departing Employees 167

39. Interlocutory Relief: A Modified Approach 171

40. Employers Beware: Ontario Passes Controversial Amendments to the Ontario Human Rights Code 175
1. The Human Rights Code Undergoes Major Renovations 175
2. Individuals Can and Must Apply Directly to the Tribunal 176
3. Applications May be Made Up to One Year Following the Incident 176
4. Tribunal Practices and Procedures 176
5. Whether Tribunal Can Award Damages for Mental Anguish 177
6. Civil Courts and Human Rights Complaints 178
7. Decisions of the Tribunal 178
8. Prevention is the Key 179

41. Undue Hardship and the Employer's Duty to Accommodate 181

42. ADGA Group Consultants Inc. v. Lane – What to do When an Employee Hides a Disability? 185

43. Dismissed Employees May Need to Relocate to Mitigate Their Damages 189

44. When Does an Employee Have NO Duty to Mitigate? The Case of Wronko v. Western Inventory Service Ltd. 191

45. The Wait is Over — The Supreme Court of Canada Closes the Floodgate to Punitive Damages Claims 193

46. How to Avoid Wallace Damages 199

47. Ontario Court of Appeal Makes it More Difficult for Employees to Win Wallace Damages 203

PART FOUR
PRACTICAL TIPS

48. How to Bullet Proof Your Job 207
1. Document Your Side of the Story 208
2. Avoid Insubordination 209
3. Don't Poison the Workplace 209
4. Hire a Ghostwriter 209
5. Know When to Make a Deal 209

49. What to do When You Get Fired 211
1. No Job Security 211
2. There is a Difference 212
3. Onus of Proof 212
4. Grounds for Dismissal 212
5. Mitigation 213
6. Get Advice 213

50. Considerations During the Holiday Season 215
1. Dismissals 215
2. Lateness/Absenteeism 216
3. Alcohol Consumption 216
4. Harassment 217
5. Conflict of Interest 217

51. How to Deal with a Workplace Disability 219

52. Top Bloopers to Avoid if You Are an Employer 223
1. Don't Forget to Use a Contract 223
2. Forgetting to Sign the Employment Contract Before the Employee Starts Work 224
3. Calling a Termination a Layoff 224
4. Unilateral Changes to the Employee's Pay or Work Duties 225
5. Don't Forget to Pay Overtime Pay 225
6. Terminating a Disabled Employee 226
7. Age Doesn't Mean Anything 226

53. The Ten Most Common Errors in Human Resources Policy Manuals 229

1. Not Including an Introduction..230
2. No Accommodation/Substance Abuse Policy 230
3. Incorrect or Vague Definition of Workplace Harassment..230
4. Overtime 231
5. Zero Tolerance Policies 231
6. Falling Behind the Legislation......................................231
7. Failing to Keep Employees Apprised of Changes...........231
8. Failing to Make it Binding..232
9. Not Sticking to It..232
10. Not Having One At All...232

54. When is a Workplace Human Rights Investigation Necessary? Practical Tips for Managers and Human Resources Professionals..235

55. A Practical Guide for Employers Defending a Wrongful Dismissal Action 239
1. Review the Claim Carefully 240
2. Choose the Right Lawyer 240
3. Pick a "Point Person"...240
4. Ask for a Legal Opinion 241
5. Co-operate with Your Counsel 241
6. Never Allege Cause if None Exists 241
7. Investigate for Other Improper Conduct.......................241
8. Avoid Defamatory Statements......................................241
9. Reference Letters 242
10. Offer to Settle...242
11. Mediation 242
12. Document Disclosure and Retention 242

56. E-Discovery in Ontario: What are Employers' Obligations?..245

57. What Employers Need to Know about Summary Judgment 249

58. Family Day: What Employers Need to Know 251
1. Background..251
2. Step 1: Understanding the Employment Standards Act Entitlement..252

3. Step 2: Evaluate your Employment Contracts or Holiday Policies in Comparison to the Employment Standards Act Standard 253
4. Conclusion 253

59. H1N1 in the Workplace 255

60. Tips for Managing Your Workplace in Times of Economic Crisis 259
1. How to Structure Severance Packages 259
2. Forget About the Non-Compete Clause 260
3. Payment Without a Release 260
4. Avoid Constructive Dismissal Claims 260
5. Deal with Disability Cases 261

61. New Rules Change Employment Litigation Landscape 263
1. Increased Cap for Small Claims Court Actions 264
2. Increased Cap and Discovery for Simplified Procedure Actions 264
3. Evidence on Summary Judgment Motions 265
4. Other Changes to Civil Actions Over $100,000 266

62. Violence and Harassment in the Workplace 267
1. What are Workplace Harassment and Workplace Violence? 268
2. What are the New Requirements for Employers? 268
   (a) Risk Assessment 269
   (b) Written Policies and Implementation Programs 269
   (c) Extension of Existing OH&S Obligations to Workplace Violence 270
   (d) Domestic Violence in the Workplace 270
   (e) Disclose Risks of Violence to Employees 271
3. What Should Employers do to Comply With the New Requirements? 271

63. Amendments to the Occupational Health and Safety Act Have an Impact on Directors and Officers of a Corporation 273

Index 277

PART ONE

Beginning the Employment Relationship

1

TEN QUESTIONS TO ASK YOURSELF WHEN HIRING

1. How Much do I Need to Know About the Applicant Before I Make an Offer?
2. How Long do I Need to Properly Assess This Candidate's Skills?
3. What Promises Have I Made?
4. What Kind of Changes Can I Expect?
5. What do I Consider to be Unforgivable?
6. How Much am I Willing to Pay to End the Relationship?
7. Do I Have Any Secrets That Must be Kept?
8. Do I Have Any Client Relationships That Need to be Protected?
9. Have I Communicated My Performance Expecttations?
10. Have I Put This All in Writing?

The beginning of an employment relationship is often a time of great optimism. It is very easy to focus on the positives (a new beginning, a fresh perspective, company growth) and to lose sight of an important aspect of hiring: risk management. To help you avoid pitfalls in the hiring process, ask yourself the following questions:

1. HOW MUCH DO I NEED TO KNOW ABOUT THE APPLICANT BEFORE I MAKE AN OFFER?

You should carefully review your company's job application forms and postings to ensure that they do not violate your province's human rights legislation. Do not request information on a protected ground (*e.g.*, age, disability) until after a conditional offer of employment has been extended and only then when you have a *bona fide* occupational requirement (a "BFOR"). If you have any doubt about what constitutes a BFOR, speak to your lawyer.

If the position for which you are hiring requires a successful applicant to have achieved a certain level of education or training, consider calling the school to ensure the applicant has actually achieved the necessary degree. Falsifying or exaggerating on résumés is an all too common practice, especially in a competitive job market.

2. HOW LONG DO I NEED TO PROPERLY ASSESS THIS CANDIDATE'S SKILLS?

Most provincial employment standards legislation, including the Ontario *Employment Standards Act, 2000*, S.O. 2000, c. 41, provide for a probationary period during which an employer can terminate an employee without providing any notice of termination or pay in lieu thereof. Review your province's legislation and consider implementing a probationary period in new employment relationships. You must specifically tell the candidate that he or she will be subject to a probationary period. It is also advisable to set out the criteria by which the candidate will be assessed. If you need longer than is provided in the applicable legislation, you can still let the candidate know that he or she will be assessed for suitability during that longer period, but you will be obligated to pay at least the statutory minimum if you intend to terminate the relationship.

3. WHAT PROMISES HAVE I MADE?

In an attempt to convince an attractive candidate to accept employment, company representatives may occasionally exaggerate the perks and opportunities associated with the position in question. This is a very risky tactic and has resulted in disappointed employees bringing successful claims against their former employers.

To avoid this unfortunate development, anyone who meets with applicants should be briefed on proper interview techniques. Ensure that the position is accurately described in any postings or offer letters and that you have been clear about the compensation associated with the job. Your recruiters must be told not to make any representations regarding length of employment or the possibility of promotion.

4. WHAT KIND OF CHANGES CAN I EXPECT?

This question is related to the issue of pre-employment representations. Before extending an offer of employment, consider where the company is going to be in one, three or even five years. If you foresee significant changes on the horizon – particularly those that might have an impact on reporting lines or staffing needs – consider warning the candidate that such changes are pending. Any offer of employment should specifically reserve the right to make certain changes to an employee's position. This clause may not be sufficient to forestall a claim of constructive dismissal but it could go a long way toward managing your new employee's expectations regarding his or her position.

5. WHAT DO I CONSIDER TO BE UNFORGIVABLE?

Every employer has a (perhaps unspoken) list of behaviours or actions that will result in a just cause termination. When hiring new employees, state specifically that you have the right to terminate the relationship without notice for cause. We recommend that you provide examples of actions that will constitute just cause, especially if you have concerns that are more specific than the traditional common law definition of "just cause", *e.g.*, dishonesty. Be sure to reserve some discretion to discipline rather than terminate. You should also indicate that the list is not exhaustive: never underestimate the ability of your employees to surprise you.

6. HOW MUCH AM I WILLING TO PAY TO END THE RELATIONSHIP?

The best time to define an employee's rights upon termination is at the beginning of the employment relationship. If you intend to pay out only the statutory minimum upon termination of employment, you must make that clear at the beginning of the relationship. Unless you specifically adopt the provisions of the provincial employment standards legislation, you will be deemed to have agreed to provide your employee with common law reasonable notice of termination, which can run between two and four weeks per year of service for non-executive employees. High-ranking executives often receive much more, even with very short service.

7. DO I HAVE ANY SECRETS THAT MUST BE KEPT?

If your new employee will be exposed to any trade secrets, inventions or confidential information, it is advisable to get a written guarantee that the employee will not disclose such information during or after employment. Although all employees have an implied obligation to refrain from disclosing confidential information belonging to their employer, disputes often arise about which information can actually be considered confidential. To avoid any confusion, we recommend that you describe the confidential information that you wish to protect and explicitly state that the employee is forbidden from disclosing it to anyone without written permission to do so.

8. DO I HAVE ANY CLIENT RELATIONSHIPS THAT NEED TO BE PROTECTED?

If you are hiring someone who will be responsible for managing client relationships on your behalf or you are recruiting new clients for your company, you may want to consider protecting those relationships by entering into a non-solicitation agreement with your new employee. Such an agreement would restrict the employee from pursuing your company's clients following the termination of his or her employment. There are certain requirements that must be met for a non-solicitation agreement to be enforceable and we strongly advise you to speak to an employment lawyer before entering into such an agreement.

9. HAVE I COMMUNICATED MY PERFORMANCE EXPECTATIONS?

As discussed above, when recruiting new employees it is tempting to emphasize the attractive aspects of a position and downplay the obligations. While it is important to communicate the benefits of working with your company, you should also ensure that you have given the candidate a true picture of your expectations for the position. If long hours and extensive travel are required, say so. If it is important to you that the successful candidate be comfortable networking and demonstrate enthusiasm for meeting new clients, communicate that as well. If the employee feels that the new position is more than he or she bargained for, frustration will quickly set in on both sides.

10. HAVE I PUT THIS ALL IN WRITING?

Although it is not uncommon for employers to hire new employees without a written contract, we do not recommend this practice. This is particularly true where the employee will have access to confidential information, trade secrets or important clients. Providing new hires with a written contract of employment, along with copies of any relevant human resources policies, is the best way to protect your interests and prevent costly misunderstandings. Both the contract and the policies should be provided to the new employee before his or her first day of work. If the employee is simply given an employment agreement when he or she reports for work, a court may later find that the employee did not have an opportunity to read and understand the agreement or that the terms of employment had already been settled. If you intend to provide the employee with a letter of hire prior to having the employment contract signed, make sure that the letter specifically references the contract and states that the employee must sign it before starting work. This is particularly true if the employment agreement contains non-solicitation or confidentiality clauses.

One of the most effective ways to minimize risk in an employment relationship is to have a process for dealing with new hires. Reviewing a checklist can be an important step in creating the process that is right for your company.

2

"Let me be clear!" - The Failure of Non-Competition and Non-Solicitation Agreements in an Age of the Overly-cautious Employer

In business warfare, an employer can suffer no greater setback than the defection of an employee to a competitor. In fact, such an employee can deliver a lethal blow to his or her former company when he or she takes business opportunities, clients and confidential information, and hands them over to "the enemy" for whom he or she is now working. Thus, non-competition and non-solicitation agreements have become a vital weapon in an employer's battle against disloyal servants.

Employers can, however, be overly-cautious when protecting their business: non-competition and non-solicitation agreements that cast too wide a net in the protection of commercial interests can be rendered inoperable. Indeed, the Ontario Court of Appeal's decision in *IT/NET Inc. v. Cameron*, [2006] O.J. No. 156 suggests that employers must clearly and narrowly define the interests they are seeking to protect when restricting the activities of employees who pursue other job opportunities. To do otherwise can be detrimental to the contract.

IT/NET Inc. was a placement services company that often contracted with the federal government. In response to a request for proposal of a government department, IT/NET Inc. would search for an individual who matched the qualifications sought and, with that individual's permission, submit a response, including the individual's résumé. The company would then enter into a contract with the client department and a parallel contract of service with the individual. IT/NET Inc. entered into such agreements with the Department of National Defence (DND) and Len Cameron. Cameron's contract included a non-solicitation clause, a non-competition clause and a confidentiality clause.

After his contract expired, Cameron contacted a competitor of IT/NET Inc., and sent the competitor a copy of his résumé. This résumé was, in turn, submitted to the DND when the Department reposted a vacancy for the position that Cameron previously held. The competitor was successful in its bid. Cameron returned to his previous position and IT/NET Inc. was left without a contract with the DND. IT/NET Inc. brought an action for breach of contract and was successful at trial. (See *IT/Net Inc. v. Cameron*, [2003] O.J. No. 4202 (Ont. S.C.J.)).

That decision was overturned. In its judgment, the Court of Appeal found that the restrictive clauses in Cameron's contract with IT/NET Inc. went "considerably beyond" what was needed to protect IT/NET Inc.'s commercial interest with the DND. Specifically, the non-solicitation clause prevented Cameron from soliciting business from "any" of the respondent's "clients or prospects", and not just from the client where Cameron had been placed. The clause also had no time limit, and parts of it were unclear. On the issue of clarity, it was difficult to determine whether "clients or prospects" referred to the present, the past or those who may become prospects over the life of the contract. The Court also found that Cameron had not breached IT/NET Inc.'s confidentiality or a duty of good faith toward his former employer.

This decision stands as a warning to employers. When committing employees to non-solicitation as well as non-competition agreements, do so carefully. Precisely define what commercial interests the agreements protect and confine that definition to the current business. Impose a reasonable time period during which the agreements will remain in force, taking into consideration the propensity of the courts to balance the needs of businesses and their former employees. Employers who follows these guidelines may bolster their tactical resources, and leave the agreements, and their business, less vulnerable to attack.

3

RESTRICTIVE COVENANTS: PROTECTING YOUR COMPANY

1. Get it in Writing
2. Ensure the Employee Gets Something in Return
3. Make it Reasonable
4. Control and Clearly Define the Scope
5. Independent Legal Advice

When hiring a new employee, it is always prudent to plan for the end of the employment relationship. This is especially important where the employee in question is an executive or will have a key role in your company. Not only can these terminations or resignations be expensive and litigious, they also create the potential for valuable information and know-how to leave the workplace and walk across the street to a competitor. There are several ways for companies to minimize the harm caused by the loss of a key employee, including restrictive covenants. However, in order to make restrictive covenants effective, they should be carefully planned and implemented.

A restrictive covenant is loosely defined as any agreement wherein an individual or company promises to refrain from engaging in certain behaviour(s). In the employment context, they generally take the form of confidentiality provisions, non-solicitation agreements and non-competition agreements. Nearly all companies should prohibit departing employees from using or disclosing confidential information gained in the course of their employment. This prohibition should be in writing and should explicitly define what information will be considered confidential and proprietary. Confidentiality clauses are often the easiest to enforce through litigation, as employees already have a common law duty to refrain from taking and using confidential information that belongs to their former employers.

Non-solicitation and non-competition clauses should be used more sparingly. Courts are generally unwilling to prevent individuals from working in their chosen field or profession as it is considered a restraint of trade. Employers who wish to restrict their former employees' activities in the marketplace should give close attention to the following considerations.

1. GET IT IN WRITING

Without a written non-solicitation/non-competition agreement, it will be much more difficult to restrain the former employee. In order to convince the court to restrict the former employee's activities, you will have to show that his or her role in the company was so essential that the employee owed and continues to owe your company a fiduciary duty and, therefore, is obliged to put its interests before his or her own.

2. ENSURE THE EMPLOYEE GETS SOMETHING IN RETURN

A non-solicitation/non-competition agreement is like any other contract as there must be value flowing both ways for a court to enforce it. This is particularly true in agreements between employers and employees where there is a recognized imbalance of power. Where an employee enters into a restrictive covenant during the course of employment but does not receive anything of value in return, the covenant will likely be found to be unenforceable. Accordingly, it is advisable to have the employee execute the restrictive agreement as a term and condition of entering into employment with your company. Where the employment relationship is already in progress, common forms of consideration include lump sum payments, promotions or stock options.

3. MAKE IT REASONABLE

The reasonableness of a non-solicitation or non-competition clause will be assessed in light of two primary factors — time and geography. The restriction should only cover the period of time and the geographic scope truly necessary to protect the employer's interests. Anything broader will be rejected by the court. For example, a five-year prohibition against competing with the former employer anywhere in North America is far too broad. However, a six-month prohibition against competing against the former employer within a 50-kilometre radius of the employee's home office will be more likely to meet the standard of reasonableness.

4. CONTROL AND CLEARLY DEFINE THE SCOPE

As noted above, reasonableness is a primary concern for courts being asked to rule on the enforceability of a non-competition or non-solicitation agreement. Before drafting a restrictive covenant for a particular employee or class of employee, sit down and think about the business interests that you truly need to protect. Limit the scope of the protection to the business in which the employee was directly involved. The restriction should be individually tailored to avoid an overly broad clause that will be unenforceable. Once you clearly understand the threat posed by a departing employee, you can create a restrictive covenant that affords limited but effective protection. For example, where a sales manager has unfettered access to customer records, a strict confidentiality clause paired with a time-limited client non-solicitation agreement can help shield the employer against a possible exodus of customers. Where the departing employee is a member of the human resources group or is a popular manager, a simple non-solicitation of employees agreement can help prevent the loss of top performers or future stars.

5. INDEPENDENT LEGAL ADVICE

As previously discussed, courts see the relationship between employers and employees as being inherently more favourable to employers. Therefore, any time you ask an employee to enter into an agreement that could affect his or her post-termination rights, be sure to afford the employee the opportunity to seek independent legal advice. The employee should be given at least three business days to consider your proposed agreement and see a lawyer.

Ensuring successful business continuity is a complex exercise that can take many forms, including assessing potential talent, nurturing top performers, recruiting star candidates and protecting your company's confidential information and client relationships. If used properly, restrictive covenants can be a valuable tool in achieving those goals.

4

Restrictive Covenants Difficult to Enforce

Restrictive covenants are often included in employment contracts where an employer has a proprietary interest they wish to protect. One type of restrictive covenant is a non-competition clause, which places geographic or temporal restraints on an employee's ability to work in a competitive business after their employment ends. These covenants can be important to an employer where an employee holds a senior position or possesses sensitive company information.

Courts have made it very clear that restrictive covenants must pass rigorous scrutiny before they will be enforced in an employment context, largely due to the power imbalance that exists between an employer and employee, and the effect restrictive covenants can have on a person's ability to re-employ.

In the recent case of *Shafron v. KRG Ins. Brokers (Western) Inc.*, [2009] S.C.J. No. 6, [2009] 1 S.C.R. 157 ("*Shafron*"), the Supreme Court of Canada confirmed that restrictive covenants must be reasonable, clear and unambiguous in order to be enforced, and that courts will rarely intervene to cure clauses that are not. Instead, as a general rule restrictive covenants that are not reasonable, clear and unambiguous will simply be held unenforceable.

In *Shafron*, the employment contract stated that the plaintiff could not be employed by any insurance broker post-employment for a period of three years within the "Metropolitan City of Vancouver". This geographic restraint was found to be ambiguous since there is no common understanding of what "Metropolitan City of Vancouver" encompasses.

The Court took this opportunity to reaffirm various principles relating to covenants. First and foremost, a covenant must be reasonable and the onus is on the party seeking to enforce the restrictive covenant to show that it is reasonable. Particular attention will be paid to the geographic and temporal scope of the clause, as well as to the activity sought to be prohibited. If any one of these elements are drafted in a manner that is overbroad or otherwise unreasonable, the clause may be found entirely unenforceable.

In order to be reasonable, covenants must be clear and unambiguous. Terms used must be commonly understood by both parties and must not be reasonably capable of more than one meaning. For example, it would likely be unacceptable if a covenant provided that an employee was prohibited from working as a real estate agent for a period of two years in Toronto and the surrounding area, as there is no common definition of what "Toronto and the surrounding area" includes.

The Court confirmed that it will not engage in "blue pencil severance", which involves striking out a portion of a covenant in order to resolve an ambiguity or cure a drafting default, except in rare cases where the portion to be removed is clearly severable, trivial and not part of the main purpose of the restrictive covenant. A court would therefore be unlikely to remove "and the surrounding area" from the previous example so that the employee is prohibited from working in "Toronto". Geography is a main component of the covenant, and altering it would change what the parties bargained.

The Court also confirmed that it is not appropriate to apply "notional severance", also referred to as "reading down", in order to make a clause legal and enforceable. For example, a court will not impose its own view and read down the clause to mean "Toronto, Etobicoke and Scarborough" as opposed to the many other possible variations.

In the *Shafron* case, the Court found the term "Metropolitan City of Vancouver" ambiguous. It determined that blue pencil severance could not cure the covenant because removing the word "Metropolitan" would change a main component of the contract that the parties had bargained. The Court also determined that notional severance, applied by the Court of Appeal in this matter (see *KRG Ins. Brokers (Western) Inc. v. Shafron*, [2008] B.C.J. No. 1968), which read down the covenant to read "the City of Vancouver, the University of British Columbia

Endowment Lands, Richmond, and Burnaby", should not be applied to restrictive covenants. (The Court also determined that this was not an appropriate case for rectification, as it was not clear the parties had ever been of the same mind with respect to the geographical scope of the covenant.) The decision of the trial judge was therefore restored and the covenant was found entirely unenforceable.

WHAT TO TAKE AWAY

Some important points for an employer to remember when drafting restrictive covenants are:

1. Make sure the language is clear and unambiguous. Ensure that both parties specifically agree on what the language means before executing.
2. Make sure the restrictions imposed are reasonable and not overreaching. Define the description of the competitive business the employee is prohibited from joining, the geographic scope and the temporal scope as narrowly as possible.
3. Tailor restrictive covenants to each individual employee based on his or her particular circumstances. There is no "one size fits all".
4. Seek legal advice regarding the enforceability of a restrictive covenant prior to entering any agreement.

5

Broader is not Better: Court of Appeal Restricts Use of Non-Competition Clauses to Protect "Trade Connections" with Clients

Developing and maintaining client loyalty is essential for a business to succeed in today's service-oriented economy. Many businesses rely heavily on their front-line employees to build solid and lasting "trade connections" with clients. But there is a hidden danger to this practice. If an employee quits or is terminated, the employee might try to take clients with him or her to a competitor or start up their own competing business. Employers often try to prevent former employees from recruiting their clients through the placement of "restrictive covenants" in the employment contract.

Restrictive covenants come in two forms. The first, called a "non-solicitation clause", prevents a former employee from actively soliciting a client away from the employer in order to do business with the former employee. The second, called a "non-competition clause", prevents an employee from participating in a business that competes with his or her former employer. This is a broad restriction that often prevents, for example, the former employee from doing business with a former client even if the employee does not actively solicit that client.

If your company uses restrictive covenants to help protect its trade connections, *H.L. Staebler Co. v. Allan*, [2008] O.J. No. 3048, a recent decision released by the Ontario Court of Appeal, indicates that courts will not enforce these covenants if they are drafted too broadly.

In this case, the defendants (who were insurance salespeople) resigned from H.L. Staebler Co. and immediately started working for Stevenson & Hunt Insurance Brokers Ltd., a direct competitor of their former employer. The defendants had developed close personal relationships with H.L. Staebler's clients. They asked these clients to take their business away from H.L. Staebler and follow them to Stevenson & Hunt. One hundred and eighteen clients agreed to move. H.L. Staebler then sued the defendants for damages resulting from the loss of these clients, claiming the defendants had violated the restrictive covenant in their employment contracts, which stated, at para. 18:

> In the event of termination of your employment with the Company, you undertake that you will not for a period of 2 consecutive years following said termination, conduct business with any clients or customers of H.L. Staebler Company Limited that were handled or serviced by you at the date of your termination.

H.L. Staebler was successful at trial. The trial judge found that the restrictive covenant was enforceable and that the defendants had violated the contract by soliciting H.L. Staebler's clients to follow them to their new employer. The trial judge awarded $2 million in damages. The defendants appealed and the Ontario Court of Appeal set aside the trial judge's decision, concluding that the restrictive covenant was unenforceable.

The restrictive covenant placed a blanket prohibition on the defendants from engaging in any kind of "business" (even business unrelated to insurance) with H.L. Staebler clients. The covenant also had no geographical limit, and therefore would restrict the defendants from doing business with H.L. Staebler clients anywhere in Canada. The Court of Appeal held that the restrictive covenant was therefore a "non-competition clause", the use of which is justifiable only in "exceptional circumstances". The Court concluded that the circumstances did not require H.L. Staebler to rely on a non-competition clause to protect its "trade connections" with its clients.

The Court noted that while the defendants had close personal relationships with H.L. Staebler clients, this was the industry norm, and in any case those relationships were not exclusive since clients were also served by other H.L. Staebler employees. The Court also noted that the defendants were "ordinary salespeople" and were not "key" employees (*i.e.*, the defendants had no "special knowledge of or influence over the Staebler business"). Given these circumstances, the Court concluded that the use of a broad non-competition clause was not justified. A "suitably restricted non-solicitation clause" would have been sufficient to protect H.L. Staebler's interests without "unduly compromising" the ability of the defendants to work in their chosen field.

If your company currently uses or plans on using a restrictive covenant in an employment contract, the Court of Appeal's decision in *H.L. Staebler Co. v. Allan* indicates that the following principles should be considered:

1. **Carefully examine the context of the employment relationship.** Whether a court will enforce a restriction placed on an employee in a restrictive covenant will depend on the type of employee and his or her relationship to the company. Broader restrictions may be justified for "key" employees who have exclusive relationships with clients or who have special knowledge or influence over your business, but may not be enforced for "ordinary" employees.

2. **Minimize the scope of the restriction.** Courts are not likely to enforce restrictions that apply for long periods of time (*e.g.*, greater than two years) or cover large geographic areas (*e.g.*, all of Ontario). Assess the risk an employee may pose to your clients if that employee were to leave and carefully craft the restrictions to provide your company with a reasonable opportunity to proactively take steps to retain those clients.

3. **Use a non-solicitation clause rather than a non-competition clause.** Non-competition clauses are enforceable only in "exceptional circumstances". In most cases, you can protect your company's "trade connections" with its clients by restricting a former employee from soliciting those clients for a reasonable period of time. If, however, the circumstances require the use of a non-competition clause, make sure the restriction only limits the employee from engaging in a "business" that directly competes with your company.

6

Substance Over Form: Establishing Independent Contractor Status is Easier Said Than Done

An employer can benefit by having its staff characterized as independent contractors. It provides an employer with greater flexibility in making personnel decisions. When an employer wishes to terminate its relationship with an independent contractor, it need only provide the amount of notice required by the contract between the parties, and if no notice is specified, the employer is not obligated to provide any notice at all. Dismissing an employee places an onerous notice obligation on an employer and, in the case of a long-term employee, satisfying this requirement can be a costly proposition.

For this reason, many employers go to great lengths to craft employment relationships that appear to be independent contracts. However, as many employers have learned, this is not an easy task. The employment relationship is viewed by the courts as inherently characterized by an imbalance of power, in which employees are seen as occupying the weaker ground. Accordingly, uncertainty about the character of an employment contract has generally been resolved in favour of the interests of employees.

The decision of the Ontario Superior Court of Justice in *Braiden v. La-Z-Boy Canada Ltd.*, [2006] O.J. No. 2791 (affirmed [2008] O.J. No. 2314 (Ont. C.A.)), exemplifies just how difficult it can be for an employer to establish an independent contractor relationship. Faced with a relationship that on the surface appeared to be an independent contract, Justice Sills found that La-Z-Boy Canada Ltd. ("La-Z-Boy") had wrongfully dismissed Gordon Braiden. The lesson La-Z-Boy learned was that it is the relationship's substance and not its form that dictates its classification.

Gordon Braiden was associated with La-Z-Boy in some capacity for 23 years. He began working for La-Z-Boy as a customer service manager in 1981, and in 1987 was transferred to the position of commissioned sales agent. It was at this time that La-Z-Boy attempted to change the nature of its relationship with Braiden. Braiden was informed that he was no longer considered an "employee" of La-Z-Boy. As a sales agent, Braiden's earnings were solely through commission and he was responsible for all his own expenses.

The relationship between Braiden and La-Z-Boy continued in this manner until the end of 1995, at which time La-Z-Boy required all of its commissioned sales agents to sign yearly "independent sales and marketing consultants" agreements ("Agreements"). These Agreements did not make substantive changes to Braiden's job description or remuneration. In addition to signing the Agreements, La-Z-Boy required its commissioned sales agents to incorporate. Braiden's incorporated company, Gordon Braiden Sales Inc. ("Braiden Sales"), became the signatory to the Agreement from 1998 onward. In 2003, La-Z-Boy decided to terminate its relationship with Braiden Sales. No severance payment was paid to Braiden or his incorporated company. Braiden and Braiden Sales brought an action for wrongful dismissal against La-Z-Boy.

At trial, Braiden advanced the position that he was an employee of La-Z-Boy on the date of termination and was entitled to reasonable notice of termination. It was the position of La-Z-Boy that Braiden, through the plaintiff corporation, was an independent contractor and entitled only to the 60-day notice period specified in the Agreements.

The Court identified a host of facts that it felt were indicative of an employment relationship:

- Braiden was indisputably an employee from 1981 until 1987.
- Braiden and Braiden Sales had little choice in signing the yearly Agreements.
- The Agreements made no substantive changes to

Braiden's duties or remuneration.
- The terms of the Agreements were imposed by La-Z-Boy without prior discussion.
- La-Z-Boy was permitted to make unilateral alterations to the terms of the Agreements.
- Braiden Sales' compensation was determined and paid by La-Z-Boy.
- Braiden Sales could not sell or promote competing and non-competing products.
- La-Z-Boy alone made decisions with respect to sales and promotional activities.
- Braiden was required to participate in all sales and promotional activities.
- Braiden was required to attend certain trade shows at his own expense.
- Braiden was required to attend meetings as scheduled by La-Z-Boy.
- La-Z-Boy exercised complete control over the designs and prices of the merchandise.
- Braiden Sales was required to maintain business records as mandated by La-Z-Boy.
- Only La-Z-Boy could accept orders solicited from customers by Braiden Sales.
- La-Z-Boy established sales performance goals and quotas.
- La-Z-Boy conducted regular sales reviews and scrutinized the activities of Braiden Sales.

Despite this evidence, the matter was complicated by the fact that on the date of termination there was no direct relationship between La-Z-Boy and Braiden. In fact, the parties had no formal relationship since Braiden Sales became the signatory to the Agreements in 1998. Furthermore, the Agreement, which Braiden acknowledged having understood and accepted, specifically described the relationship as independent.

In rejecting La-Z-Boy's argument, the Court noted that it is well settled that a company's labelling of an employee as an "independent contractor" is not determinative of the character of the relationship. At the same time, this principle – that the characterization of an employment relationship does not depend on the technical structure of the parties – led the Court to conclude that the lack of a formal relationship between Braiden and La-Z-Boy was equally non-determinative of the character of their relationship.

The Court extended the general principle emphasizing substance over form in concluding that the entitlement to notice is unaffected by the fact that the contracting party was an incorporated company. The Court noted that it could have found Braiden Sales to be the relevant employee entitled to reasonable notice but, nonetheless, found Braiden himself to be an employee based on the conduct of the parties toward each other. Integral to Justice Sills's conclusion was that the Agreements specifically required the ongoing participation of Braiden as a necessary "principal" of Braiden Sales. Furthermore, during the dismissal process, La-Z-Boy continually referred to Braiden as the dealer's "sales and marketing consultant". To Justice Sills, these facts demonstrated that La-Z-Boy really considered Braiden to be their sales agent, as opposed to Braiden Sales.

As La-Z-Boy found out, it is difficult to reclassify a former employee as an independent contractor. It is not enough to notify the employee that their employment has come to an end, to call them an independent contractor, or to even employ them through a corporate company. The essential question a court will ask itself is whether the relationship in question bears greater resemblance to one of employment or independent contract? Accordingly, to have an employee classified as an independent contractor, an employer must do more than formally distance itself from the employee. The employer must take steps to distinguish the substance of the relationship from one between an employer and employee.

It is important to point out that the Court's reasoning was coloured by its view that La-Z-Boy's actions were undertaken solely to avoid the employer obligations associated with a contract of employment. The evidence showed that La-Z-Boy's actions were taken in response to a determination by the Employee Health Tax and Workplace Safety and Insurance Board that La-Z-Boy's commissioned sales agents fell within its definition of "employees". Although employers are certainly free to engage in independent contractor relationships in the interest of avoiding the obligations that accompany employees, the decision in *La-Z-Boy* seems to suggest that where an employer wishes to convert an employee into an independent contractor it should have a good faith reason for doing so.

The main difficulty the Court seems to have had with La-Z-Boy's actions was the perception that it had attempted to gain the benefits of an independent contractor relationship (lesser obligations) while retaining the benefits of an employment relationship (greater control). In the end, the Court concluded that La-Z-Boy could not have it both ways. Accordingly, unless a change to an employee's formal employment status is accompanied by an equal change in the degree of control exercised over that employee, the relationship will continue to be characterized as an employment relationship. Accordingly, an employer looking to effect a change in the employment status of an employee should:

- Provide the employee with some input into the terms of any new employment arrangement;
- Ensure that the employee receives some benefit in exchange for agreeing to have his or her employment status reclassified; and
- Treat the former employee as an independent contractor by allowing the employee greater freedom in managing his or her affairs.

The *La-Z-Boy* case is an important reminder to employers about just how difficult it is to convert an employee to an independent contractor. What must be remembered is that it is the substance of the relationship, and not its form which determines its character.

7

TIPS FOR CREATING A PROPER INDEPENDENT CONTRACTOR RELATIONSHIP

1. The Fourfold Test *most import.
2. The Control Test
3. The Permanency Test
4. The Organization Test

Many companies attempt to avoid the risks and headaches associated with running a workplace by designating workers as "consultants" or "independent contractors". However, creating a true independent contractor relationship requires far more than a change in title and companies that miss the mark can face serious consequences. A finding that the person retained to perform work for your company is, in fact, an employee could give rise to obligations to provide reasonable or statutory notice of termination, overtime, vacation pay, holiday pay and to make all appropriate deductions in respect of income tax, Canada Pension Plan, Employment Insurance and Workplace Safety and Insurance Board. In short, improperly characterizing a worker as an independent contractor could cost you a great deal of money. So, how can you minimize the risks associated with creating an independent contractor relationship?

Unfortunately, the law in this area is not exactly straightforward. Although there are many factors taken into account by courts when assessing whether or not a worker is an independent contractor, it is not always clear which characteristics are determinative. As is so often the case in employment law, context is everything. It is also important to realize that various courts and government agencies may come to different legal conclusions depending upon the facts of a particular case. Generally, there are four tests used by courts and administrative tribunals to determine whether or not an independent contractor relationship exists.

1. THE FOURFOLD TEST *[handwritten: MOST PRACTICAL ✓]*

This test focuses on four specific questions:
1. Who has control over the manner in which the work will be performed and when and where it will be performed?
2. Who has ownership of the relevant tools?
3. Is there a chance of profit for the contractor?
4. Is there a risk of loss to the contractor?

A person will be held to be an employee where the company has control over the performance of the work, provides the work equipment and where the worker is paid a fixed amount of compensation, regardless of the outcome of the project or the company's profitability.

2. THE CONTROL TEST

Does the company have the control and direction over the manner in which the work is performed and when and where the work is performed? If the answer is "yes", then the worker will likely be treated as an employee.

3. THE PERMANENCY TEST

Do the terms of the relationship indicate a sense of permanency between the parties? For example, did the company provide the worker with training, supervision and guidance? Did the worker make changes in his or her life in order to work for this particular company?

4. THE ORGANIZATION TEST

This test focuses on whether the worker can be seen as a true part of the company's business organization. An independent contractor will generally not perform work that is integral to the company's operations. Rather, his or her work will be ancillary to the company's business.

It should be noted that, of the above-noted tests, the Fourfold Test and the Control Test are the most prominent. However, it is quite common for adjudicators to use elements from each test in determining whether or not an independent contractor relationship has been established.

What steps can you take to ensure that your independent contractor does not become your next (and possibly most expensive) employee?

1. Have a clear, written contract confirming that the person is not an employee. You may also want to include an indemnity provision allowing you to recover any moneys that are subsequently found to be due and owing by your company to the Canada Revenue Agency, Employment Insurance Commission, Canada Pension Plan or the Workplace Safety and Insurance Board.

2. Do not take statutory deductions from payments to the independent contractor. Doing so will be treated as an admission that the alleged contractor is actually an employee.

3. Do not provide vacation pay, statutory holiday pay, overtime pay or any health-care or employee benefits.

4. Do not provide a company uniform, business cards, a company vehicle or, if possible, any company equipment at all.

5. Do not restrict the worker from accepting work from other sources. Exclusivity or economic dependence will be seen as indicative of an employment relationship.

6. Avoid setting hours or days of work. Scheduling should be at the discretion of the worker and subject to the requirements of the contract.

7. Avoid providing the worker with bookkeeping or invoicing services or administrative assistance.

8. Although the worker should not be subject to performance reviews or discipline, the contract should have a provision that permits the company to terminate the agreement for cause.

9. The worker should have a company, sole proprietorship or a partnership established with a GST number and should submit the appropriate tax return reflecting his or her independent contractor status.

10. The contract should contain a very clear termination clause that can be exercised by either the contractor or the company at any time.

Although there are many benefits to be gained from creating an independent contractor relationship, it is important to realize that employers can face significant costs if they do not do so properly. Employers are well-advised to keep the legal tests in mind when structuring an independent contractor agreement in order to minimize the risk of financial loss.

8

EMPLOYEES V. DEPENDENT CONTRACTORS V. INDEPENDENT CONTRACTORS

1. The Facts
2. Dependent Contractors
3. Findings
4. What Employers Should Know

In a recent decision, the Ontario Court of Appeal has confirmed that somewhere between employee status and independent contractor status exists the category of "dependent contractors". In *McKee v. Reid's Heritage Homes Limited*, [2009] O.J. No. 5489, the Court outlined how dependent contractor status is defined in relation to existing categories. This decision has serious implications for employers, as dependent contractors will be entitled to reasonable notice of the termination of their services in the same way as an employee. By contrast, employers are not required to provide notice to independent contractors.

1. THE FACTS

In 1987, Elizabeth McKee signed a sales and advertising agreement on behalf of her business, Nu Homes, with the defendant Reid's Heritage Homes Limited ("RHH"). Pursuant to the agreement, McKee was to advertise and sell 69 homes for which she would charge a fee of $2,500 per home sold. The agreement provided that RHH would have exclusive use of Nu Home services, with the exception of certain other businesses owned by the principle of RHH. The Agreement provided that either party could terminate the agreement for any reason upon 30 days' notice.

After the first 69 homes were sold, McKee continued to sell homes for RHH without a new agreement in place. RHH supplied stationery and forms for selling homes, and McKee was given the title of "Sales Manager". RHH paid McKee through Nu Homes. McKee hired, trained and managed her own sub-agents with whom she split her commissions on their sales, without intervention, direction or interference from RHH. McKee invoiced RHH and paid her subagents through her corporation.

In 2004, RHH's sales force was restructured and in 2005, McKee was told her subagents would have to work for RHH as "direct employees". Negotiations regarding the terms of McKee's own relationship with RHH broke down. McKee sued RHH for wrongful dismissal. She was 64 years old at the time.

The trial judge found that McKee was an employee of RHH, as her activity of selling homes was an integral part of the defendant's business. Given her position, years of service and age, in light of the limited availability of comparable employment for someone of her experience, training and qualifications, she was awarded 18 months' severance in lieu of notice. This decision was appealed by RHH.

2. DEPENDENT CONTRACTORS

In the course of the appeal, the Court addressed whether there exists an intermediate position of "dependent contractor" between employee status and independent contractor status. The Court confirmed such a category exists, and took this opportunity to define what it means.

The Court found that dependent contractor status may exist where someone is not an employee, but where a certain minimum economic dependency is present between the individual and the employer. This will usually exist where the person works exclusively, or nearly exclusively, for the employer. Importantly, the Court confirmed that workers classified as dependent contractors will be owed reasonable notice upon termination.

Determining whether someone is a "dependant contractor" is a two-step analysis. First, it must be determined whether a person is an employee or a contractor. The Court confirmed the following important questions in making this determination:

1. Whether or not the agent was limited exclusively to the service of the principal;
2. Whether or not the agent is subject to the control of the principal, not only as to the product sold, but also as to when, where and how it is sold;
3. Whether or not the agent has an investment or interest in what are characterized as the "tools" relating to his or her service;
4. Whether or not the agent has undertaken any risk in the business sense or, alternatively, has any expectation of profit associated with the delivery of his or her service as distinct from a fixed commission;
5. Whether or not the activity of the agent is part of the business organization of the principal for which he or she works. In other words, whose business is it?

If the agent is found to be an employee, the analysis is complete. However, if the agent is deemed to be a contractor, the next question is whether the contractor is dependent or independent. If a contractor works exclusively for the business, and is therefore economically dependent on the business, the contractor will be considered dependent. Because there is a relationship of dependency, the Court stated that dependent contractors are owed reasonable notice upon termination, akin to an employee.

3. FINDINGS

Based on the particular facts of this case, the Court did not disturb the lower Court's finding that McKee was an employee (see [2008] O.J. No. 5877 (Ont. S.C.J.)). The Court acknowledged she worked for RHH exclusively, was subject to RHH's control as to where she sold homes, what promotional methods she was to use, what to sell and how much to sell it for. Additionally, she performed her sales function in model homes provided by RHH, used stationery and forms supplied by RHH, as she was financially dependent on RHH as she relied on fixed commissions without any further chance for profit and she did not risk any significant capital in her sales operation. Finally, the sales force of which McKee was a member was a crucial element of RHH's business. The fact that McKee operated through her own business and that she hired subagents who reported to her did not outweigh the other factors.

4. WHAT EMPLOYERS SHOULD KNOW

This case encompasses important issues for employers. The Court has clearly stated that workers who are not employees may be either dependent contractors or independent contractors. Where a contractor works exclusively for the employer, or is otherwise financially dependent on an employer, the employer may be obligated to provide reasonable notice upon termination of the working relationship. Where the contractor's status is independent, no notice is owed.

This has potentially significant financial ramifications for employers who engage contractors. Steps can be taken to minimize risk – in particular, extra care must be taken to outline responsibilities and roles of the parties in their governing contract, and contracts that expire must be renewed or replaced immediately.

9

THE EMPLOYEE SIGNED THE CONTRACT, BUT... ARE YOU SURE IT'S BINDING?

The classification of workers as employees versus independent contractors continues to be scrutinized by the courts. The Ontario Court of Appeal has weighed in on this subject and declared that simply having a worker sign a contract that classifies him or her as an independent contractor is not sufficient. Rather, the nature of the relationship itself must be considered in order to accurately classify the worker.

If you are an employer that seeks to reclassify an existing employee as an independent contractor or plans to otherwise alter a fundamental term of the employment contract for a current employee, you should be mindful of the Ontario Court of Appeal's decision in *Braiden v. La-Z-Boy Canada Ltd.*, [2008] O.J. No. 2314.

Gordon Braiden ("Braiden") began working at La-Z-Boy Canada Limited ("La-Z-Boy") in 1981 as a customer service manager. From July 1986 to August 1987, Braiden worked as a sales representative trainee. La-Z-Boy then advised Braiden that effective August 30, 1987, he would become a commissioned sales representative for the company. The employment relationship continued in this fashion for almost a decade, at which point La-Z-Boy decided to enter into annual written Agreements with its sales representatives. La-Z-Boy's intention was to convert all commissioned sales representatives to independent contractors. It was Braiden's understanding that refusing to sign the Agreement would probably cost him his job. The first such Agreement was executed by Braiden in 1996. Similar Agreements were executed by Braiden annually from 1996 to 2003. To further complicate matters, La-Z-boy required Braiden to incorporate a company. As a result, the 1998 to 2003 Agreements were between La-Z-Boy and Braiden's company.

The trial judge concluded that despite La-Z-Boy's attempts to classify Braiden as an independent contractor, the nature of the relationship was that of employee and employer. Little significance was attached to the technical structure of the arrangement between the parties. Instead, the trial judge focused on the extent of control held and exercised by La-Z-Boy. The Court of Appeal agreed with the conclusions of the trial judge saying the key factor was that Braiden was carrying on the business of La-Z-Boy.

Classifying the relationship as employee and employer opened the door to Braiden's claim for reasonable notice of termination or payment in lieu. When Braiden started working at La-Z-Boy his contract did not contain a provision dealing with notice of termination. This meant that Braiden was entitled to reasonable notice of termination under the common law. La-Z-Boy sought to limit Braiden's entitlement under the common law by introducing a provision for the first time in the 1996 Agreement, which provided that Braiden could be terminated on 60 days' notice. The 1996 Agreement, and those that followed, all provided that Braiden could be terminated on 60 days' notice. La-Z-Boy terminated Braiden in 2003 on 60 days' notice, relying on the notice provision in the Agreement.

On appeal, Braiden successfully argued that the revised employment Agreement failed because there were no benefits that flowed to him under the Agreement. It is well-established law that in order for a contract to be binding, each party to the contract must receive some benefit from the other. In legal terms, this exchange of benefits is called consideration. Where consideration is absent, there is no contract. While this is a basic principle of contract law, the Court of Appeal indicated it is of particular importance in the employment context, saying:

> The requirement of consideration to support a change to the terms of an agreement is especially important in the employment context where, generally, there is inequality of bargaining power between employees and employers. Some employees may enjoy a measure of bargaining power when negotiating the terms of prospective employment but once they have been hired and are dependent on the remuneration

of the job, they become more vulnerable. ([2008] O.J. No. 2314 at para. 49).

The Court next addressed the issue of whether forbearance from firing constitutes good consideration. Braiden was given a choice to either sign the new agreement or lose his job. He of course signed the Agreement and in exchange he received continued employment. The Court of Appeal held that this was not sufficient consideration to justify Braiden being bound by the modified terms of the Agreement, namely the inclusion of the 60-day notice period. In its reasons, the Court cited with approval its earlier decisions in *Hobbs v. TDI Canada Ltd.*, [2004] O.J. No. 4876 and *Francis v. Canadian Imperial Bank of Commerce*, [1994] O.J. No. 2657:

> ... [A] change in the notice period is a significant modification of the employment agreement, additional consideration is required to support such a modification and continued employment does not constitute something of value flowing to the employee...

> ... Francis makes it clear the law does not permit employers to present employees with changed terms of employment, threaten to fire them if they do not agree to them, and then rely on the continued employment relations as the consideration for the new terms. (See [2008] O.J. No. 2314 at para. 57.)

The Court of Appeal did accept that if an employer provides consideration beyond mere continued employment, the employee may be bound by the modified terms of the agreement.

In summary, it is not always sufficient to simply present an employee with a contract and have the employee sign it. This will not always result in a binding contract that you, as the employer, can rely upon. If you want the contract to be enforceable, you should ensure you take the following steps:

- Provide the employee with the contract well in advance of the employee's first day on the job.
- Draw the employee's attention to the termination clause and make sure that the employee fully understands the terms of the contract.
- Have the employee sign the contract before he or she starts work.

If you have done all this and then later seek to alter the terms of the employment contract for an existing employee, ensure that the modified contract provides some benefit to the employee. Ask yourself, what is the employee getting in exchange for signing the new contract? Some examples of the types of benefits that might flow to the employee include a promotion, a bonus or a raise. Where the employee receives a benefit in return for signing the new contract, it is likely to be enforceable.

10

THE CASE OF THE ENFORCEABLE TERMINATION CLAUSE – CLARKE V. INSIGHT COMPONENTS (CANADA) INC.

In times of economic recession and downsizing, as was recently experienced in Ontario, a termination clause is an integral part of an employment contract. A termination clause limits the amount of severance an employee is entitled to when his or her employment is terminated without cause. In the absence of a termination clause, a downsized employee is entitled to "common law" reasonable notice of termination, the amount of which is typically far greater than the minimums provided in the *Employment Standards Act, 2000*, S.O. 2000, c. 41 (the "ESA") and which varies depending on each employee's particular circumstances. A termination clause therefore provides the employer with greater certainty regarding the costs of downsizing employees. Of course, that certainty is only provided when the termination clause is enforceable, and there are many ways for termination clauses to be found unenforceable by a court.

Fortunately, the decision in *Clarke v. Insight Components (Canada) Inc.*, [2007] O.J. No. 5671 (Ont. S.C.J.), affirmed [2008] O.J. No. 5025 (Ont. C.A.), offers employers clear guidance about how to ensure termination clauses in employment contracts remain enforceable.

In *Clarke*, the plaintiff joined the defendant in 1995 and signed an employment contract that did not contain a termination clause. In 2000, a company-wide policy stated all employees at the plaintiff's level should have a termination clause in their contracts. In April 2001, the plaintiff was promoted to managing director for Canada and his compensation was significantly increased. Two weeks after he began his new role, the plaintiff signed a memorandum of understanding that outlined the terms of his position, including his improved salary and the new termination clause, which stated, at para. 18:

> **Termination of Employment**— Your employment may be terminated for cause at any time in which event you shall be entitled to only the amount of your salary and vacation pay earned up to the effective date of termination. Your employment may be terminated without cause for any reason upon the provision of reasonable notice equal to the requirements of the applicable employment or labour standards legislation. By signing below, you agree that upon the receipt of your entitlements in accordance with this legislation, no further amounts will be due and payable to you whether under statute or common law.

A well-known legal rule is that a change to the terms of an employment contract requires some form of extra payment (what lawyers call "consideration"), which most often takes the form of more money. The trial judge in *Clarke* found that the plaintiff was provided with consideration for the addition of the termination clause to his employment contract because the plaintiff received an increase in compensation at the same time the termination clause was added.

The trial judge also found that the termination clause was unambiguous because it clearly limited the plaintiff's entitlements on his dismissal without cause to the payments he would receive under the applicable legislation – in this case the notice pay and severance pay under the ESA.

The trial judge therefore concluded that the termination clause was enforceable. When the plaintiff was dismissed without cause, he was not entitled to reasonable notice at common law and was only entitled to receive notice pay and severance pay under the ESA as provided for in the termination clause. The plaintiff appealed but the Ontario Court of Appeal upheld the trial judge's decision, saying, at para. 11:

> Simply put, when the appellant agreed to accept promotion to the position of managing director with all the benefits that position entailed, on the findings of the trial judge which was supported by the evidence, he knew that the termination clause was a necessary part of his employment package.

There is no better time than the present for employers to take note of the guidance provided by the Court in *Clarke*. As the economy improves and firms look to hire new employees, forward-looking employers will be planning to limit the cost of future downsizing during the next downturn in the business cycle. While employers should always seek advice from a lawyer before introducing a termination clause to employment contracts, here are some practical tips to keep in mind:

1. **Make sure the termination clause language is crystal clear.** Since courts recognize that employers have more bargaining power than employees, contracts are typically interpreted in favour of employees, which means judges will likely throw out termination clauses if they find any ambiguity in the contractual language.

2. **Make sure the employee is made aware of the termination clause and provide an opportunity to obtain legal advice.** Courts recognize that employees do not necessarily read contracts before signing them. Termination clauses are typically not enforced by judges where the employee was not aware of the clause or was not given an opportunity to seek independent legal advice. Eliminate any uncertainty by specifically explaining the termination clause to the employee and giving the employee time to consult a lawyer before he or she signs the contract. In addition, make sure the employee signs the contract before his or her start date.

3. **Make sure the employee receives consideration.** Providing a new employee with employment is typically sufficient consideration for a termination clause. For current employees without a termination clause in their contract, courts have not allowed employers to rely on termination clauses that have been unilaterally added to a contract by the employer. Make sure the employee is provided with sufficient payment in exchange for introducing the termination clause.

PART TWO

The Employment Relationship

11

WHY YOUR PLANT NEEDS A PERFORMANCE MANAGEMENT PROGRAM

1. Irregular or Tardy Reviews
2. Leaving No Room for the Exercise of Discretion
3. Dishonest or Misleading Reviews
4. Insufficient Guidance or Instruction
5. Reviewing Performance and Salary Simultaneously
6. Poor or Non-Existent Documentation
7. No Employee Acknowledgment

Performance reviews and performance management programs are two of the most essential elements of any employment relationship. However, because they often require delivering bad news or criticism, many managers and employers overlook or even avoid their implementation.

There are two aspects to performance management: scheduled assessments and disciplinary interventions. No matter what the size of the workplace, it is essential for the employer to have procedures in place to regularly review an employee's performance and to address problems as they may arise. The need for effective performance management is twofold. First, it helps the employer maintain standards of quality and efficiency by correcting inappropriate behaviour. Employers are entitled to maintain a safe, efficient and courteous workplace. In order to effectively do so, it is often necessary to reprimand employees for inappropriate behaviour and remind them of their obligation to abide by the employer's policies and procedures.

Second, performance management programs serve to protect the employer's interests in the event that litigation results from termination. When a performance management program is administered in a fair and standardized fashion, it has the effect of documenting the employer's relationship with each employee, thus creating a reliable and thorough record for use in court.

The first step in creating or using an effective performance management system is to decide what your expectations are with respect to the workplace as a whole and from specific employees or positions. It is a good idea to write down those expectations, both for your own reference and for the purposes of communicating with employees. When listing your expectations, it is wise to be mindful of your statutory obligations as an employer under the relevant employment standards, occupational health and safety, and human rights legislation.

The next step is to ensure that your employees understand, or have had ample opportunity to understand, the standards they are expected to meet in performing their duties and interacting with co-workers. Communications regarding appropriate workplace behaviour and performance standards can take the form of internal memoranda, human resources policy manuals, job descriptions, disciplinary letters, training sessions and meetings between management and employees. Formal messages from the employer are not the only means of educating employees about workplace standards. Equally important is the tenor and content of day-to-day interactions between management and staff. Supervisors should be instructed to familiarize themselves with all applicable workplace policies, procedures and manuals.

The final step is applying your own performance management policy. This is the stage where most employers experience difficulties. What are the most common pitfalls and how can you, as an employer, take steps to avoid them?

1. IRREGULAR OR TARDY REVIEWS

Performance reviews should occur on a regular schedule that is known to both employees and management. Failure to abide by a set schedule undermines the impact of the reviews and hampers their ability to monitor and improve performance. If a disciplinary issue occurs, it should be addressed as promptly as possible. Employers who are slow to respond to workplace infractions can be found by courts to have condoned the offending behaviour.

2. LEAVING NO ROOM FOR THE EXERCISE OF DISCRETION

It is always advisable to have a transparent and predictable discipline process, *i.e.*, a first offence results in a verbal warning, a second offence merits a written warning, etc. However, employers should be wary of relinquishing their own discretion and should explicitly reserve the right to skip a step in the discipline process where the offence is severe or to decline to escalate the matter where the offence is minor. The employer should always be in a position to consider all of the relevant circumstances when applying disciplinary measures.

3. DISHONEST OR MISLEADING REVIEWS

It is not uncommon for employment lawyers, to hear from clients who claim to have terminated an employee for "incompetence", only to discover that the employee's personnel file contains a series of glowing annual reviews. It is essential that performance reviews accurately reflect the state of the workplace, otherwise they do nothing to help the employee improve and will severely hamper any efforts by the employer to sustain a dismissal for cause. An example of the pitfalls of overly positive reviews is the decision in *Canada Council for the Arts v. Public Service Alliance of Canada*, 2003 Can LII 52692, [2003] C.L.A.D. No. 409 (Ont. C.A.), where the grievor was dismissed on the grounds that she allegedly failed to meet the requirements of her position. The arbitrator reviewed the grievor's performance reviews and concluded that there was no evidence to support the employer's contention that she did not perform her duties competently. In fact, her reviews were quite positive. The arbitrator upheld the grievance and made the following comments (at para. 97):

Encouragement of an employee is to be commended, but a desire to be positive does not excuse a failure to warn of the possibility of termination such that an employee does not really understand the extent of the employer's dissatisfaction.

4. INSUFFICIENT GUIDANCE OR INSTRUCTION

Equally hazardous can be a lack of guidance or suggestions on how to improve. Employers who criticize employees without also providing instructions as to how they can better meet expectations can create a risk of an employee complaining that he or she was treated in bad faith or, worse, was the subject of workplace harassment.

5. REVIEWING PERFORMANCE AND SALARY SIMULTANEOUSLY

A very common error made by employers is to conduct performance reviews at the same time as the employee's annual salary review. This practice is not advisable. Most salary reviews result in a raise, even if only to adjust for the cost of living. Constructive criticism and negative feedback will not likely register with the employee if they are accompanied by a raise.

6. POOR OR NON-EXISTENT DOCUMENTATION

Most employers who make use of performance management programs have standard forms. Unfortunately, few employers monitor the manner in which those standard forms are completed by supervisors and managers. A performance management form that has not been completed, is illegible or is ambiguous is of no use to the employer. Supervisors should receive training on the correct use of performance management forms and should be held accountable when the forms are not completed appropriately.

7. NO EMPLOYEE ACKNOWLEDGEMENT

It is not uncommon for employees to allege that they did not receive copies of their performance reviews or disciplinary letters. All such forms and communications should contain a space for the employee's signature, acknowledging that the employee has received the document. Some employees are reluctant to sign the acknowledgement on the ground that they disagree with the contents of the review. In these situations, it is advisable to provide the employee with an opportunity to record his or her objection to the review. Not only does this allow the employee to feel as though he or she has had a chance to provide another side of the story, but it also serves as evidence that the employee did indeed receive the feedback in question and records the employee's response at the time the review was conducted.

For many in the human resources field, the term "performance management" has a dubious reputation. It is often seen solely as a method for exiting problem employees from the workplace. While performance management can certainly aid employers in building a "just cause" termination, it can also be a valuable tool to help ensure that the employer's standards for appropriate and efficient workplace behaviour are upheld.

12

THE DOS AND DON'TS OF PERFORMANCE MANAGEMENT

Recently, a new client called and described a problem they were having with one of their long term employees. This employee (let's call her "Deborah"), had been with the company for seven years. Deborah had never been a star but she always managed to stick around, generally by switching positions every few years. Deborah was earning roughly the same amount as when she started and qualified for our client's standard employee bonus every year. She had a few warning letters on file regarding her attendance but no record of further discipline. Our client advised us that they did conduct annual performance reviews but that they were not taken very seriously by employees or management. All employees generally received a "satisfactory" grade.

Deborah had recently started working under an ambitious young manager. The manager, unhappy with Deborah's inability to meet deadlines and sloppy work product, began to coach Deborah on her performance. Deborah responded poorly and complained loudly to her co-workers about her "inexperienced" and "pushy" boss. The manager responded by issuing a disciplinary letter to Deborah. Upon receiving the letter, Deborah stormed out of the workplace. She has since refused to return, and alleges that she is being harassed by her new manager.

What went wrong? And how can it be fixed?

It is important to remember that performance management is an essential part of any functional employment relationship. It is essential for employers to have procedures in place to regularly review employees' performance and to address problems as they arise. The need for effective performance management is twofold. First, it helps the employer maintain standards of quality and efficiency by correcting inappropriate behaviour. Second, performance management programs are a risk-management tool. When a performance management program is administered in a fair and standardized fashion, it has the effect of documenting the employer's relationship with each employee, thus creating a reliable and thorough record for use in court.

The failure of Deborah's employer to document her performance issues and communicate its expectations has left it vulnerable. Any allegations of poor performance are now a matter of "he said/she said". So what can our client do to address the issue?

The problem must be tackled on two levels. Deborah now presents a serious concern. Since she has alleged that she is being harassed, her allegations should be investigated by a member of the human resources department or an independent party. If the investigation reveals no substance to the allegations of harassment, her performance coaching should begin in earnest. Deborah must be made to understand the expectations her employer has for her performance and her new manager should be supported in her efforts to ensure that Deborah meets those expectations. Realistically speaking, however, the employment relationship has soured and will likely end in litigation.

In dealing with the workforce as a whole, our client must first decide what its expectations are with respect to employees and/or positions. These expectations should be set out in writing, both for the employer's reference and for the purposes of communicating with employees. The next step is to ensure that its employees understand, or have had ample opportunity to understand, the standards they are expected to meet in performing their duties and interacting with co-workers. Communications regarding appropriate workplace behaviour and performance standards can take the form of internal memoranda, human resources policy manuals, job descriptions, disciplinary letters, training sessions and meetings between management and employees. Formal messages from the employer are not the only means of educating employees about workplace standards. Equally important is the tenor and content of day-to-day interactions between management and staff. All supervisors should be instructed to familiarize themselves with all applicable workplace policies, procedures and manuals.

Most importantly, our client must change its existing practice with respect to performance reviews. Managers must be retrained on the proper procedure for evaluating performance and providing feedback to employees under their supervision. Each manager should be advised that failure to administer a proper performance management program will be seen as a failure to meet his or her own performance expectations. When creating and implementing performance management programs, there are several common missteps to avoid:

- Irregular or tardy reviews: performance reviews should occur on a regular schedule that is known to both employees and management. Employers who are slow to respond to workplace infractions can be found by courts to have condoned the offending behaviour.

- Leaving no room for the exercise of discretion: employers should explicitly reserve the right to skip a step in the discipline process where the offence is severe or to decline to escalate the matter where the offence is minor. Your managers should always be in a position to consider all of the relevant circumstances when applying disciplinary measures.

- Dishonest or misleading reviews: it is essential that performance reviews accurately reflect the state of the workplace; otherwise they do nothing to help the employee improve and will severely hamper any efforts by the employer to sustain a dismissal for cause. This is certainly the case with Deborah's employer, who has only a file full of "satisfactory" reviews to support its allegation that Deborah's performance was lacking.

- Insufficient guidance or instruction: employers who criticize employees without also providing instructions as to how they can better meet expectations can create a risk of an employee complaining that he or she was treated in bad faith or, worse, was the subject of workplace harassment.

- Reviewing performance and salary simultaneously: most salary reviews result in a raise, even if only to adjust for the cost of living. Constructive criticism and negative feedback will not likely register with the employee if they are accompanied by a raise.

- Poor or non-existent documentation: a performance management form that has not been completed, is illegible or is ambiguous is of no use to the employer. Supervisors should receive training on the correct use of performance management forms and should be held accountable when the forms are not completed appropriately.

- No employee acknowledgement: it is not uncommon for employees to allege that they did not receive copies of their performance reviews or disciplinary letters. All such forms and communications should contain a space for the employee's signature, acknowledging that the employee has received the document, even if the employee does not agree with its contents.

For many in the human resources field, the term "performance management" has a dubious reputation. It is often seen solely as a method for exiting problem employees from the workplace. While performance management can certainly aid employers in building a "just cause" termination, it can also be a valuable tool to help ensure that the employer's standards for appropriate and efficient workplace behaviour are upheld.

13

WHY WORKPLACE HARASSMENT INVESTIGATIONS FAIL

1. The Investigators
2. Lawyers
3. Not Protecting the Participants
4. The Scope of the Investigation
5. Zero Tolerance
6. Lack of Flexibility
7. Remedial Action

Most of us appreciate the need to conduct a workplace investigation following the occurrence of a harassment incident.

Some investigations are fairly straightforward, even routine, for an experienced human resources professional to handle, but some cases are much more complicated and emotionally charged either because of the nature of the allegations or the people involved. These investigations are typically time-consuming, expensive and upsetting. Very often, the goal will be solely to resolve the matter as easily and as quickly as possible with the hope of minimizing disruption of the normal workplace operations. Rarely is there any analysis done following the investigation to determine whether the investigation itself was successful beyond simply resolving the complaint. Resolving the complaint should only be one of the goals of any investigation.

Equally important are considerations relating to protecting the complainant (emotionally and physically), protecting the reputation of the accused, maintaining a workplace that is respectful and where employees feel valued and safe and ensuring that the company's business is interrupted as little as possible.

So, what are the things that can cause an investigation to fail? Obviously, there are a multitude of reasons why an investigation can miss the mark, but these are some of the most frequent reasons:

1. THE INVESTIGATORS

Choosing the wrong people to conduct the investigation almost guarantees an outcome about which you will not be entirely satisfied. Who should you retain to conduct the investigation will depend on the particular facts of the case. You should not assume the same person or persons should conduct every investigation. The person(s) you should choose should understand your organization and the nature of your business. The person has to have credibility and be seen as being impartial and with no vested interest in the outcome. In some cases, you will want a woman to conduct the investigation. In other cases, you may be better off with a man. You may need to have two people conduct the investigation as opposed to one. It is preferred to always conduct an investigation with another person, for the simple reason that there are two people who will observe all the witnesses and hear the evidence.

2. LAWYERS

Lawyers do not always make the best investigators. Although they are skilled in gathering evidence and preparing a case, those are not the only talents that you are looking for. The best investigators are those who are not rigid and who are sensitive and emotionally open to understanding the human dynamics at play. Regrettably, lawyers can also play a negative role when they are only providing advice to you or the investigators during an investigation. Regardless of the advice that you may get to the contrary, remember that each investigation will have its unique circumstances and generally, there are no fast and hard rules about what you should do for every circumstance that may arise. Being sensitive to the people involved and using good common sense will usually get you by quite well.

3. NOT PROTECTING THE PARTICIPANTS

Investigators need to be flexible in their approach and need to be alert to any issues relating to the safety and well-being of the participants. In some cases, removing one or more of the participants (complainant, accused, witness) may be necessary to maintain the integrity of the investigation and the protection of your employees. The challenge will always be to make the best decision depending on the circumstances. Refusing to remove the accused can have devastating effects on the complainant in particular and can adversely influence the entire investigation.

Improperly removing a complainant or the accused can result in either a human rights complaint or civil litigation and may destroy any possibility of returning the individuals to the workplace following the completion of the investigation.

4. THE SCOPE OF THE INVESTIGATION

It is critical to control the scope of the investigation. There are serious consequences for the employer in either case where the investigation is too narrow or too broad.

You will need to get to the root cause of the problem and not only deal with the symptoms. A superficial investigation will not usually resolve the problem and exposes the workplace and the employer to further disruption. Conversely, an overly broad investigation can result in permanent damage to the workplace culture and cause lasting problems for peoples' reputations and their ability to perform their duties.

Litigation usually follows where the scope of the investigation has not been properly determined.

5. ZERO TOLERANCE

"Capital punishment" should not be the penalty for every incident of harassment, although there can be a zero tolerance approach with respect to tolerating harassment in the workplace. The approach to discipline should be progressive depending on the seriousness of the incident and the harm caused, among other things.

Importantly, investigators cannot have a zero tolerance mindset in terms of discipline when conducting their investigations. The lens from which they must view this behaviour must be more progressive and more sensitive to the many issues surrounding the investigation and the participants. The real danger with a zero tolerance mindset is that employees will generally be more reluctant to participate in the investigation, which will ultimately make proper resolution more difficult.

6. LACK OF FLEXIBILITY

Every workplace harassment investigation will be different. Investigators need to be flexible with the procedure they follow, which will usually be dictated by the particular circumstances of the case. Who will be interviewed, the order of the interviews, when and where the interviews will be conducted and the time frame all require flexibility in order to ensure a fair and complete investigation. Lack of flexibility will inevitably result in incomplete evidence.

7. REMEDIAL ACTION

Investigators must be prepared to make recommendations with respect to appropriate remedial action following the completion of the investigation. Although some would argue that the role of the investigator should be limited to gathering and reporting the evidence, the better approach is for the investigator(s) to assess credibility, make the findings of fact and recommend remedial action. The investigator is always in the best position to understand what has happened and what needs to be done to correct the problem. By avoiding this role, investigators fail in their responsibility to assist the employer in achieving a progressive resolution.

Every investigation will be different and will present unique challenges. Provided that you recognize this inescapable fact and you are committed to conducting a fair and impartial investigation and avoid the mistakes that have been reviewed above, you are more likely to achieve the proper resolution.

14

EXPERIENCE COUNTS WHEN CONDUCTING A WORKPLACE INVESTIGATION

Anyone who has ever conducted a workplace investigation will know that it is difficult to conduct a perfect investigation. There are usually bumps along the way and the investigator must make difficult decisions. What is now required of a good investigator in addition to strong communication skills is a sound understanding of due process requirements. The fact is, a lack of due process can almost always result in a flawed investigation, which ultimately will adversely affect the conclusions that were reached by the investigator during and at the conclusion of the workplace investigation.

In *Stone v. SDS Kerr Beavers Dental*, [2006] O.J. No. 2532, the judge found in favour of the plaintiff employee after he concluded that the workplace investigation that was conducted by an inexperienced human resources person was flawed. What seemed to upset the Court the most was that Stone, the accused, was not given a full opportunity to explain his actions or to rectify an unsatisfactory situation. Stone was given only a very vague description of the harassing behaviour. The alleged victim's name was not provided. Even though he was told that there was more than one complainant, Stone was not told the number of complainants and none were identified. One of the most ridiculous parts of the investigation was where the investigator provided to Stone a copy of the harassment policy and asked him whether any of his conduct during the time in question might fall within the policy. The judge noted that the investigation was the first one conducted by the human resources person and that her inexperience in handling human resources issues played a significant role in management's response to Stone.

This case would make good reading for anyone preparing to embark upon an investigation. The following checklist provides details about how to approach a workplace investigation.

1. **Do you have a complaint?**

    Not all anonymous complaints should be investigated. As well, if you have a reluctant complainant, consider creative solutions that may not involve an investigation such as a transfer or education and training.

2. **Who should conduct the investigation?**

    This is a critical question. It should not be the lawyer who represents the company. In some cases, it should be the internal human resources person, but in most cases, an external, experienced investigator who is impartial is the type of person you want.

3. **What will be the scope of the investigation?**

    These investigations have a tendency to mutate. Try to keep control of the scope of the investigation and keep asking yourself "Do I need to speak to this person in order to prove or disprove this particular complaint?" An overly broad and unstructured investigation tends to cause more disruption in the workplace, will take more time and will cost the company more money.

4. **Full disclosure.**

    Although the investigation is supposed to be "confidential" almost everyone misunderstands what that means. The accused and the complainant have a right to know what is being said about them. All allegations and the identity of witnesses must be disclosed. Witnesses do not have the same substantive rights as the complainant and the accused.

5. **Legal representation.**

    Although it is an internal investigation, lawyers for the complainant, accused and perhaps even the witnesses should be permitted to participate by being present during questioning. Refusing an accused's request to have his or her counsel present could certainly be viewed as unfair and high-handed. Although counsel should be permitted to attend, actual participation should be limited and counsel should not be allowed to interfere with the conduct of the investigation.

6. **Avoid delay.**

    Conduct the investigation quickly, make a decision and communicate the decision to the complainant and the accused. Delay causes stress and a disruption in the workplace.

7. **Provide support.**

    Participants in the investigation may need emotional support. Access EAP (Employee Assistance Programs) or provide a paid leave of absence, if necessary.

8. **Evaluate what the employer has done.**

    If the employer has condoned the behaviour this needs to be considered in evaluating the conclusions and the proper corrective action.

9. **Education.**

    How many times have you distributed your harassment policy? How often have you provided your employees with training? This is not a one-shot deal. It should be an ongoing process. Simply redistributing your policy every six months is a great way to keep sending the message to your employees.

10. **Zero tolerance is gone.**

    There are different levels of severity of harassment and therefore, termination is not always the most suitable form of discipline. Remember also that courts are sympathetic to dismissed employees and the court will adopt a contextual analysis in determining whether an employee who is found guilty of harassment should be dismissed for cause.

15

INVESTIGATING HARASSMENT IN THE WORKPLACE MUST BE PROMPT

1. Conducting a Proper Investigation
2. Prepare the Complainant for Possible Future Litigation

One of the most difficult situations faced by human resources professionals are those involving allegations of workplace harassment. Unchecked harassment can quickly poison a workplace, and can result in expensive and potentially embarrassing litigation. It is therefore vitally important that human resources professionals conduct prompt and proper investigations of every harassment complaint.

The consequences of an inadequate harassment investigation can be severe. *Piresferreira v. Ayotte*, [2008] O.J. No. 5187 (Ont. S.C.J.), varied on appeal [2010] O.J. No. 2224 (Ont. C.A.), is a recent example of the significant fallout of an improper harassment investigation. In this case a manager verbally abused and physically shoved a subordinate in the workplace. In an attempt to ward off any complaint by the employee, the manager drafted a performance plan, labelling the employee as a problem employee and requiring her to work even more closely with the manager to improve her skills. The employee complained, but human resources failed to properly investigate the complaint, failed to apologize for what had occurred (or require the manager to apologize) and actually required the employee to meet with the manager to review her performance plan. The employee developed a severe case of anxiety and depression and became physically unable to work. She sued the employer and was awarded more than $500,000 at trial in damages for assault and battery, intentional infliction of emotional distress, negligent infliction of emotional distress (due to the improper harassment investigation) and constructive dismissal. The Court of Appeal overturned the decision of the trial judge, in part finding that the tort of negligent infliction of mental suffering was not available against the employer. Nevertheless, the case continues to stand as a reminder of the significant risk to employers related to an improper harassment investigation.

1. CONDUCTING A PROPER INVESTIGATION

When conducting a harassment investigation, human resources professionals need to balance a number of often competing interests. Here are some suggestions about how to conduct a proper investigation:

1. **Have written allegations** – Having the employee put the allegations in writing will help focus the complaint and will force the complainant to stick to his or her story.

2. **Choose an independent investigator** – The investigator should be independent of both the complainant and the accused and should just gather the facts; the investigator should not be the person to decide whether harassment occurred and what disciplinary action should be taken; this should be left to management.

3. **Interview all relevant witnesses** – Both the complainant and the accused should be interviewed, and they should be asked to list any relevant witnesses that the investigator should interview.

4. **Move quickly and keep it confidential** – An investigation should be initiated and completed as soon as possible, and should only involve those directly affected by the complaint.

5. **Prepare a report** – The investigator should prepare a report that explains the complaint, the witnesses interviewed and the factual findings. The report should not make recommendations for any action to be taken.

6. **Take the appropriate action** – Management should review the report, decide whether harassment occurred and promptly take corrective action, which could include an apology, reporting changes, suspension or in very serious cases, termination.

2. PREPARE THE COMPLAINANT FOR POSSIBLE FUTURE LITIGATION

If the result of an investigation results in the termination of the accused, the accused may sue the employer for wrongful dismissal. If this occurs, a recent Court decision has confirmed that the accused can require the complainant to testify on behalf of the employer during the discovery process (see *Ciardullo v. Premetalco Inc.*, [2009] O.J. No. 3625 (Ont. S.C.J.)). The complainant should be informed of this possibility and be reassured that he or she will receive the employer's support.

16

WHEN YOUR BOSS IS A BULLY

1. Communicate with Your Manager
2. Document the Behaviour
3. File an Internal Complaint
4. File an External Complaint
5. Commence a Civil Action
6. Consider Resigning

Despite all the new-age management books that try to provide guidance to managers about how to motivate and treat their employees fairly, some managers still don't get it. How can you identify when your boss is a bully? What should you do to deal with such conduct?

In many cases, bullying behaviour by a supervisor or manager is due to a lack of training for the job. It often happens that being a good worker does not translate to being a good manager. Bullying behaviour can include yelling, rude behaviour, severe criticism, threats, harassment (sexual or racial are the most common) and even physical assaults. Usually the behaviour is frequent and affects your ability to properly perform your duties.

Obviously, managers have the right and an obligation to manage their workforce. However, when managing turns into harassment or any other form of bullying, it becomes important for you to take steps to stop the behaviour. Considering that the bully in these circumstances is your boss, how do you get your manager to stop such conduct while at the same time avoiding your own dismissal? Here are a few suggestions.

1. COMMUNICATE WITH YOUR MANAGER

Tell your manager politely that you consider his or her behaviour to be inappropriate. Request that the conduct end immediately. Hopefully, a verbal communication will change the way the manager is acting toward you. If not, you may consider communicating with your manager in writing, with or without a copy to his or her supervisor. No doubt this approach is a lot more aggressive, so you need to be certain of your position.

2. DOCUMENT THE BEHAVIOUR

Remember that it will usually boil down to a credibility issue between you and your boss. If you keep detailed notes of the conduct, when and where the conduct occurred, along with the names of any witnesses, this may help you later.

3. FILE AN INTERNAL COMPLAINT

Check to see what corporate policies are in place to deal with the kind of behaviour being engaged in by your manager. The best example is a sexual harassment or workplace harassment policy. Usually, these policies deal with conduct that is defined as discrimination and are particularly focused on race, sex, disability, sexual orientation and other types of discrimination on prohibited grounds. What this means is that the conduct, in order to fall within the policy, must have a human rights violation aspect to it. Otherwise, it may not fall within the policy and you will have to seek another alternative. However, some workplace harassment policies are broad enough to cover "personal harassment", in that the policy specifically prohibits any conduct that causes emotional, psychological or physical discomfort and does not have to be based on a human rights ground of discrimination.

4. FILE AN EXTERNAL COMPLAINT

This should only be done in circumstances where you have already taken steps to stop the bullying behaviour (such as communicating with your manager or filing an internal complaint) but the manager or the company have failed to take your complaint seriously. Not all bullying behaviour can give rise to an external complaint. If your complaint is based on conduct that is discriminatory in nature, for example, sexual or racial harassment, you may file a complaint with a human rights commission. Usually there is a limitation period for filing a complaint, so you should consult directly with the commission to avoid missing the date for filing your complaint. There may also be remedies under workers' compensation and occupational health and safety legislation, depending on the specific facts of your case.

5. COMMENCE A CIVIL ACTION

Starting a lawsuit is expensive and in most cases will mean that you will have to leave your current job. Again, depending on the nature of the bullying behaviour and how severe the consequences of the conduct have been for you, you may have the option of claiming constructive dismissal, entitling you to sue for reasonable notice damages. The idea here is that the conduct must be serious and display an intention by the employer to no longer be bound by the employment contract. In most cases, such a claim will be difficult to prove. Another possibility is a claim for intentional infliction of mental suffering or for assault. Usually significant medical evidence will be required to substantiate such a claim.

6. CONSIDER RESIGNING

In some cases, the bullying behaviour causes significant emotional and psychological harm to the victim. In these circumstances, and especially where the company has failed to respond to the complaint quickly, it is probably wise to simply resign from your job. Even though a resignation will disentitle you to any compensation, peace of mind is probably your best alternative.

17

HOW TO COPE WITH THE HOSTILE EMPLOYEE

1. Look Beyond Technical Skills
2. Conduct More Than One Interview Before Hiring
3. Conduct Proper Reference Checks
4. Implement a Probation Term
5. Document Performance or Attitude Problems as They Occur
6. Conduct All Meetings With Hostile Employees with a Company Witness Present
7. Consider Whether There Are Any Extenuating Circumstances Causing the Employee's Behaviour
8. Terminate Early if Circumstances Warrant Dismissal

A clerical employee refuses to share an office fax machine with his co-workers. Every time co-workers approach the company machine, they are verbally abused by the employee, who claims "de facto" ownership although he has been repeatedly warned to be courteous to co-workers and to share its use.

Another employee continuously underperforms, has difficulty getting along with co-workers, adversely affects the relationship between the company and its customers and refuses to attend meetings with his supervisor unless an agenda is prepared in advance of the meeting and a witness is present.

Usually these scenarios turn into multiple legal proceedings either before the courts, human rights commissions, workers' compensation tribunals and/or labour boards. There is very little that an employer can do to prevent an employee from lodging a number of different legal complaints under several different pieces of legislation. In some cases, an employer may be obligated to defend several claims at the same time at significant expense. This is even more aggravating and emotionally distressing where the employee has only marginal service or where the complaints are obviously frivolous. Although in some cases the employer may be able to delay one proceeding while another proceeds, this is not always the case. Too often both cases will proceed with a significant risk of conflicting decisions.

So how can an employer either avoid or minimize the consequences brought on by a hostile employee? Here are some suggestions.

1. LOOK BEYOND TECHNICAL SKILLS

Avoid hiring employees on the basis of simply the skills that they bring to the job. In today's workplace, technical skills are not enough. An employer needs an employee who is honest and communicates well. Also important are traits of initiative, integrity and compassion. Call it emotional intelligence or just plain common sense, but some employers are realizing the importance of these qualities above technical skill.

2. CONDUCT MORE THAN ONE INTERVIEW BEFORE HIRING

Several interviews with different people may take extra time but in comparison to a lengthy legal battle, the choice is obvious.

3. CONDUCT PROPER REFERENCE CHECKS

Hostile employees usually leave behind a trail of litigation. Former employers can provide important insights on the job applicant's skills, personality and ability to get along with co-workers. It is not uncommon that applicants exaggerate their skills and at the same time "overlook" listing the name of an employer that they have either departed from on bad terms or commenced litigation against. Pay serious attention to any "gaps" in the chronology of employment.

4. IMPLEMENT A PROBATION TERM

The purpose of a probation term is to allow the employer to assess the employee prior to confirming full-time employment status. In the event that the employee proves to be incompatible with the corporate structure, or where performance standards are not met, the employer can usually terminate with little or no choice or payment in lieu of notice. Most probation terms are only three months in duration, but they can be longer. Six months is not unusual and, in any event, a shorter probationary term can be extended, depending on the wording of the term.

5. DOCUMENT PERFORMANCE OR ATTITUDE PROBLEMS AS THEY OCCUR

Where obvious problems with performance or attitude arise, verbal communication is rarely sufficient when dealing with a hostile employee. Clearly written communication is necessary, with a specific warning of possible termination in the event there is no consistent improvement. Always be sure to provide the employee with a copy of the written reprimand.

6. CONDUCT ALL MEETINGS WITH HOSTILE EMPLOYEES WITH A COMPANY WITNESS PRESENT

Even with clearly written documentation provided to the employee, if a meeting is held just between the employee and a representative of the company, there is a strong likelihood that the hostile employee will dispute what was actually discussed at the meeting. Have a witness record what is said during the meeting.

7. CONSIDER WHETHER THERE ARE ANY EXTENUATING CIRCUMSTANCES CAUSING THE EMPLOYEE'S BEHAVIOUR

In some cases, substance abuse, a medical problem or a personal life crisis is the cause of the employee's unreasonable conduct and it can be reasonably expected that, with assistance, the employee will resume normal behaviour.

8. TERMINATE EARLY IF CIRCUMSTANCES WARRANT DISMISSAL

If common sense tells you that you are dealing with a hostile employee, recognize it and deal with the problem promptly. Avoid transferring the employee to another department. Document the occurrences and consider dismissal if there are no signs of improvement. Rarely do these situations change for the better, and the longer it continues, the greater the risk for the company and to other employees.

18

Workplace Disputes Fuel Retention Problems

1. Workplace Harassment
2. Failure to Comply with Statutory Obligations
3. Poor Hiring Practices
4. Harsh Treatment at the Time of Departure
5. The Duty to Accommodate
6. Constructive Dismissal
7. Create Workplace Policies

If you ask any workplace guru about what an employer needs to do in order to improve retention, the answer usually involves a discussion about showing the employee that he or she is respected and a dialogue about worklife balance or incentive compensation.

If you ask an employment lawyer about retention, the answer will definitely be different and will most likely focus on employer practices that discourage loyalty and that make retention more challenging.

Retention is definitely an important issue for most employers. The financial cost and adverse effects on productivity and on employee morale, are just some of the reasons "turnover" is a bad word for most companies.

The workforce is less committed to their employer and are generally more willing to move to a different company for financial or lifestyle reasons. But in many cases, employers are to blame for an employee's lack of loyalty and willingness to move, which ultimately can create a larger retention issue for the employer. So what are some of the most obvious workplace disputes that cause retention issues? What should you do to avoid these issues?

The top seven workplace disputes to avoid are discussed below.

1. WORKPLACE HARASSMENT

Workplace harassment can poison the working environment to the point where employees lose respect for management and for the company, and where employees become either unable or unwilling to report to work. Whether the type of harassment involves sex, race, disability or involves bullying by a manager or a co-worker, it can have a devastating impact on the victim and on the co-workers who are involved directly as witnesses or indirectly as observers. Obviously, a victim of harassment will lose respect and loyalty for the company. However, the entire workforce can be adversely affected where senior management is involved, where the company has condoned the behaviour or failed to take steps to prevent the conduct from reoccurring.

Employers need to be proactive to avoid this type of conduct in the workplace. As an employer you need to have a workplace harassment policy, and all employees, including managers, should receive training on the policy. Any complaints must be responded to promptly.

When a complaint is received it is important, in most cases, to conduct an independent investigation and to take appropriate corrective action. As an employer, you should be willing to repeat harassment training or redistribute the harassment policy on a regular basis.

2. FAILURE TO COMPLY WITH STATUTORY OBLIGATIONS

Employers that ignore statutory obligations under the *Occupational Health & Safety Act* and the *Employment Standards Act* that result in either injury to their employees or in unlawful pay practices will also face hiring and retention challenges.

Few employees would overlook dangerous work conditions in order to stay employed. Fatalities or serious injuries at the workplace are emotionally devastating for everyone at the workplace. Employers need to ensure the safety of their workplace, along with proper supervision at all times.

Equally, employees are less willing to accept employment practices that result in lower wages, such as failure to pay holiday pay, vacation pay or overtime pay. Failure by an employer to comply with minimum statutory obligations under the *Employment Standards Act* is unlawful and will not engender loyalty among your employees. It can also lead to litigation with the Ministry of Labour, resulting in significant payment orders and penalties.

3. POOR HIRING PRACTICES

Failure to use a proper hiring letter or contract can create serious problems for the employer at the time of termination. Short-term employees are still entitled to notice and may even be entitled to rely on their length of service at their previous job when calculating their entitlement to reasonable notice if they are fired by your company.

A well-thought-out letter of hire can avoid significant acrimony over employment status, compensation and termination issues. Although a more formal and lengthy written contract can adequately address more issues, a properly detailed hire letter may suffice. By far the greatest number of disputes that arise from the initial hiring relate to the terms with respect to probationary status, compensation in the form of bonuses or incentive pay and termination/resignation obligations. Clarity around these issues can avoid unnecessary departures or disputes arising from a termination or resignation. It is far more prudent to negotiate employment terms at the commencement of the relationship as opposed to after a dispute arises.

4. HARSH TREATMENT AT THE TIME OF DEPARTURE

A lot can be learned about an employer's human resources practices by how they treat their employees at the time of departure. Although the protocol about how to treat a departing employee may vary depending on the circumstances of the departure, an employer should always treat the employee professionally, honestly and with respect.

Co-workers who observe their employer engaging in unfair treatment, such as bad-mouthing the employee to co-workers or refusing to pay outstanding wages, will form a negative opinion about their employer.

Employers should have a written policy that states how to conduct a termination interview or how to deal with a resignation, as well as a clear practice on the appropriate steps to follow in each case. Although every termination or resignation is different and as a result may require a modified approach, using a standardized, well-organized plan will limit the risks associated with a termination or resignation.

5. THE DUTY TO ACCOMMODATE

Perhaps the most frequent issue facing employers today is the duty to accommodate employees with a disability. Courts have consistently expressed the view that employers must treat employees fairly and with respect during the accommodation process. Employers will seldom be able to prove undue hardship or cause during the accommodation process. Courts have recognized the inherent vulnerability of employees who are being terminated while suffering from a disability. With an aging workforce and a likely increase in the frequency of disability claims, it is imperative that employers develop an accommodation policy that recognizes and accepts the obligation to accommodate an employee to the point of undue hardship and that allows for flexibility and communication throughout the accommodation process.

6. CONSTRUCTIVE DISMISSAL

Employers are increasingly responding to competition by reorganizing their workforce and redistributing job duties. Regrettably, employees still perceive that they have a right to their jobs and to the duties attached to their jobs. Courts have recognized an employer's need for flexibility when it comes to organizing its work functions and as a result, constructive dismissal claims are more difficult for the employee to sustain.

However, if employers want more flexibility and want to reduce the risks that are related to job changes and reorganization, employers should reserve the right to make unilateral changes in the written employment contract or be willing to provide the employee with reasonable notice of any change to a material term of the contract. Employees generally do not like change; however, employers that embrace a strategic approach to introducing changes to the terms of employment, including a sound communication strategy, will avoid some of the risks associated with constructive dismissal claims.

7. CREATE WORKPLACE POLICIES

Employers should use policies as a means of communicating to their employees about their rights and obligations. Policies should be incorporated into the terms of the employee's employment contract, be written in plain English and should be repeatedly distributed, if appropriate.

Sound corporate policies will assist the employer to manage expectations flowing between the employer and the employee. The effect of well-drafted corporate policies will minimize the risks associated with the inconsistent exercise of management discretion while at the same time provide greater certainty for employees.

19

EMPLOYEES IN CRISIS: HOW TO DEAL WITH A SUICIDAL OR UNSTABLE EMPLOYEE

1. Take it Seriously
2. Remove the Individual From the Workplace
3. Secure the Workplace
4. Provide Assistance

In an ideal world, a workplace is a place of cooperation, productivity and professionalism. Employees bring their skills and ambition to the office and check their personal problems at the door. Of course, the reality is that people are occasionally overwhelmed by issues in their home life and cannot prevent these concerns from seeping into their workplace behaviour. This is particularly true when the employee is suffering from mental illness. Although many see mental illness as a rare or extraordinary occurrence, approximately 20 per cent of all Canadians will suffer from mental illness at least once in their lives. (See Health Canada, *A Report on Mental Illnesses in Canada*, Ottawa, Canada, 2002. http://www.phacaspc.gc.ca/publicat/miic-mmac/pdf/men_ill_e.pdf, p. 15.) As a result, employers need to know how to recognize and accommodate mental illness in the workplace, especially when an employee reaches a crisis point.

If an employee's behaviour gives you a reasonable basis to believe that the employee is not fit to work because of a mental illness, it is your right – and perhaps your responsibility – to advise the employee that you have serious concerns about his or her ability to perform the essential functions of his or her position and that the employee should see his or her physician and refrain from returning to the workplace until the employee has obtained a medical note clearing him or her for work. If necessary, arrange for an independent medical assessment.

On rare occasions, the issue may present itself in a more urgent manner. Stress, burnout, an unexpected death in the family or the sudden manifestation of a mood disorder can all result in aggressive or self-destructive behaviour in the workplace. Unfortunately, these episodes are often impossible to foresee and can be dangerous for both the ill employee and his or her co-workers. So how should you respond when faced with a critical situation like a threat of suicide or violence?

1. TAKE IT SERIOUSLY

Contrary to popular belief, people do not threaten to kill themselves just to get attention. Every mention of suicide or self-harm should be treated as an urgent matter. Similarly, threats of violence against co-workers, supervisors or members of the public need to be dealt with firmly and immediately. Educate your employees about the limits of acceptable workplace behaviour. Make sure they know that they can and should report any such incidents to their supervisor or to human resources.

2. REMOVE THE INDIVIDUAL FROM THE WORKPLACE

Employers are obligated to create and maintain a safe workplace for their employees. If you have reason to believe that your employees are in jeopardy, it is your responsibility to take steps to protect them. A suicidal employee poses a serious risk to himself or herself and to others. The employee should be asked to leave the workplace immediately. Where necessary, consider involving the police or health-care workers.

3. SECURE THE WORKPLACE

It is advisable to request that the disturbed employee return any keys, pass cards or access codes that would allow the employee to re-enter the workplace. Clearly communicate to the employee that he or she is not permitted to return to work until he or she is cleared to do so by an appropriate medical professional. If the employee has threatened his or her co-workers with violence, consider improving protective measures such as surveillance cameras or security guards.

4. PROVIDE ASSISTANCE

Many employers have an employee and family assistance program that provide support and counselling to the suicidal or distraught employee. If your company provides such a program, it should be offered to the employee as soon as possible. If your company does not have an employee assistance program (EAP), you may consider helping the employee find an appropriate medical professional.

Crisis management is not the end point of dealing with an employee who is suffering from mental illness. Like any other disabled employee, a mentally ill employee must be accommodated to the point of undue hardship. More than any other type of disability, mental illness requires that the employer work closely with the employee and medical professionals to reintegrate the disabled employee into the workplace. It is advisable to obtain a written authorization from the employee giving you information regarding the employee's diagnosis, symptoms, treatment and prognosis, as this will allow you to spot any red flags and intervene before the employee reaches a crisis situation again. When it is time to return the employee to the workplace, you may consider having the employee sign a reinstatement agreement that confirms the employee will continue to receive medical assistance or take medication until the employee's physician advises him or her to stop and that, should the employee cease treatment against medical advice, the employee will face immediate dismissal.

As with any sort of crisis management, training is the key to preventing or minimizing the occurrence of suicidal or violent behaviour in the workplace. Human resources staff should make an effort to educate employees about employee assistance programs and ensure that each employee has contact information for the program's confidential counselling services. Expectations regarding appropriate workplace behaviour should be clearly communicated – preferably in your employee handbook – and employees should be told that they are expected to report any inappropriate incidents to their supervisors or to human resources. Supervisors and managers should receive training about how to deal with unstable employees and should also be encouraged to be observant of employee behaviour. A supervisor who has a good relationship with the employees under his or her watch will be more likely to observe unusual or troubling behaviour at an early stage, when prevention is still possible.

20

BUSINESS, PLEASURE OR BOTH? COMPANY RETREATS AND COMPENSATION ISSUES

Company retreats can provide many benefits to employers. They often encourage bonding between employees, strengthen loyalty to the company and provide opportunities for intensive training. They can also serve as a "thank you" gesture to hard-working employees. However, company retreats also pose several unique challenges, particularly in the area of employee compensation – both during the employment relationship and after termination.

While the individual is still employed, there is the challenge of properly accounting for the reward. The Canada Revenue Agency has issued a policy statement to the effect that "hospitality rewards" such as lunches and trips that are given to employees as thanks or recognition for a job well-done are a taxable benefit to the employee and must be reflected in payroll records. Most employers seek to offset the potential tax consequences to the employee by grossing up the value of the trip and absorbing the resulting tax.

Another significant issue is accounting for the value of the trip or retreat at the time of termination. Consider the following scenario: one of your employees resigns to accept another opportunity and, following his or her resignation, sends a letter advising that he or she still intends to attend the company retreat. The retreat is scheduled to take place in a tropical location and is made available to the company's top sales performers. The former employee argues that he or she has qualified for the trip and is entitled to either attend or receive the value in cash, notwithstanding the fact that the employee had resigned from his or her employment. Your company sees the primary function of the retreat as an opportunity to provide additional training and mentorship to top performers, not as compensation for achieving certain sales benchmarks. Unfortunately, you do not have a written policy setting out the nature and purpose of the trip. Management refuses the former employee's request and the company is served with a statement of claim seeking the grossed up value of the retreat.

So what are the merits of the former employee's claim? Is the employee actually entitled to compensation for the lost opportunity to take the trip? The answer may surprise you. Because your policy did not specifically state that the retreat was a work event designed to train and mentor employees and, further, because achieving certain sales goals is a prerequisite for attendance, the employee has a strong case for the fact that the trip was a bonus rather than a work seminar. Courts in Ontario have held that such work-related trips can constitute an integral part of an employee's compensation, even where there is a policy that states that a person must be an employee at the time of the event in order to attend.

Fortunately, there are some practical steps you can take in order to minimize your company's risk with respect to such retreats and vacations seminars. First, have a concise and unambiguous written policy that deals with the company retreat. This policy should clearly state the preconditions for attendance, as well as the purpose of the event. Be sure to describe the retreat as a company event that is intended to provide employees with training and mentorship opportunities. Second, ensure that your employees have been provided with a current copy of your written policy, as it can only be binding upon them if they have been made aware of its terms. Third, when planning the retreat, take steps to make it a meaningful work experience. Schedule seminars that provide training, mentorship or opportunities for problem-solving. If you are going to take the position that it is a work event, it should be planned and executed as such. Attendance at seminars and meetings should be mandatory.

Your written policy should also make it apparent that the opportunity to attend the retreat in the first place is a privilege, not a right. It should clearly state that the scheduling, value, duration and nature of the retreat is entirely within your discretion and may be cancelled at any time and for any reason. Reserve the right to direct employees not to attend wherever appropriate. Finally, the policy should explicitly state that employees who resign or whose employment is terminated for any reason prior to the date of the retreat are not permitted to attend, nor are they entitled to any compensation for the lost trip.

Company retreats have the potential to foster closer ties between employers and employees and can encourage camaraderie and creativity in the workforce. However, as with nearly everything in the workplace, human resources professionals and employers must plan carefully in order to avoid unexpected risk.

21

OVERTIME ISSUES IN YOUR WORKPLACE: HOW TO PREVENT UNFORESEEN CLAIMS FOR OVERTIME PAY

The issue of hours of work and overtime gained prominence when Ontario revamped its requirements for employees working in excess of the statutory maximum. Employers were required to re-examine their practices regarding overtime and hours of work in order to comply with the legislative changes to the *Employment Standards Act, 2000*, S.O. 2000, c. 41 (the "ESA"), which took effect on March 1, 2005.

Perhaps because of the heightened awareness surrounding the issue, many employment lawyers' clients have seen a rise in claims for unpaid overtime hours. In most of these claims, the clients were not even aware that the employee in question considered himself or herself to be entitled to overtime pay, or that the employee had been spending so many hours at work. Overtime claims are often for relatively large sums and are particularly common in wrongful dismissal claims, where there is no employment relationship left to salvage. Most importantly, overtime claims are difficult to defend. The employer often has no documentary or anecdotal evidence to counter the employee's account of hours worked. So how can you protect your company from surprise claims for outstanding overtime pay?

First, know the legislation. The ESA provides that employees who work more than 44 hours in each week are entitled to overtime pay in the amount of 1.5 times their regular rate of pay. The regulations to the ESA provide that certain employees are exempt from the overtime provisions of the Act. Most notably, an employee whose work is managerial in character and who may perform non-managerial tasks on an irregular basis is not entitled to overtime pay.

The ESA, does not explain what constitutes managerial responsibility but case law indicates that the title of "manager" is not sufficient to prevent entitlement to overtime pay. The employee must have responsibility for such areas as hiring and firing, business planning, administration and discipline. The fact that the employee also performs some non-managerial tasks does not automatically mean that the employee is no longer exempt but it will make it more difficult for the employer to argue that the employee should not receive overtime pay.

Some employers mistakenly believe that employees who receive an annual salary are not entitled to overtime pay. Whether or not an employee is entitled to overtime pay is based only on the employee's duties and responsibilities. Where an employee is not paid on an hourly basis, the employer must calculate the employee's effective hourly rate (based on 44 hours per week), and then provide the employee with 1.5 times that rate for each hour of overtime.

Another important step toward protecting your company is to have a system for monitoring and authorizing employees' hours of work. Employment agreements and any relevant human resources policies should state that employees are not permitted to work overtime unless it is pre-authorized. Employees should also be informed that working unauthorized overtime could result in discipline.

In addition, all supervisors should be thoroughly briefed about the company's policy on overtime and hours of work. Schedules should be prepared regularly and in a consistent manner. Wherever possible, it is advisable to have each employee sign off on the weekly schedule, acknowledging that it is an accurate reflection of the hours the employee worked. Supervisors should keep a close eye on employees' hours of work and immediately raise concerns regarding excessive hours. It may even be necessary to have the supervisor sweep the premises at closing time and usher out any lingering employees.

It is important to note that employees are entitled to collect overtime pay for all hours "worked" in excess of the statutory maximum. The ESA, states that work is considered to be completed on the employer's behalf when the work is, in fact, performed - even if the employment contract limits an employee's hours of work. Practically speaking, this means that the employer must pay the employee for every hour spent at work - whether or not the employee had permission to be there.

Of course, employees must satisfy the Employment Standards Branch or court that they actually worked the hours claimed. To do so, employees are typically forced to rely on their memories, diaries, calendars or the recollections of co-workers. These sources can be faulty and are vulnerable to attacks on credibility. For security reasons, many workplaces now have electronic pass cards. These pass cards permit employers to track employees' movements, and can be a valuable tool in assessing claims for overtime pay. However, there is no reason to wait until you receive a claim to make use of the tracking features of your pass card system. Make it a practice to check the logs to see who is leaving work later than they should be or spending long hours in the office. Be particularly mindful of employees who come in on their days off.

Although these measures may seem overly cautious, an overtime claim is an easy way for an employee or former employee to collect from their employer. Even though claims for unpaid wages under the ESA, are limited to $10,000 and must be made within two years, a claim for outstanding overtime in a civil case can be much higher because courts usually reject the limitations in the legislation. Your best protection is to be aware of the overtime issue and to ensure that your supervisors, who have the most and best access to employees, are actively enforcing company policy.

22

REQUESTS FOR MEDICAL INFORMATION MUST RESPECT PRIVACY

A decision of the Ontario Divisional Court has highlighted the judiciary's unwillingness to grant employers unfettered access to their employees' medical information, even when employees are returning from a medical leave of absence. Indeed, the Court has held that where an employer's request is broad or invasive, the employee is entitled to withhold information. Employers must consider this decision as imposing a limit on their ability to subject their employees to unwarranted questions concerning health.

In *Ontario Nurses' Assn. v. St. Joseph's Health Centre*, [2005] O.J. No. 2874 (Ont. Div. Ct.), the Court was asked to determine the extent to which an employer could demand a medical assessment of an employee's fitness to return to work after medical leave. In January 2001, the employee, a registered nurse, took a leave from work at St. Joseph's Health Centre to undergo gynecological surgery. Since May 2001, she had been healthy and willing to return to work without restriction.

The Health Centre required the employee to fill out a form that authorized the release of information from her physician, and required her to provide other specific medical information. The employee did not consent to this release, on the basis that the Health Centre's demands invaded her privacy. In turn, the Health Centre refused to permit the employee to return to work.

The matter was taken to arbitration pursuant to a collective agreement. The arbitrator, without any information concerning the precise reasons for the employee's medical absence, ordered that she respond to the questions. A second arbitration was subsequently required to determine whether the employee answered all of the questions put to her. The arbitrator found that she did not. Although the arbitrator noted that the employee's absence was a result of a physical ailment, he ordered the employee to answer two outstanding questions that would have required the employee to submit to an extensive mental fitness examination by a third party psychologist or psychiatrist. The employee sought judicial review of the arbitrator's second decision.

Justice Lane, for the majority, held, at para. 20, that "employers are entitled to seek medical information to ensure a returning employee is able to return to work safely and poses no hazard to others." An employee has an initial obligation to present some brief information from the doctor declaring the employee's fitness to return. If the employer has "reasonable grounds" to believe that the employee's medical condition presents a danger to herself or others, additional information can be requested with an explanation to the employee. The request must be related to the reasons for absence, and cannot be a broad inquiry with respect to health.

Justice Lane also stated, at para. 21, that "a psychiatric or psychological examination is a highly intrusive and sensitive procedure and should only be available to employers in cases where the necessity for it has been firmly established." Where the employee was concerned, the outstanding questions referred to mental health and not physical fitness. By the time of the second arbitration, it was clear that the reasons for the employee's absence related to physical and not mental health issues, and, as such, at para. 22, "there [was] no basis in evidence supporting a reasonable and probable ground for believing that the condition which led to the absence had any potential psychiatric or psychological consequences for the [employee]'s ability to perform her job." Thus, no psychological or psychiatric information or examination was appropriate.

In this context, Justice Lane found that the arbitrator made two errors when he ordered the remaining questions to be answered. The first error was that he did not analyze the known facts and determine why the questions were still appropriate when the employee's mental health was never at issue. Secondly, the arbitrator failed to appreciate that the questions would have required the employee to submit to a third party psychological assessment, and not simply an examination from the physician with whom she was acquainted. This was an unwarranted escalation.

Having allowed the application for judicial review, Justice Lane remitted to the arbitrator the task of fixing the employee's entitlement to compensation for being kept out of the work.

This case stands for the proposition that an employer may not request that an employee answer far-reaching health-related questions when an employee returns to work from leave. A request for a mental diagnosis to determine fitness to return to work is wholly inappropriate, especially when the reason for the medical absence was known and did not implicate the employee's mental or emotional state. While the employer is entitled to seek medical justification as to fitness, the employer's questions must directly pertain to the medical reason for the leave, and may not touch upon unrelated health matters.

23

IDENTIFYING AND MANAGING DISABILITY FRAUD

1. Seek Legal Advice
2. Conduct a Proper Investigation
3. Review Company Policies
4. Keep Communicating
5. Use Surveillance Very Cautiously

As human resources professionals, you know that managing and minimizing absenteeism has always been a priority for employers. One of the most complex challenges to minimizing absenteeism is employee disability fraud. Disability fraud refers to a situation where an employee falsely claims a workplace injury or disability. It can also refer to a scenario where an employee initially suffers a genuine injury or illness but then malingers, refusing appropriate treatment and staying out of the workplace for longer than is necessary.

Managing absenteeism due to disability is a tricky proposition. Many managers freeze when confronted with anything other than a very straightforward disability issue. There are good reasons to be wary. Courts and human rights commissions in Canada are very hard on employers who put undue pressure on ill employees to return to the workplace. *Keays v. Honda Canada Inc.*, [2005] O.J. No. 1145 (Ont. S.C.J.), varied *Honda Canada Inc. v. Keays* [2008] S.C.J. No. 40 (S.C.C), is a particularly well-known example of an employer faced with an employee with chronic illness and absenteeism. The Supreme Court of Canada recognized that employers have the right to expect regular attendance and the right to information regarding the employee's condition where the employee is chronically absent. There are many other court decisions, however, in which an employer has suffered serious consequences for mismanaging a disability issue. So what can you do if you suspect that your employee has filed a false claim?

1. SEEK LEGAL ADVICE

If it is an alleged workplace injury that you are dealing with, it is advisable to consult a lawyer who specializes in workers' compensation cases and find out what documentation needs to be filed with the provincial workers' compensation board or agency and how to file your objection. If the alleged disability arises from a non-workplace injury, then your focus will be on determining whether a fraudulent claim can be proven.

2. CONDUCT A PROPER INVESTIGATION

So how should you proceed? In a word, cautiously. Avoid making a quick decision or jumping to conclusions. You must do a proper investigation. Although filing a false claim for sick pay or disability benefits is akin to theft or dishonesty, dismissing an employee who has a *bona fide* disability can result in serious legal liability. It is essential that you are in a position to justify any such termination with objective proof of fraud.

3. REVIEW COMPANY POLICIES

Always review the provisions of your company's policy or practice manual on handling disability claims. If your company allows employees to leave work without any confirmation of illness or to re-enter the workplace without adequate medical documentation confirming the illness, you have established a precedent that employees are not necessarily required to support sick days with medical notes. This will make it much more difficult for you to argue that your employee's failure to adequately support the employee's time off for illness is just cause for dismissal.

Your company should have a clear policy with respect to leaving the workplace, calling in sick and returning to work after an illness. Requesting satisfactory medical evidence is always a good idea. The medical evidence should confirm the date the employee was seen by the doctor, the employee's prognosis and the time required for recovery. Having your employee sign a prior written authorization to allow you to communicate directly with his or her doctor is also helpful. In addition to having a clear policy in place, your company should also have a system for tracking employee absenteeism. A pattern of absenteeism can often provide evidence of a false claim.

4. KEEP COMMUNICATING

While an employee is off work due to disability, keep the lines of communication open. The level of communication that is appropriate may vary depending on the nature of the illness. Advise the employee that the company cares about him or her and wants to be kept updated about the employee's prognosis. You should also be clear that it is important to you that employees attend regularly at work unless they are unable to do so due to sickness or other urgent situations. It is advisable to document all of your conversations with the employee regarding his or her absence. If there are issues regarding the employee's credibility or inconsistencies in his or her claims, these notes will be very useful.

5. USE SURVEILLANCE VERY CAUTIOUSLY

Surveillance is an extraordinary measure and should be used sparingly. Even though the employee would only be monitored while he or she is out in public, surveillance is likely to be viewed by the courts as an intrusive action. Therefore, you should always be prepared to demonstrate that you had reasonable suspicion of fraud before ordering surveillance. Surveillance is also problematic because it can invite employers and managers to substitute their own judgment for that of the employee's doctor. If you see an allegedly disabled employee engage in what looks like heavy lifting, you may be tempted to assume that the employee is lying about his or her back problem. In reality, you may have very little information about the employee's limitations or even the object the employee is moving (not all large objects are heavy). Consider having a physician review any surveillance before forming an opinion about whether or not the activities recorded are inconsistent with the employee's alleged disability.

Before any decision is made, you must provide the employee with an opportunity to respond to your suspicions. This should be in the form of a face-to-face meeting and you must notify the employee of any facts you are relying on to support your allegations. Be prepared to postpone termination or take it off the table entirely if you receive a reasonable explanation or even an expression of remorse. You should always consider possible mitigating factors such as the employee's length of service, absenteeism record, position with the company or family circumstances. Occasionally, mental health issues may be in play. Feigning disability or failing to justify absence from work could be a manifestation of depression or serious issues in the employee's home. Employers should be careful not to terminate employment when the employee is in an exceptionally vulnerable situation.

If you do decide to proceed with termination, the termination should be for just cause. To minimize risk, you may wish to consider providing a "without prejudice" payment in exchange for the employee executing a release in favour of your company. The release should contain an express acknowledgement by the employee that there has been no violation of the employee's statutory rights.

Disability fraud is uncommon. However, since it can be very expensive it is important to incorporate fraud detection strategies into your disability management practices. The key is to approach potential disability fraud cases with caution and careful attention to detail. By properly managing this challenge, you can avoid the costly consequences of wrongfully terminating an employee who suffers from a legitimate disability.

24

VIDEO SURVEILLANCE AND BIOMETRICS IN THE WORKPLACE: BALANCING SECURITY WITH PRIVACY AND RELIGIOUS INTERESTS

1. Provide Employees With Notice
2. Prove There is a Legitimate Objective
3. Restrict the Scope of Surveillance
4. Limit the Use of Surveillance Records
5. Limit Retention and Access
6. Accommodate Religious Beliefs

We all know that ensuring the safety and security of the workplace is essential for all employers. The difficulty for employers comes in finding ways to achieve this objective in an efficient and cost-effective manner. Many different forms of security measures are available. Hired security guards are highly visible deterrents to unauthorized access and theft, but can be prohibitively expensive. Pass card systems are readily available, but can be manipulated or breached by wrongdoers with the technical know-how.

In recent years, many employers have turned to more advanced technologies to satisfy safety and security needs. Video surveillance is a common tool used by employers. While video surveillance has been available for many years, the more recent introduction of digital technology has made video surveillance cheaper and more secure, and therefore more accessible to many employers. Digital video surveillance can have a significant deterrent effect, and most importantly it can record and store massive amounts of video footage that can be later relied upon to investigate a security or safety-related workplace incident.

Some employers have also introduced biometric scanning technologies to limit and track access to the workplace. Biometric scanners digitally scan unique physical characteristics (examples include a person's iris, fingerprint or hand geometry) and therefore can limit access to the workplace to only those authorized persons whose unique physical characteristics are stored in the company's computer system.

Employers do not, however, have an unfettered right to use video surveillance and biometric scanning as they see fit. The use of these technologies involves the collection and storage of employees' personal information, which raises issues of both employee privacy and, perhaps surprisingly, religious interests. The passage of the federal *Personal Information Protection and Electronic Documents Act* in 2004 (cited as S.C. 2000, c. 5), places limits on employers' collection and use of employee information. Furthermore, both the courts and labour arbitrators have recognized that employees have workplace privacy and religious interests that compete with, and therefore must be balanced against, the employer's use of mechanisms to control and supervise the workplace.

There is no easy formula for determining what steps an employer must take to balance employee privacy and religious interests with greater workplace safety through the use of these technologies. Each situation will turn on the particular circumstances, and therefore employers should seek professional legal advice. However, the following general principles have been considered by courts and labour arbitrators and offer a useful starting point for employers thinking of introducing video surveillance or biometric technologies in the workplace:

1. PROVIDE EMPLOYEES WITH NOTICE

Covertly using surveillance technologies without notice to employees is generally deemed to be unreasonable except in cases of illegal activity (*e.g.*, employee fraud). Providing advance notice, particularly in the unionized workplace, helps allay employee fears associated with surveillance and biometric systems and can promote meaningful and informed discussions between management and employees regarding how the new system can be implemented to minimize the impact on employee privacy or religious interests.

2. PROVE THERE IS A LEGITIMATE OBJECTIVE

Employers should be prepared to provide proof that the surveillance technology is being used to further a legitimate objective. That means if the stated objective is to deter theft or ensure only authorized access to the workplace, there should be proof that theft is actually a problem or that there is a serious risk of harm if unauthorized persons gain access to the workplace.

3. RESTRICT THE SCOPE OF SURVEILLANCE

The use of direct and constant surveillance of employees in the workplace has been characterized as "workplace spying" and is generally considered unreasonable. The proper balance between privacy and security is often struck by limiting video surveillance to fixed positions that promote the employer's objective (*e.g.*, placing video surveillance or biometric scanners only at entrance and exit points to ensure authorized access to the workplace, or placing video surveillance only in storage facilities to deter theft).

4. LIMIT THE USE OF SURVEILLANCE RECORDS

Systematically reviewing surveillance recordings to try to "find" problems is usually frowned upon. Generally speaking, employers should only review surveillance recordings when investigating particular workplace incidents.

5. LIMIT RETENTION AND ACCESS

Since both video surveillance and biometric data often contain sensitive information about individual employees, such data should be kept secured at all times and access should be limited to only a few members of management. The retention of video recordings should be limited in time to allow for the investigating of recent incidents, and should thereafter be destroyed. Biometric data should not be retained after termination of employment.

6. ACCOMMODATE RELIGIOUS BELIEFS

Employers should explore alternatives to biometric scanning systems for those employees who object to their usage on religious grounds. In *407 ETR Concession Co. v. C.A.W. Canada, Local 414*, [2007] O.L.A.A. No. 34, several employees were terminated for refusing to enrol in a biometric hand identification system introduced by the employer to enhance security in the workplace. The labour arbitrator found that the terminated employees sincerely believed that if they submitted to biometric scanning they would be tainted with the "mark of the beast", risking their damnation. The employer's failure to accommodate such beliefs was held to violate human rights legislation. In such circumstances, employers should explore alternatives to accommodate these religious beliefs, such as a pass card access system used in conjunction with the biometric system.

25

COURT WEIGHS PERIODIC CRIMINAL RECORD CHECKS

It has become common practice for many employers to require job applicants to agree to a criminal record check before starting a new job. Requesting a criminal record check is generally seen as reasonable because the employer is attempting to assess the character and trustworthiness of a job applicant who is, for all intents and purposes, a stranger.

Some employers, however, go a step further and require their employees to agree to periodic criminal checks throughout the employment relationship. A recent court decision in a case between the City of Ottawa and the Ottawa Professional Firefighters union indicates that this practice may unreasonably infringe on employee privacy rights.

In that case, the City of Ottawa implemented a policy requiring all of its firefighters to consent to a criminal record check every three years. The policy stated that failure to consent would lead to discipline up to and including dismissal. The union challenged the policy, alleging that it unreasonably infringed on firefighters' privacy rights under the *Municipal Freedom of Information and Protection of Privacy Act*, R.S.O. 1990, c. M.56 ("MFIPPA"). The arbitrator agreed with the union and concluded that the policy was unreasonable.

The arbitrator pointed out that employees have a right under the MFIPPA to keep information regarding their criminal history private unless they give written consent to its release. The arbitrator held that it may be reasonable to oblige an employee to consent to periodic criminal checks where the employee's position is safety or security-sensitive: for example, where the job requires an employee to work with vulnerable clients, such as young children or persons with disabilities, or where the employer's operations require tight security, such as at a police department, an airport or a bank. The arbitrator concluded that there was insufficient evidence to conclude that the firefighter job was so safety or security sensitive to justify forcing firefighters to waive their privacy rights every three years.

There are two lessons to be learned from this case. First, an employer should carefully select the classes of employees it wishes to subject to ongoing background checks, and should be prepared to provide sufficient evidence that the employees selected occupy safety or security sensitive positions. Second, the judicial system is becoming increasingly sensitive to protecting employee privacy. Some judges have permitted employees to bring lawsuits against their employers to recover damages for invasion of privacy. In this environment, it is therefore generally wise for an employer to seek consent before trying to obtain personal information about its employees.

PART THREE

Ending the Employment Relationship

26

A New Meaning for "Just Cause"

One of the more interesting cases on just cause was brought to light in 2006. In *Whitehouse v. RBC Dominion Securities Inc.*, [2006] A.J. No. 667 (Alta. Q.B.), an Alberta Court found that RBC had just cause for dismissing James Whitehouse ("Whitehouse") after it was discovered that Whitehouse had drunkenly brought a prostitute into the office after business hours. Whitehouse brought an action for damages arising from wrongful dismissal. RBC counterclaimed for damages to its reputation.

At the time of dismissal, Whitehouse was 51 years old and held the position of vice-president and investment advisor with RBC. Prior to his dismissal, Whitehouse had worked for RBC for 16 years. Whitehouse managed $125 million of his clients' capital and earned $424,500 in commissions in the year before his termination. On January 22, 2004, Whitehouse was advised that he was being terminated for cause.

On January 20, 2004, Whitehouse had been out drinking heavily when he went looking for a prostitute and met a woman named Cassandra Stolarchuk ("Stolarchuk"). Whitehouse paid Stolarchuk a portion of the agreed price of $200 up front. At his suggestion, the two travelled by taxi to his office in the Canada Trust Tower in downtown Calgary, arriving just before 10:30 p.m. Whitehouse used his pass card to enter the building and to access the elevator to get to the 16th floor where RBC had their offices. Stolarchuk used the washroom located in the lobby, where she consumed some cocaine, and then was led into the interior offices by Whitehouse. At some point while the two were in the interior offices, they had a dispute over the payment of the balance owed to Stolarchuk. According to Whitehouse, the services contracted for were not performed. Whitehouse demanded that Stolarchuk leave the building and Stolarchuk demanded that Whitehouse pay her the balance before she would leave. Whitehouse testified that as no services had been gained, he was disinclined to pay the balance. The result was that they returned to the lobby area and Whitehouse left the building, leaving Stolarchuk behind. At this point, Stolarchuk would have had access to any files or papers on the reception desk or in the file cabinet behind it. Stolarchuk used her time in the lobby to leave a message, recorded at 10:41 p.m., on another phone in the office. That message was as follows, at para. 9:

> Hi, I don't know what time it is at night, but I'm here in your RBC Investment offices, RBC Canadian Securities Incorporated. A man who works in your office named Bill brought me up here. I'm a hooker from 3rd Avenue and he picked me up in a taxi and brought me up here to do me in his office. He's not paying me the rest of my money, so therefore he's left me in your building at night. Your phones say night on them in here. I don't know where he is. I don't know how to get out. He's left me up here in the office building. So I'm sure you'll have many questions for me tomorrow. You can call me at 889-1602. My name is Cassandra. And I'm not joking around about this.

At some point after leaving this message, Stolarchuk left the premises without seeing Whitehouse again.

The next day, news of the incident spread rapidly around the bank. Stolarchuk also paid a visit to the bank in order to collect the balance allegedly owed to her by Whitehouse. By this time, the branch manager and Whitehouse's immediate supervisor were setting up a meeting with Whitehouse. In this meeting, Whitehouse denied having brought a prostitute into the office until it was revealed to him that there was videotape evidence of the incident. Shortly after this admission, Whitehouse was terminated for cause and escorted out of the building. On his way out, the branch manager suggested to Whitehouse that he call Stolarchuk and pay her. If she continued to visit the offices, the bank would give her Whitehouse's home telephone number. At some point, Whitehouse met with Stolarchuk and paid her the balance.

The judge dismissed Whitehouse's claim for wrongful dismissal. The Court found that RBC had just cause for dismissing Whitehouse as his conduct put client and corporate confidentiality at risk. Whitehouse further compounded his misconduct when he lied to his superior the following day. Had there been no tape or entry logs, the inference from his answers is that he would have denied the entire incident. According to Justice McMahon, at para. 36, "this was not a single testosterone driven mistake by a 25 year old. This man was 49 years of age. He was married with a young family." Justice McMahon found Whitehouse's conduct to be reprehensible and he found that RBC was justified in summarily dismissing Whitehouse. Whitehouse argued that a lesser penalty was appropriate, such as a warning, assistance for his alcohol addiction or a suspension. Justice McMahon disagreed. He found that Whitehouse's conduct in the incident showed a lack of integrity, deficient judgment, dishonesty, untrustworthiness and careless disregard for client and corporate confidentiality and therefore warranted immediate dismissal.

The judge dismissed RBC's counterclaim for defamation and damages to its reputation as there was no specific evidence to show that there was damage to RBCs business or reputation. The Court found that any risk of damage flowing from the incident was removed by the employer's immediate dismissal of the employee.

This case is significant for employers as it shows that there are situations where Canadian courts will allow for summary dismissal. While there is no doubt that the facts of this case are unique, it shows that breaches of client confidentiality will be taken seriously by the courts. Despite the seemingly endless obligations for employers to accommodate their workers, the Court found that in the circumstances of this case RBC did not have an obligation to give Whitehouse a second chance.

27

WHEN IS OFF-DUTY CRIMINAL CONDUCT CAUSE FOR TERMINATION?

As an employer, you may consider drug dealers, child molesters and the like as undesirable employees. When it comes to the attention of an employer that one of its employees has been charged or convicted with a crime of moral turpitude, the first instinct in many cases may be to terminate the employee immediately. Subject to any human rights considerations, an employer can always terminate an employee charged or convicted with a crime without cause by providing reasonable notice or pay in lieu of notice. However, an employer must look very closely at the specific facts of the situation before terminating for cause in such circumstances, as only in rare cases will off-duty criminal conduct be sufficient cause for termination.

It is well established in Canadian case law that an employer may dismiss an employee for off-duty conduct, where the particular facts of the case warrant dismissal. However, in order to justify cause for termination, an employer must show that the employee's off-duty conduct was prejudicial to the employer because it represented a serious threat to the employer's reputation and legitimate business interests. Generally, this approach means that an employer cannot make a decision to terminate for cause based on the morality or immorality of the employee's conduct. Instead, the decision to terminate must be based on whether the employee's conduct is sufficiently business-related to the extent that the conduct is prejudicial to the employer's business reputation.

The impact that an employee's off-duty criminal conduct may have on an employer's business will be influenced by a number of factors, including the nature of the employer's business, the employee's position, the nature of the criminal conduct and whether there is a reluctance or refusal to work with the employee as a result of the criminal conduct. In most cases an employer has an uphill battle when trying to justify dismissal for criminal conduct that took place entirely outside the workplace. It is even more challenging when the employee has only been charged with a criminal offence but has not yet been convicted of the offence.

In *Kelly v. Linamar Corp.*, [2005] O.J. No. 4899 (hereinafter *Kelly*), a decision of the Ontario Superior Court of Justice, an employer's decision to terminate an employee for cause three days after the employee was charged with possession of child pornography was upheld.

On January 21, 2002, a search warrant was executed at the home of Philip Kelly ("Kelly"). As a result, he was charged with possession of child pornography and released on a recognizance of bail. Unfortunately for Kelly, news of his arrest was highly publicized in the local media. Kelly's employment with Emtol Manufacturing Ltd., a subsidiary of Linamar Corporation was terminated on January 24, 2002.

Linamar, an automotive parts manufacturer, is the largest employer in Guelph, Ontario, a community of approximately 100,000. In 2002, Linamar employed approximately 8,000 employees in Guelph at its various divisions. Linamar was, and still is, well-known in the community of Guelph as a good corporate citizen. Of particular importance was the fact that Linamar's philanthropic activity was directly focused toward children. Linamar actively supported a multitude of programs for children in the community, including sponsoring their attendance at cultural events, sponsoring sports teams and partnering with local schools to implement innovative educational programs.

Over his 14-year career with Linamar, Kelly had worked in five different divisions, and was known to many within the Linamar group of companies. At the time of his termination, Kelly was the materials manager at Emtol. In that role, Kelly supervised 10 to 12 employees either directly or indirectly. He was part of the Plant Operating Committee and regularly interacted with the other managers at Emtol, as well as with the materials managers at the other Linamar divisions. As materials manager, Kelly had regular contact with suppliers and customers.

News of Kelly's arrest and the repulsive nature of the charges against him became known throughout Emtol and Linamar as a result of radio and newspaper reports. Over the three days following Kelly's arrest, he reported to work and his employer conducted an investigation into Kelly's alleged conduct. After several meetings with Kelly, the employer reached the conclusion that Kelly had been involved in inappropriate conduct in relation to children. Given the employer's profile in the community and its commitment to children's programs, Emtol and Linamar concluded that Kelly's misconduct, which was broadcast to the community at large, had a negative impact on the company's legitimate interests. Accordingly, Kelly was terminated for cause.

Also contributing to the decision to terminate for cause were the concerns raised by employees regarding working with Kelly, as well as threats to Kelly's safety. On September 18, 2003, Kelly pleaded guilty to possessing child pornography, and on November 12, 2003 he was sentenced to three months to be served conditionally in the community. The identity of Kelly's employer was published in the newspaper subsequent to his termination, and the loss of his employment was referred to as a mitigating factor at the time Kelly was sentenced. Although the Court determined that it was not necessary to rely on the subsequent conviction and publication of the employer's identity in order to find cause, Justice Herold did indicate that these were factors that, if necessary, would favour a finding that there was after-acquired cause for termination.

In determining that the employer had just cause to terminate Kelly, Justice Herold confirmed that although the basis for the termination was the allegation of criminal charges, the employer only had to prove just cause on a balance of probabilities. As with any termination for cause, the employer must conduct a thorough investigation and give the accused employee the opportunity to respond to the allegations. Justice Herold was satisfied that Emtol and Linamar took the appropriate steps to investigate the matter and that a lot of consideration had been given to the matter.

It is important to note that the criminal conduct took place entirely outside the workplace, and there was no suggestion that Kelly downloaded or viewed child pornography from his work computer. The *Kelly* decision does not mean that every employee charged or convicted with possessing child pornography or some other crime of moral turpitude can be dismissed for cause. Each case must be considered on its own facts. The basis of the cause in this case was the potential reputational damage to a high profile employer in a relatively small community.

The *Kelly* decision is a helpful decision for employers as it confirms that in certain cases it is not necessary to wait for the outcome of the criminal proceedings before terminating, particularly where the nature of the charge is potentially prejudicial to the employer's reputation. The *Kelly* decision also sends a message, particularly to managers, that if you are going to engage in immoral criminal conduct in your private life, you do so at the risk of jeopardizing your employment.

28

DISLOYALTY CAN RESULT IN DISMISSAL

1. Employee Tips
2. Employer Tips

What degree of loyalty do you owe your current employer? Can you have a part-time job or is it even safe to look for another job while you are already employed? Can you get fired for not disclosing to your boss that you are contemplating setting up your own business?

There is no doubt that a conflict of interest or even a potential conflict of interest may constitute cause for dismissal. However, whether a conflict or potential conflict exists and whether there are any mitigating factors that should be considered that would not justify a dismissal is the subject of considerable debate and litigation.

What typically occurs is that the employee is either looking for another job, is thinking about setting up his or her own competing business or has engaged in some form of activity that may prejudice the interests of the current employer.

One of the leading cases that deals with a conflict of interest involved the Windsor Star Newspaper ("Windsor Star"). In *Atkins v. Windsor Star*, [1994] O.J. No. 623 (Ont. Gen. Div.), the newspaper decided to dismiss a salesperson who was selling advertising space when they discovered that the employee had created an interest publication that promoted a non-profit fisherman's association. The idea behind the publication was to promote the association; the costs of the publication would be covered by the advertising in the publication. The concern for the Windsor Star was that some of the advertisers in the association's publication were businesses with advertising contracts with the Windsor Star. From the employee's point of view, he did not see how his tabloid could be competing with the Windsor Star's daily newspaper and considered his involvement in the Fisherman's Association was merely an extension of his hobby of fishing.

In finding in favour of the employee, the Court concluded that the Windsor Star did not have just cause for dismissal. Of particular importance for the Court was that the Windsor Star had not spelled out its expectations in a written employment contract and the fact that there was nothing dishonest in the employee's activities. The employee was simply promoting a recreational activity on his own time without using or interfering with any of the resources of the Windsor Star. There was no evidence that advertisements sold for the publication reduced or interfered with the advertising revenue of the Windsor Star. The absence of any warning to the employee that his activities were unacceptable to the Windsor Star and could result in his summary dismissal if continued, was a convincing factor for the Court.

1. EMPLOYEE TIPS

Employees should keep these tips in mind when considering a conflict of interest:

1. As an employee, you owe a duty of loyalty and good faith to your employer. This means that you cannot engage in any activities, even during evenings or weekends, and certainly not during normal working hours, that conflict with your obligations to your employer or with the interests of your employer.

2. You probably can look for a job without telling your boss about it, but once you accept a new job, particularly with a competitor, you should disclose it to your current employer.

3. You cannot promote your own interests during normal business hours. You should avoid using any company equipment, including the computer, telephone or fax

machine in order to promote your non-work activities. You cannot use confidential information for your own purposes.

4. Be honest with your current employer. Any attempt to conceal your activities or any lack of honesty when confronted with your activities will support a dismissal for cause.

2. EMPLOYER TIPS

Tips employers should keep in mind when considering a conflict of interest are:

1. Use a written contract.

    Most companies use at least a written offer letter that outlines the terms of employment, if not a more formal written contract. The contract should contain a specific clause that requires employees to devote their full time and attention to the performance of their duties and an obligation to disclose any other activities.

2. Provide the employee with an opportunity to respond.

    As an employer it is far more prudent to disclose to the employee your concerns and make sure that you have the facts straight before you decide to dismiss for cause.

3. Be objective.

    You need to consider the severity of the activity and the impact that it will have on your company. Do not overlook the particular circumstances relating to the employee. A more senior employee will have less wiggle room than a lower level employee. A long-service employee is generally more difficult to dismiss for cause than a short-service employee.

4. Be practical.

    Litigation is expensive and proving cause for dismissal is becoming increasingly difficult. If practical, give the employee a written warning to stop the external activities or else they will face being dismissed with cause. If the employee refuses or conceals continuous activities, then you will have a much stronger case if you decide to proceed with a termination at a later date.

29

WHEN IS A WORKPLACE ROMANCE CAUSE FOR TERMINATION OF EMPLOYMENT?

It is likely inevitable that workplace romances will develop. The workplace is a primary venue for social interaction. However, the law gives employers the right to place parameters on workplace romances. The law looks at the power imbalance between managers and employees and discourages romance between managers and employees. A romantic relationship between a manager and an employee is incompatible with the manager's duties and responsibilities to the employer. For this reason, a romantic relationship between a manager and an employee will sometimes constitute just cause for termination of employment.

The principle that a romantic relationship between a manager and an employee may be cause for termination of employment was recently put to the test at a trial before the Ontario Superior Court of Justice in Guelph. Our firm had success in representing the employer in the case of *Cavaliere v. Corvex Manufacturing Ltd.*, [2009] O.J. No. 2334 (Ont. S.C.J.). The company frowned upon a plant manager engaging in a sexual relationship with a subordinate employee. The plant manager had a pattern of behaving as a sexual predator toward young women in the workplace. The company took a hard line approach regarding the plant manager's conduct and was vindicated in the result. The trial judge accepted that the plant manager's behaviour was entirely inappropriate and the termination of his employment was justified.

The company is a major employer in the municipality in which it operates. It prides itself on being a good corporate citizen. It supports local events and charities in the community. It also sponsors many local sports teams and donates to children's performing arts programs. The trial judge considered these factors in determining that the company was concerned about its reputation in the community and potential civil liability arising from the plant manager's inappropriate conduct.

The plant manager ("F.C") began working at the company on October 5, 1987, as a machine operator. He progressed through the ranks of the company and was ultimately promoted to the position of plant manager. His employment was terminated on June 14, 2006. During the course of his employment, F.C. engaged in at least two sexual relationships with subordinate employees. After the first relationship was brought to the attention of the company, it transferred F.C. to one of its other facilities and demoted F.C. to a more junior position. After the first demotion, F.C. again climbed through the management ranks. Ultimately, he failed to stop engaging in sexual relationships with the young women with whom he worked. The events in F.C.'s employment history that the trial judge found to be the most troubling to his case were the following:

- F.C. engaged in a sexual relationship in 1997-1998 with a subordinate employee ("A.R."). She reported to him directly. A.R.'s husband also worked for the company. A.R.'s husband initiated a complaint to the company regarding the sexual relationship. As a result of the complaint, F.C. was ordered transferred to another facility and demoted.

- F.C. recommended A.R. for a promotion. He did not disclose his conflict of interest when making the recommendation. A.R. received the promotion, which also included her being transferred to the same facility as F.C.

- F.C. received a second disciplinary transfer and demotion in May 2004. At that time, he received a letter that stated "future instances of inappropriate conduct with female employees shall also be grounds for immediate termination of employment for cause without further notice or warning".

- F.C. commenced a sexual relationship in 2005 with a subordinate employee ("M.N."). She reported to him indirectly. M.N.'s husband also worked for the company. M.N.'s husband initiated a complaint to the company regarding the sexual relationship.

- F.C. was suspended pending the investigation into the complaint filed by M.N.'s husband. F.C. was told not to have any contact with any of the company's employees until further notice. F.C. went to M.N.'s house while he was on suspension to convince her husband to withdraw his complaint.

The trial judge provided his verbal reasons on May 8, 2009. In his decision, the Honourable Mr. Justice C. Herold stated that because of the power imbalance between the plant manager and the subordinate employee, the subordinate employee was not freely consenting to the sexual relationship. He found, therefore, that the conduct was unwelcome conduct. The subordinate employee felt constrained from objecting to the conduct.

In addition, the trial judge relied on the reasoning of the Ontario Court of Appeal in *Bannister v. General Motors of Canada Ltd.*, [1998] O.J. No. 3402 and *Simpson v. Consumers' Assn. of Canada*, [2001] O.J. No. 5058. The trial judge held that as a plant manager, F.C. had two positive duties to the company. First, he was obligated to protect members of the workforce from offensive conduct. Second, he was obligated to protect the company from civil suits brought by individual complainants. The trial judge was satisfied that F.C. breached these duties by engaging in a sexual relationship with a subordinate employee. The company had just cause to terminate his employment.

In summary, this case supports the position that sexual relationships between managers and their subordinates are problematic for the employer. There is always a question as to whether the relationship is consensual. Furthermore, it is quite simply not the type of behaviour that an employer is entitled to expect from its managers. The managers are expected to protect the employer from complaints by individual employees. Similarly, managers are expected to protect employees from offensive conduct. These responsibilities are not compatible with engaging in sexual relationships with subordinate employees.

If you have concerns about inter-office relationships between managers and employees in your workplace, some things you can do are:
- Develop and implement a sexual harassment policy. The policy should provide examples of behaviour that crosses the line and the penalties for violation.

- Have every employee sign that they have received and read a copy of the sexual harassment policy. Have every employee sign a renewal every year.
- Provide sexual harassment training to all levels of employees.
- Encourage managers to disclose that they are engaged in a personal relationship with an employee. This ensures that you can effectively manage the risk associated with such a relationship and any repercussions that might flow from the relationship.

RODRIGUES V. POWELL (2007): AN EXAMINATION OF AFTER-ACQUIRED CAUSE

Employers are generally advised against terminating an employee without notice when there is insufficient evidence of just cause. This is trite law for counsel and, indeed, most employers. *Ex post facto* justification, or simply "after-acquired cause", may be relied upon by the employer to ground a dismissal in certain circumstances – in fact, the Ontario Superior Court of Justice had the opportunity to decide such a case. However, reliance on after-acquired cause should not be regarded as a fail-safe mechanism for employers who neglect to properly investigate an employee's misconduct prior to his or her dismissal. The courts will remain skeptical about an employer's assertion of after-acquired cause, and depending on when the employer's knowledge of such cause arose, asserting it may prove to do more harm than good.

The decision of the Ontario Superior Court of Justice in *Rodrigues v. Powell*, [2007] O.J. No. 2931 (*Rodrigues*) is an example of an employer successfully relying on after-acquired cause. As noted by Justice Echlin in his decision, the facts in *Rodrigues* were somewhat complicated, but the issues were not.

Cesar Rodrigues ("Rodrigues") was a member of Local 675 of the Carpenters, Drywall and Allied Workers Union, and had been employed for five years as a senior business representative of the Central Ontario Regional Council of Carpenters, Drywall and Allied Workers ("CORC").

Rodrigues was a vehement union organizer who had, in the conservative language of the Court, "strong and firmly held beliefs in the positive value of trade unionism." He saw an opportunity for enhanced unionization of drywallers in southern

Ontario, and had aspirations of spearheading a new, province-wide drywall council. When Rodrigues's idea was met with resistance by the vice-president of Local 675's parent union, Rodrigues took it upon himself to covertly pursue the secession of Local 675 from his employer, CORC.

Ucal Powell ("Powell") was Rodrigues's immediate supervisor at CORC. In early 2003, Powell was advised that there were allegations of criminal activity occurring within CORC, and that Rodrigues had been specifically named. CORC did not conduct a full and proper investigation into these allegations. In April 2003, Powell confronted Rodrigues with the allegations, and after reviewing them with him, informed Rodrigues that his employment was being terminated without cause. When Rodrigues asked for specific reasons for the dismissal, Powell responded simply by saying, "You're a big boy – you know why."

After his dismissal, Rodrigues continued his efforts to create the new council. In late April 2003, he participated in a meeting of Local 675 members, during which he moved to transfer sums of up to $2.5 million to a lawyer as non-refundable retainers with a view to "cover the costs of the lawyer to sever our ties with the council." These moneys were never transferred, however, as the Local was placed under supervision before Rodrigues was permitted to draw any funds. He also (unsuccessfully) encouraged the mass resignation of CORC's business representatives.

CORC conceded that it had "good business reasons" for dismissing Rodrigues; however, it was not until later that it became aware of grounds sufficient to amount to just cause. Therefore, the sole issue at trial, with respect to Rodrigues, was whether CORC had after-acquired cause to justify his dismissal.

The first instance of after-acquired cause put forth by CORC involved the assertion that Rodrigues had directed and participated in criminal acts that were directly connected with his employment – namely, the purchasing and pouring of cooking oil on drywall at sites that employed non-unionized labourers, and tailing a non-unionized drywaller and subsequently puncturing all four tires on his car.

Unsurprisingly, Rodrigues denied participation in all criminal allegations; however, the Court found him to be "completely incredible and unworthy of belief."

The second instance of after-acquired cause that was relied upon asserted that Rodrigues' actions in pursuing the secession of Local 675 was a breach of his fiduciary duties to his employer, CORC.

The Court found it incredible that Rodrigues would devote more than two years of his career with CORC, to whom he "owed a duty of loyalty, good faith, honesty and the avoidance of conflict of duty and self-interest", to promoting the secession of Local 675 from CORC, all the while receiving handsome paycheques from CORC. The departure of Local 675, which represented approximately 30 per cent of CORC's membership, would have had a devastating impact on CORC, both financially and practically speaking.

Rodrigues had put his own interests before those of his employer, and his actions following his dismissal only lent further credence to the fact that he was single-minded in his desire to form a new council.

The Court noted that CORC's investigation into Rodrigues's misconduct was "less than stellar and certainly not up to the Canadian standards", but was ultimately satisfied that there was sufficient after-acquired cause to ground his dismissal without notice.

The Supreme Court of Canada's contextual approach from *McKinley v. BC Tel*, [2001] S.C.J. No. 40, is still the leading analysis for determining whether just cause for dismissal exists. It examines the nature and extent of the misconduct and the surrounding circumstances to determine whether a dismissal is warranted. It is a test of proportionality. In other words, it asks: was the employee's conduct so inexcusable that the employment relationship has suffered irreparable harm as a result? In *Rodrigues*, the plaintiff's criminal activity and dogged pursuit to form a new drywall council caused CORC to lose confidence in him – it was not a situation that called for rehabilitation.

The decision in *Rodrigues* raises some interesting questions and concerns about the success of future litigants who seek to rely on after-acquired cause.

HOW TO APPROACH AFTER-ACQUIRED CAUSE

The first issue that employers will want to address is when the alleged conduct, which would amount to just cause in law, was first discovered – in other words, was it shortly after the employee's termination of employment, or only after the employee's claim for wrongful dismissal was filed?

Asserting after-acquired cause, in any event, raises obvious suspicions why the employer was not aware of the employee's misconduct until after the employee was dismissed. Consequently, the courts generally assign less weight to assertions of after-acquired cause unless it pertains to very serious misconduct. The effectiveness of after-acquired cause is diminished even further when the timing of the allegation appears to be nothing more than a last gasp attempt at defending a wrongful dismissal claim.

The second issue to address is whether the employer had any knowledge at all of misconduct *prior* to the employee's dismissal. Take, for example, an employer who is aware of an employee falsifying an expense report by $100, but does not confront the employee about it or otherwise condones the behaviour. For one reason or another, the employee is then summarily dismissed without cause and commences an action for wrongful dismissal. If the employer subsequently discovers that, in fact, the employee had falsified thousands of dollars worth of expense reports, the employer may face an uphill battle relying on after-acquired cause as a defence in that litigation. In that scenario, the employer may be considered to have condoned any related conduct that occurred prior to its becoming aware of the false expense report claim for $100, and will likely not be permitted to rely on that conduct as after-acquired cause for dismissal.

The limited circumstances in which assertions of after-acquired cause are successful should not be regarded as a failsafe mechanism available to employers who neglect to fully investigate into an employee's misconduct prior to his or her dismissal. Before any termination occurs, the employer must be certain that it has done everything reasonably possible to become aware of all the relevant facts – and the fact that an investigation is conducted is not always going to be enough. The termination of one's employment is the harshest form of discipline available in employment law. If the investigation into allegations of misconduct is conducted in an inexperienced or inadvertently biased manner, the courts will be acutely critical and are likely to favour the employee.

A third consideration is whether, and in what circumstances, an employee ought to be given the opportunity to respond to allegations of misconduct. Normally, it is best practice to confront an employee with concerns about his or her wrongdoing in order to ascertain the employee's version of the events – or indeed, to gauge the likelihood of reform – before making the decision whether or not to terminate the employment relationship. Asserting after-acquired cause effectively denies the employee that meaningful opportunity, particularly if a wrongful dismissal claim has already been made. In very limited circumstances, such as with a dismissed employee who is receiving a salary continuance, it may be in the employer's best interest to allow that employee an opportunity to respond to findings that amount to after-acquired cause, before moving directly to a cessation of further continuance payments and procuring what otherwise would be a breach of contract.

As a practical matter, there are also significant risks associated with relying on after-acquired cause. Employers who are unsuccessful in their assertion of after-acquired cause are more likely to have significant costs awarded against them, and increase their potential for "*Wallace*" damages by proceeding in bad faith. "*Wallace*" damages are named after the description of the head of damages in *Wallace v. United Grain Growers Ltd. (c.o.b. Public Press)*, [1997] S.C.J. No. 94 (S.C.C.), where the Supreme Court of Canada recognized that dismissals that occur in bad faith will call for unique damages. In other words, the manner in which the dismissal was handled by the employer may result in an increased damage award.

In *Rodrigues*, the employer's assertions of after-acquired cause were ultimately successful. However, it is surprising that Justice Echlin chose to categorize the allegations of criminal activity involving Rodrigues as "after-acquired cause" when, in fact, the employer was aware of the extent of the criminal allegations *prior* to Rodrigues's dismissal (and indeed put the allegations to him), yet chose to terminate him without cause and without conducting a full investigation. It begs the question, what information about Rodrigues's criminal activity was acquired after the fact that was not known to CORC prior to Rodrigues's dismissal? This is not clear from the judgment. The only *truly* after-acquired cause was Rodrigues's breach of his fiduciary duties to CORC, which, in any event, the Court appeared to take even greater exception to. Had Rodrigues not also been found to have significantly breached his fiduciary duties to his employer, and CORC was forced to rely solely upon the allegations of criminal involvement as after-acquired cause, the outcome may have been much different.

The lesson to be taken away from *Rodrigues* is a simple one. After-acquired cause is available to employers, but it is fuelled with suspicion and its use is highly cautioned. The *McKinley* contextual approach is still the leading analysis for determining whether there are grounds for just cause. As an employer, your best opportunity to ensure that you have all the relevant facts and have explored all possibilities occurs while the employee is still in your employ. If you have suspicions about an employee's conduct that could constitute just cause for termination, then investigate it fully – do not simply attempt to resolve the problem by terminating the employment relationship without cause. Know the whole story, allow the employee the chance to respond and proceed accordingly. Acting precipitously will only impede your chances of success at trial.

31

UPDATE ON CONSTRUCTIVE DISMISSAL

Employees who allege that they have been constructively dismissed by their employers bear a heavy burden of proof. In order to obtain damages for constructive dismissal, an employee must prove that the employer made unilateral changes to their employment contract and that these changes were a fundamental breach of the employment relationship. The decision in *Chapman v. Bank of Nova Scotia*, [2007] O.J. No. 2044 (Ont. S.C.J.) ("*Chapman*") demonstrates the substantial challenge a plaintiff faces in bringing an action for constructive dismissal.

In the *Chapman* case, Justice Conway was required to determine whether a plaintiff (Chapman) was constructively dismissed by the Bank of Nova Scotia and, if so, the length of reasonable notice that would be appropriate.

Chapman was employed with the bank for 36 years. During that time he advanced through various positions and was relocated to Saskatchewan, Calgary and Toronto. He eventually took a position as senior vice-president Ontario Region. The plaintiff was keen to reach his goal of one day becoming an executive vice-president and appeared to have had many conversations with Bruce Birmingham, a human resources executive, about "starting down the road to [executive vice-president] level compensation". To Chapman, this meant making an annual salary of $250,000 and earning 30,000 stock options per year.

In 2001 Chapman began earning $242,000 and was told he would be eligible to receive 30,000 stock options that year. Chapman acknowledged at Court that he was never promised that this salary would continue indefinitely.

The plaintiff saw his salary increase as a sign that he was on his way to becoming an executive vice-president. The bank, however, interpreted Chapman's 2001 salary increase as a discretionary raise. In subsequent years, Chapman was granted fewer than 30,000 stock options, which lowered his overall level of compensation. At the end of 2001 Chapman received the $242,000 salary but was only granted 20,000 options. In 2002 Chapman received 6,724 options. In 2003, he was granted 4,008 options. In some years Chapman accepted these cuts and in other years he filed complaints with the bank's human resources department. Chapman eventually left his position with the bank. He claimed he was constructively dismissed because the bank failed to pay him the salary he expected.

The Court concluded that the plaintiff had not been constructively dismissed. There was no evidence of any agreement to keep Chapman's salary at $242,000 plus 30,000 stock options. Furthermore, Chapman acquiesced to salary changes over the years. Accordingly, the parties had not agreed to an exact remuneration and the plaintiff's salary was found to be variable. Therefore, the bank could not be said to have breached a fundamental term of Chapman's contract by granting different numbers of stock options each year.

The *Chapman* case is a good example of the difficulty a plaintiff can have convincing the court the he or she has been constructively dismissed. Where an employee's income varies each year it will be difficult to prove that a change in remuneration is a fundamental breach of the employment relationship. Furthermore, a plaintiff cannot claim that there was a breach of a contractual term unless there is clear evidence that the parties agreed to the term in the first place.

Though it is difficult for an employee to prove that he or she has been constructively dismissed, an employer's best bet is to avoid becoming party to constructive dismissal proceedings in the first place. The following recommendations can help you reduce your organization's risk of being sued for constructive dismissal:

1. First and foremost employers can reduce their risk of litigation by fostering communication between employees and human resources specialists, especially with respect to the terms of employment contracts. Encourage employees to ask questions when they are unclear about aspects of their contract.

2. Wherever possible, contractual terms should be reduced to writing and worded as clearly as possible.
3. If an employee's remuneration fluctuates from year to year be sure to outline how the remuneration will be calculated and explain the reasons for the fluctuation.
4. If any part of the remuneration is provided on a discretionary basis be sure to make this clear in the contract.
5. Where an employee's income includes stock options be sure to include a clause limiting the employee's entitlement to options on termination. It is important that there is consistency between the wording in the contract and the stock option plan if you want to limit an employee's rights during the notice period.

Human resources specialists should be sure to keep records when an employee raises questions or concerns about the terms of their contracts. In the *Chapman* case, the plaintiff had many conversations with one particular human resources specialist who subsequently retired. The remaining human resources personnel were not aware of these conversations. Had records of these discussions been kept, the bank might have better understood Chapman's expectations and concerns. Not only will keeping these records help other members of your human resources department understand an employee's expectations, they also provide a record that could be used in court to clarify both the discussions that took place and the parties' positions with respect to the employment contract.

32

WHY CONSTRUCTIVE DISMISSAL CLAIMS FAIL

Employees may allege constructive dismissal when their employers make fundamental changes to a term or condition of their employment contract. In order to obtain damages for constructive dismissal, a plaintiff must convince the court that the employer made changes to an existing term of the contract. The plaintiff must also prove that the altered term was of fundamental importance to the contract. A term will not be considered fundamental unless its breach frustrates the performance of the contract. The courts have awarded damages for constructive dismissal in cases where employers have made changes to an employee's key responsibilities, compensation package or where employees were subjected to hostile work environments.

An employee who alleges that he or she has been constructively dismissed by his or her employer bears a heavy burden of proof. The decisions in *Chapman v. Bank of Nova Scotia*, [2007] O.J. No. 2044 (Ont. S.C.J.) ("*Chapman*"), *Otto v. Hamilton & Olsen Surveys Ltd.*, [1993] A.J. No. 646 (Alta. C.A.) ("*Otto*") and *Rasanen v. Lisle-Metrix Ltd.*, [2002] O.J. No. 291 (Ont. S.C.J.) ("*Rasanen*") demonstrate the substantial challenge a plaintiff faces in bringing an action for constructive dismissal. In each of these cases, the plaintiffs were unsuccessful in arguing that unilateral changes to their compensation packages entitled them to damages for constructive dismissal.

In the *Chapman* case, discussed in the previous article, Justice Conway was required to determine whether a plaintiff (Chapman) was constructively dismissed by the Bank of Nova Scotia and, if so, the length of reasonable notice that would be appropriate.

The Court concluded that the plaintiff had not been constructively dismissed. There was no evidence of any agreement to keep Chapman's salary at $242,000 plus 30,000 stock options. Accordingly, the parties had not agreed to an exact remuneration and the plaintiff's salary was found to be variable. Therefore, the bank could not be said to have breached an actual term of Chapman's contract by granting different numbers of stock options each year. The Court noted that the size of the reduction to Chapman's overall compensation was not substantial enough to be considered a fundamental breach. The plaintiff received a decrease of only 3.7 per cent in his overall compensation package between 2002 and 2003. Chapman acquiesced to salary changes over the years and he could not reopen past reductions in salary in his case for constructive dismissal. The judge reasoned that the decreases to Chapman's compensation could not have been so fundamental to his employment contract if he continued to work for the company through the years.

The *Chapman* case is a good example of the difficulty a plaintiff can have convincing the court the he or she has been constructively dismissed. Where an employee's income varies each year it will be difficult to prove that a change in remuneration is a fundamental breach of the employment relationship. Furthermore, a plaintiff cannot claim that there was a breach of a contractual term unless there is clear evidence that the parties agreed to the term in the first place.

In the *Otto* case, employees Otto and Comin summarily resigned their positions after their employer made changes to their compensation packages. The employer withheld a five per cent contribution to the plaintiffs' RRSP plan. The RRSP contribution would have amounted to approximately $200 per employee per month. The employer also reduced the the plaintiffs' vacation time from six weeks to four weeks. The capitalized value of the rollbacks was a mere six to eight per cent of the plaintiffs' total compensation. These changes were made after the employer suffered a two year loss of $225,000. After investigating the company operations, the employer discovered that it was paying significantly more employee benefits than any of its competitors. The changes to remuneration were instituted as a cost-cutting measure to help the company remain competitive. The plaintiffs took the position that these changes constituted a fundamental breach of the employment contract.

The Alberta Court of Appeal found that Otto and Comin were not constructively dismissed from their positions. The changes that were made to the plaintiffs' compensation were relatively minor. The Court characterized the change to remuneration as a periodic adjustment in compensation that depended on the profitability of the company. These minor changes did not constitute a fundamental breach of the employment contract. The Court concluded that the non-payment of a relatively minor portion of compensation in a continuing employment relationship would not usually amount to constructive dismissal. In reaching these conclusions, the Court also relied on the fact that the employer made it clear that it intended for the contract of employment to continue.

In the *Rasanen* case, the plaintiff was dismissed from his position as sales and marketing manager with Lisle-Metrix Ltd. Rasanen's employment contract limited the reasonable notice period to six months. Prior to his dismissal, the employer made several changes to Rasanen's employment contract. For instance, Rasanen's bonus was changed to a discretionary bonus. Although the plaintiff was not happy with this change, he accepted it and continued working for the employer. Rasanen's base salary was reduced. In subsequent years, the plaintiff also noticed that he had fewer people reporting to him.

Rasanen tried to argue that his employer unilaterally broke the fundamental terms of his employment contract. As a result of this breach, Rasanen submitted that he should not be bound to the contractual terms regarding reasonable notice. Rasanen argued that when employers breach fundamental terms of the contract, the employee is no longer bound by the remaining terms, including the reasonable notice clause.

The Court rejected Rasanen's reasoning. With respect to the changes made to the employee's salary, the Court found that the employment contract provided for an annual salary review. Therefore, the parties had contracted for the possibility that the salary could be subject to change. More importantly, the plaintiff could not claim that the changes made to his contract were fundamental breaches because he continued to work for the employer. The Court concluded that where an employer makes changes to the terms of employment an employee may choose to accept these changes and continue to work. In the alternative, the employee may treat the contract as wrongfully terminated and resign. If an employee continues working after the changes have been made, the employee will be considered to have condoned the changes and will be precluded from claiming that there was a fundamental breach of the contract.

Making a case for constructive dismissal is usually difficult for employees. Plaintiffs will be unsuccessful in their claim if the employer can show that the parties contracted for the possibility of changes to the terms of the contract. If an employee has condoned changes to the employment contract by continuing to work for the employer, the employee will be stopped from subsequently claiming constructive dismissal. Finally, employees are usually hard-pressed to prove that their employment contract was fundamentally breached. They must show that the breach was such that they would be denied the value of the contract or that they would be unable to perform the contract as a result of the breach.

Though it is difficult for an employee to prove that he or she has been constructively dismissed, here are some tips for avoiding these types of claims:

1. First and foremost employers can reduce their risk of litigation by fostering communication between employees and human resources specialists with respect to the terms of employment contracts.

2. Contractual terms should be clear and should allow the employer some flexibility to make changes to key contractual terms without the employee's consent.

3. If an employee's remuneration fluctuates from year to year, be sure to outline how the remuneration will be calculated and explain the reasons for the fluctuation.

4. If any part of the remuneration is provided on a discretionary basis be sure to make this clear in the contract.

5. Where an employee's income includes stock options, be sure to include a clause limiting the employee's entitlement to options on termination. The contract should be consistent with the language in the stock option plan. As an employer, you will want to limit the employee's rights during the notice period.

6. Human resources specialists should be sure to keep records about when employees raise questions or concerns about the terms of their contracts. In the *Chapman* case, the plaintiff had many conversations with one particular human resources specialist who subsequently retired. The remaining human resources personnel were not aware of these conversations. Had records of these discussions been kept, the bank might have better understood Chapman's expectations and concerns. Not only will keeping these records help other members of your human resources department understand an employee's expectations, they also provide a record that could be used in court to clarify both the discussions that took place and the parties' positions with respect to the employment contract.

If there is reason to believe that an employee's salary may have to be changed from year to year, the employer should make this clear in the contract. This can be accomplished by including a clause that provides for an annual salary review. Ensure that the employee is aware that the salary may be subject to review and, where possible, explain how or why such reviews will be conducted. If employees are aware that their salary may be subject to change they will be precluded from relying on a salary change as grounds for constructive dismissal.

33

TERMINATION IN DISGUISE: LEGAL LAYOFFS REQUIRE BOTH A CONTRACTUAL RIGHT AND A GENUINE INTENTION TO RECALL

Employers in several industries experience significant fluctuations in business throughout the year. Temporary layoffs can save an employer money in unnecessary wage payments while avoiding the obligations associated with dismissing employees when business is slow and hiring new employees when business picks up again. However, employers do not have a general right to temporarily lay off employees. The decision of the Manitoba Court of Queen's Bench in *Rodger v. Falcon Machinery (1965) Ltd.*, [2006] M.J. No. 384, illustrates the criteria an employer must satisfy to legally lay off an employee. In that case, the Court found that William Rodger ("Rodger"), an employee of 13-and-a-half-years, had been constructively dismissed when he was laid off for an indefinite period of time.

Falcon Machinery ("Falcon") was a family-owned and operated company in the business of custom steel manufacturing. Rodger began working in 1993 as a steel fabricator but performed various other jobs during his time at Falcon. Rodger was laid off for the first time in February 2005. Rodger was provided with a record of employment, which stated that he had been laid off due to a shortage of work and that his expected date of recall was unknown. Furthermore, he was told by the president of Falcon that he would not be recalled any time soon. Shortly thereafter, Rodger retained legal counsel and a demand letter was sent to Falcon asserting that he had been terminated. In response to the letter, Falcon proposed that he return to work for a one-year period at the same salary and benefits but in a different position. Rodger refused to take the replacement position and commenced an action for wrongful dismissal.

The central issue in the case was whether Rodger had been laid off or wrongfully terminated. A layoff is considered a breach of the contract of employment unless the contract expressly or impliedly provides that an employee can be laid off temporarily without pay. In asserting a contractual right to lay off Rodger, Falcon relied on a paragraph in Rodger's employment application form, which stated, at para. 3, that "should it be necessary for a lay off the employee or the employer must give one working day's notice." Rodger argued that his employment contract did not allow for a layoff and that the application form did not constitute a term of the employment contract. The Court agreed with Rodger and concluded that a term in "an application form lacks contractual force since no contract is in existence at the application stage." Furthermore, despite Rodger acknowledging that he believed he could be temporarily laid off due to the nature of the industry and Falcon's past practice, the Court concluded that Rodger's 13-and-a-half-year history without a layoff negated the existence of an implied contractual right.

The Court went a step further and concluded that even if Falcon had the right to lay off Rodger, their actions could not be characterized as a temporary layoff but were effectively a termination or dismissal. Central to this determination was Falcon's failure to demonstrate an intention to recall Rodger. No assurances were made to Rodger that his job would resume at a future date and no reference was made to the prospect of any future work. Conversely, the Court identified a multitude of facts that suggested that Falcon's intention was just the opposite:

- Rodger was told by the president of Falcon that he was unlikely to be recalled any time soon.

- Although Falcon claimed that business was slow, there was conflicting evidence about the company's financial circumstances at the time.

- Falcon had only laid off a total of eight individuals in the preceding five years, and none with Rodger in February 2005.

- Rodger's normal duties were reassigned to other Falcon employees.

- The president of Falcon expressed concerns about Rodger's performance, effort and attitude.
- Falcon sent documentation to its life insurance provider indicating that Rodger was terminated.

Accordingly, the Court concluded that the cessation of employment was meant to be permanent and, thus, the purported layoff was in reality a termination or constructive dismissal. The Court also noted that had Falcon's actions constituted a temporary layoff, its offer to Rodger to return to work for a one-year period (while he looked for another job) would have amounted to a constructive dismissal. The Court awarded Rodger nine months' pay in lieu of notice.

The Court also dealt extensively with the issue of mitigation. Most significantly, it held that Rodger did not fail to mitigate his damages by refusing Falcon's offer to work for one year. Rodger was not required to accept the offer for two main reasons. First, the terms and conditions of the proposal were not sufficiently certain, including a failure to outline the work duties Rodger would be performing. Second, the employment relationship had been eroded to such an extent that the parties could not be expected to work together in harmony. On this point, the Court found it relevant that Rodger was a long-term employee who was told in a "curt and rather insensitive manner that he no longer had work". As a result, it was understandable that Rodger might feel humiliated and reluctant to accept the proposal.

The Court also emphasized that once an employee has left the employer, it becomes more difficult for a court to envision situations where the employee must return to the employer, upon the employer's request, in order to mitigate his or her damages. In particular, once an action for wrongful dismissal has been commenced the parties cannot be reasonably expected to work together in a relationship of "mutual understanding and respect". Accordingly, the importance of treating employees with dignity in the context of a layoff cannot be overstated. Furthermore, *Rodger* teaches us that employers cannot utilize a layoff and recall to effectively alter an employee's job, nor will that employee be required to accept the altered position for the purpose of mitigation.

The decision in *Rodger* is another example of increasing judicial attentiveness to employers attempting, in times of economic adversity, to avoid responsibility for providing employees with reasonable notice by calling the termination a temporary layoff until further notice. A layoff by name alone will likely be considered a constructive termination. The ability to temporarily lay off employees can be a tremendous cost-saving tool for employers. Employers who wish to have this tool available would be wise to turn their minds to it at the time of contracting (*i.e.*, spell it out) and not rely on the court to imply a layoff term on the basis of industry standards or past practice. Furthermore, in communicating a layoff to an employee, the employer must demonstrate an intention to recall the employee sometime in the future and should indicate when the employee might expect to be recalled. Finally, employers must be aware that courts have difficulty understanding how an indefinite term layoff can amount to anything but a termination of employment. Nonetheless, any claim to a right to lay off an employee for an indefinite period is futile unless spelled out in the contract of employment.

34

CHANGING EMPLOYMENT CONTRACTS

As human resources professionals, you have all been faced with the difficult challenge of implementing changes to an employee's terms of employment. Making such changes is wrought with peril as it can increase the risk of an employee claiming he or she was "constructively dismissed".

For many years, it was understood that a "constructive dismissal" occurs when the employer changes a fundamental term of employment without giving the employee reasonable advance notice of the change.

In *Wronko v. Western Inventory Service Ltd.*, [2008] O.J. No. 1589, a very surprising decision, the Ontario Court of Appeal redefined the law of constructive dismissal by removing the employer's ability to change a term of employment by providing reasonable advance notice of the change.

In *Wronko*, the plaintiff's contract included a termination clause that provided him with two years' severance. The defendant gave the plaintiff two years' notice that the termination clause would be changed to reduce his severance entitlement. The plaintiff continued his employment but voiced his opposition to the proposed change. Two years later, the defendant advised the plaintiff that the new termination clause was in effect, and that if he did not accept the new term, "we do not have a job for you."

The plaintiff rejected the change and sued, claiming he was constructively dismissed and was therefore entitled to two years' severance.

The plaintiff was unsuccessful at trial. The trial judge concluded that the plaintiff was not constructively dismissed because the defendant had provided the plaintiff with reasonable notice of the change to the termination clause.

The Court of Appeal sided with the plaintiff. The Court held that an employer cannot legally change a fundamental term of employment by providing advance notice of the change. The Court set out three options when an employer seeks to change a fundamental term of employment:

1. The employee may accept the change;
2. The employee may reject the change and sue; or
3. The employee may make it clear to the employer that he is rejecting the change. The employer can then terminate the employee (with reasonable notice) and offer re-employment on the new terms. However, if the employer does not terminate the employee and continues to allow the employee to work under the original terms, the employer will be presumed to have acquiesced to the employee's rejection of the change.

Since the plaintiff had told the defendant he was rejecting the proposed change, and since the defendant allowed the plaintiff to continue in his job for two years, the Court concluded that the defendant had implicitly agreed to not change the termination clause. The Court held that the plaintiff had been terminated when the defendant later changed the clause, therefore the plaintiff was entitled to two years' severance.

The *Wronko* decision significantly increases the risk of a lawsuit when an employer seeks to implement changes in the terms of employment of its employees. So what can you do to limit your employer's risk of liability? While you should obtain professional legal advice, you may wish to consider the following options:

1. **Provide consideration for the change.** Changes to an employment contract can be legally made where the employee is given something in return (*e.g.*, a signing bonus).
2. **Provide "working notice" along with an offer of re-employment under the new terms.** Terminate the employee by providing "working notice" while at the same time offer re-employment under the new terms starting at the end of the working notice period. By

providing reasonable working notice, you will save the expense of having to immediately sever the employee and secure a replacement. Immediately offering re-employment under the new terms should soften the blow to morale caused by the notice of termination. And if the employee rejects the offer of re-employment, you will have time to find a replacement employee at the end of the working notice period.

The *Wronko* decision represents a significant change to how the law has been interpreted in the past. Employers will now need to be much more careful in making changes to any material term of an employment contract if they hope to achieve the desired outcome. Until this case is overturned or varied, employers will not be successful in altering the terms of an employment contract by simply providing reasonable notice of the change.

35

VIDEO SURVEILLANCE OF AN EMPLOYEE CAN CONSTITUTE CONSTRUCTIVE DISMISSAL

Defining an employee's right to privacy is currently a hot topic in employment law. Recently, the Ontario Superior Court took a step toward safeguarding an employee's right to privacy, determining that the unjustified covert video surveillance of an employee can constitute constructive dismissal. Employers who are using or considering using video surveillance to monitor employees will want to carefully consider the decision in *Colwell v. Cornerstone Properties Inc.*, [2008] O.J. No. 5092 (*"Colwell"*).

Colleen Colwell ("Colwell") was a commercial manager at Cornerstone Properties ("Cornerstone"). She discovered that a hidden camera had been placed in her office by her direct supervisor, Trent Krauel ("Krauel"). Krauel claimed that the camera was installed for the purpose of detecting theft by the maintenance staff. While there had been some instances of theft at Cornerstone, Colwell had never had anything stolen from her office. Krauel stated that he trusted Colwell, that he wanted her to remain in her position and that she was not a suspect. Colwell could not understand why, if she was not a suspect, she had not been informed about the existence of the camera. The situation was compounded by the fact that the camera in Colwell's office was the only one that had been installed in the Cornerstone office and by Krauel's absurd explanation that he believed the thieves might use her office to "review the loot". Krauel maintained his right to install the camera and refused to apologize. Colwell felt psychologically violated and sought medical assistance for stress. She decided to leave her employment and sued Cornerstone for constructive dismissal.

The Court concluded that Colwell had been constructively dismissed. In the facts of this case, the Court found that Colwell's employment contract contained an implied term that the parties would treat each other in good faith and fairly, not only during termination, but throughout the existence of the contract. The Court found that the actions of the employer, both in installing surveillance equipment and in providing an unreasonable explanation for the surveillance, poisoned the workplace and justified Colwell leaving her employment. The Court wrote, at para. 33:

> The cost to human dignity caused by such surveillance, coupled with the unbelievable explanation subsequently provided, left Mrs. Colwell in a position of being unable to rely upon the honesty and trustworthiness of her immediate supervisor... .
>
> .....
>
> Not only had her privacy been violated, but so had her contract of employment in that all trust had evaporated.

The Court awarded Colwell damages equivalent to a notice period of seven months but declined to make an award for aggravated damages given that the law in the area of invasion of privacy is still developing.

The *Colwell* case is only one example of unwarranted surveillance and invasion of privacy, yet it prompts a broader inquiry. To what extent do employers have the right to use surveillance to monitor their employees?

Employers should note that an employee's right to privacy is dependent on where the employee works. The law differs depending on whether a workplace is unionized, federally regulated or neither. However, the following are general guidelines for employers in determining whether video surveillance is appropriate:

- Surveillance must be reasonable: it must have a reasonable basis and be conducted in a reasonable manner.
- Employers should resort to video surveillance only when a video is likely to be effective in meeting a specific need and there are no other less intrusive alternatives that would meet that need.

- Employers should be wary of covert surveillance. Open surveillance, conducted with employee consent, is vastly different from installing hidden cameras and will be more easily justified. As the *Colwell* case illustrates, courts will not be sympathetic to employers found secretly spying on employees without an airtight reason for doing so.

In this rapidly developing area of law, employers should consult legal counsel before installing video surveillance equipment. Employers should tread carefully given the trend toward recognizing and protecting an employee's right to privacy.

36

LONG-TERM DISABILITY BENEFITS MUST CONTINUE AFTER DISMISSAL

Employers will be held responsible for the provision of long-term disability benefits to employees who are terminated before or while experiencing a disability. This has been made clear through a line of decisions stemming from courts in British Columbia and Ontario. The following discussion highlights those decisions and provides suggestions to employers concerning the manner in which they can avoid areas of liability.

In *Asselstine v. Manufacturers Life Ins. Co.*, [2003] B.C.J. No. 1692 (B.C.S.C.); varied [2005] B.C.J. No. 1152 (B.C.C.A) ("*Asselstine*"), the plaintiff employee received notice of termination from the defendant, University of British Columbia ("UBC"), after she was diagnosed with multiple sclerosis. Following the end of her employment, she made an application for long-term disability benefits under UBC's insurance plan. This application and subsequent appeals were denied by the benefits administrator, The Manufacturers Life Insurance Company ("Insurance Company"). Thus, she brought an action against UBC and the Insurance Company for specific performance of the insurance contract. She also claimed aggravated and punitive damages, alleging that the defendants breached a contractual duty of good faith in the handling of her application.

The Court held that the plaintiff had established her eligibility for benefits. It found that the Insurance Company placed "undue emphasis on unreliable, incomplete and flawed evidence and disregarded pertinent information, to the detriment of the plaintiff" (see [2003] B.C.J. No. 1692 at para. 193). Medical evidence supporting the plaintiff's claim was inappropriately rejected or ignored in light of conflicting evidence that was detrimental to her claim. The Insurance Company also improperly relied on a medical report that did not consider a number of factors, including the plaintiff's medical condition during the relevant period and her physician's statements and opinions. In this context, the Court held further that the defendants did breach a duty of good faith to fairly consider her application.

The Court awarded the plaintiff aggravated damages in the amount of $35,000 for the anxiety and mental, emotional and financial stress to which she was subjected as a result of the benefit claims process. At para. 213 ([2003] B.C.J. No. 1692), punitive damages of $150,000 were also awarded "as a reminder that it is not in the economic interest of the insurer to engage in similar conduct in future similar situations." Notably, the employer, UBC, was held liable for damages along with the Insurance Company, which directly adjudicated the plaintiff's application. On appeal, however, the Court overturned this finding of joint liability, and held UBC solely responsible for the actions of the insurer. Indeed, the Court noted that the Insurance Company was not a party to a contract with the plaintiff and performed a function as agent of its principal, UBC.

As a precedent, *Asselstine* thus imposes a significant burden on employers to monitor the adjudication process of third party benefit providers contracted to insure the health of employees. This burden continues during the notice period following termination. Interestingly, although the judgment in *Asselstine* arises from British Columbia, it is an extension of Ontario cases, including *Re Stelco Inc.*, 2005 Ont. S.C.J. [Commercial List]; *Zorn-Smith v. Bank of Montreal*, [2003] O.J. No. 5044 (Ont. S.C.J.) ("*Zorn-Smith*"); and *Prinzo v. Baycrest Centre for Geriatric Care*, [2000] O.J. No. 683 (Ont. S.C.J.), varied [2002] O.J. No. 2712 (Ont. C.A.) ("*Baycrest*"). In the former two cases, Ontario courts held the defendant employers responsible for denying disability benefits during the notice period. In the latter case, the court demonstrated its disapproval of employees denied benefits through high-handed conduct. *Asselstine* should be read with these judgments in mind as a further indication of the courts' sympathetic disposition toward disabled employees.

In *Honda Canada Inc. v. Keays*, [2008] S.C.J. No. 40 (S.C.C.) ("*Honda*"), the Supreme Court of Canada signalled a shift away from the general sympathy toward disabled employees. Nevertheless, employers must still be vigilant in monitoring the condition of employees on a leave of absence and applying for long-term disability benefits. The lower court decisions continue to provide guidance in this regard.

In *Re Stelco Inc.*, the plaintiff employee, a 44-year-old security officer, had been dismissed from her employment by the defendant, Stelco Inc., as a result of chronic absenteeism. The Court heard evidence that the plaintiff's poor attendance record was a result of recurring health problems including polyarthritis, depression, fibromyalgia, insomnia, hypothyroidism and hypoglycaemia. The defendant refused to provide short- and long-term disability benefits during the plaintiff's period of salary continuation.

The plaintiff thus brought an action for wrongful dismissal, claiming entitlement to a longer notice period with corresponding salary and benefits. She was awarded a notice period of 12 months in light of her employment and personal circumstances. Moreover, the Court found that she would have been entitled to long-term disability benefits during this period, and that she would have taken advantage of those benefits. Stelco Inc., not the insurer, was liable to pay the long-term disability benefits forgone, as it was Stelco Inc. that breached the contract of employment.

In *Zorn-Smith*, the plaintiff brought an action for wrongful dismissal against the defendant bank. She became ill after being assigned to a financial services manager position for which she had no training or prior experience. She went on disability leave when she was unable to focus and began suffering from sleep disturbance, exhaustion, irritability and loss of appetite. Her physician later diagnosed her with an adjustment disorder, and indicated that a modification of her workplace would facilitate her return to work.

Nevertheless, the bank cancelled the plaintiff's long-term disability benefits. Moreover, under threat of termination, the bank offered to employ the plaintiff on a part- or full-time basis. It relied on the advice of a medical advisor who had not consulted the plaintiff's physician and had not spoken to or examined the plaintiff. In his assessment, the advisor also required the plaintiff to meet a higher standard of disability than what was mandated by the insurance contract.

The plaintiff refused to work, and the bank terminated her employment. In her action for wrongful dismissal, intentional infliction of mental distress, and loss of benefits, she was awarded a notice period of 16 months that included an extended period on account of "*Wallace*" damages. As stated earlier, "*Wallace*" damages are an increased damages award in wrongful dismissal cases because of the manner in which the dismissal was handled by the employer. In its judgment, the Court stated that the bank had engaged in bad faith conduct that included advising the plaintiff while on disability leave that she was to return to work or face termination, refusing to take responsibility for effects of its work environment on the plaintiff's health, failing to contact the plaintiff's physician and failing to advise the plaintiff of the specifics of an appeal of her denial of benefits. Once again, the Court held the defendant liable to pay her long-term disability benefits to the end of her period of disability. The Court also awarded $15,000 in damages for intentional infliction of mental distress.

In *Baycrest*, the Court considered the circumstances of a disabled plaintiff whose employment was terminated after 17 years of service. She sustained injuries after falling in the defendant employer's parking lot and took disability leave. During her period of absence, the employer's representatives contacted her by phone and mail, and made harassing, misleading and intimidating comments while urging her to return to work on a modified basis. This behaviour continued even after the plaintiff's counsel requested that all contact be directed through him. Upon the plaintiff's return to work, the representatives discussed termination and erroneously implied that her conduct was harming the residents of the employer's geriatric care centre. Approximately one month later, the plaintiff received notice of termination.

The Court awarded the plaintiff 18 months' notice for wrongful dismissal and $15,000 in damages for mental distress. Where the latter award was concerned, the Court stated, at para. 22, that "certain acts of harassment by the employees of the defendant were so extreme and insensitive that they constituted a reckless and wanton disregard for the health of the plaintiff...." Punitive damages of $5,000 were also assessed. The Court of Appeal reduced the notice period to 12 months and overturned the award of punitive damages, but upheld the award of damages for mental distress.

Finally, the decision in *Honda* concerned a plaintiff who was fired by his employer after he refused to meet with Honda's occupational health specialist. The plaintiff suffered from chronic fatigue syndrome ("CFS") and was frequently absent from work as a result. He retained counsel to reach a suitable working arrangement with his employer. The meeting with the specialist was ordered after Honda unilaterally ended the plaintiff's human rights accommodations and asserted that Honda's physicians could find no justification for the plaintiff's absences.

In his action for wrongful dismissal, the plaintiff was awarded 24 months' notice of termination by the trial judge. This included a nine-month extended notice period on account of *Wallace*, which extension was granted in light of Honda's conduct in misrepresenting medical opinions and arranging a medical assessment in bad faith, the impact of the dismissal on the plaintiff's health and Honda's retribution against the plaintiff's pursuit of accommodation under the Ontario *Human Rights Code*. He was also awarded $500,000 in punitive damages. After referring to a number of factors to justify this award, the trial judge stated ([2005] O.J. No. 1145 at para. 62) that "[i]t would appear to me that Honda ran amok as a result of their blinded insistence on production 'efficiency' at the expense of their obligation to provide a long-time employee reasonable accommodation that included his own physician's participation." The plaintiff was not awarded compensation for lost disability benefits as a result of a technical failure in his pleadings. The Court of Appeal reduced the quantum of punitive damages to $100,000 but upheld the other aspects of the award.

On appeal, the Supreme Court of Canada overturned the decision of the trial judge and Court of Appeal on the issue of *Wallace* damages and punitive damages. The Supreme Court recognized that merely listening to expert medical advice cannot be considered "hardball". Rather, an employer is entitled to create a disability program and requiring employees to provide a note supporting their absence from work cannot be equated to malicious intent to discriminate. Accordingly, no *Wallace* damages or punitive damages were warranted on the facts of this case. The Supreme Court reduced the notice period to 15 months.

Taken together, these cases provide clear examples of what can go wrong when terminating an employee who is claiming disability benefits. Here are some suggestions about how to minimize your risks:

1. Treat each case independently based on the facts of the particular case. Avoid a standard, formalized approach that neglects the particular facts involving the employee you are currently dealing with. Ask yourself the question "Are we treating this employee fairly?"

2. Do not rely exclusively on your third party insurer. If there is a dispute between the employee and your third party insurer, have an independent medical examination (IME) performed.

3. Provide the employee with any assistance required in applying for short-term disability (STD) and long-term disability (LTD) benefits.

4. Understand your limitations on knowing the full extent of the employee's illness. As the employer, you are not entitled to know the nature or prognosis of the employee's medical history. You are entitled to receive information that confirms that the employee is medically fit to perform the essential duties of the job and what, if any, restrictions there are with respect to the performance of these duties.

5. Keep working on the file. Inaction is also a problem that should be avoided. Leaving an employee on payroll who refused to report to work because of an alleged but unproven disability is equally problematic. Deal with the issues in a timely and thoughtful fashion to avoid a future problem with this employee.

37

TURF WARS – TIPS FOR THE DEPARTING EMPLOYEE

1. Review Your Employment Contract
2. Provide Your Employer with Notice of Resignation
3. Are You a Fiduciary?
4. Disclose Your Prior Obligations to Your New Employer
5. Never Remove Customer Information
6. Protect Customer Interests
7. Plan Your Departure Carefully

Companies are increasingly suing departing employees who are unlawfully soliciting the business of customers. Virtually any type of business where you have direct contact with customers and are selling either products or services can give rise to litigation if you try to take this business with you when you leave. Financial services, insurance and placement industries are examples of areas where competition is fierce in a consolidating marketplace. Litigation is expensive and time-consuming and can become a very big distraction for you as a departing employee.

This is what you should know about leaving your job and taking your former employer's business:

1. REVIEW YOUR EMPLOYMENT CONTRACT

Do you have a written employment contract? If you do, it will likely spell out what your obligations are at the time of your departure with respect to your resignation, non-disclosure of confidential information and non-competition/non-solicitation. The contract can impose upon you conditions that are more restrictive than what a court would normally impose. It will be important for you to get advice and find out whether your contract is enforceable. If you signed your contract after you began your employment, or if the restrictive clauses are too broad, they may not be upheld. If you do not have a written employment contract, it is incorrect to assume that you have no obligations to your former employer. For example, you will be prohibited indefinitely from using or disclosing confidential corporate information even in the absence of a written employment contract.

2. PROVIDE YOUR EMPLOYER WITH NOTICE OF RESIGNATION

Your employer is entitled to reasonable notice of your resignation. Your written employment contract will probably deal with this but in the absence of a written contract, you still have the obligation to provide notice. It is incorrect to assume that means only two weeks' notice. In some cases, notice could be several months, depending on your position, length of service and the time it will take your employer to find a replacement.

Once you provide your employer with notice, your employer can waive the notice by paying you your salary in lieu of notice and ask you to leave immediately. That will not override your ongoing obligations to your employer.

3. ARE YOU A FIDUCIARY?

A fiduciary is usually regarded as an employee who is in a position of trust and who has independent decision-making authority, which makes the fiduciary's employer vulnerable to his or her decisions. If you are an executive or senior manager with decision-making authority, including hiring and firing, and you have access to confidential information, you are probably a fiduciary. In some cases, you may be viewed as a "key employee", which will result in you having fiduciary obligations even though you may not be a senior manager or executive. If you are a fiduciary or key employee, you can compete with your former employer but you are restricted from directly soliciting your former employer's customers for a reasonable period of time, and you can never use or disclose confidential corporate information. What will be a reasonable amount of time varies in each case but 12 to 18 months is usually viewed as reasonable.

If you are not a fiduciary or a key employee, you will be considered a "mere employee" and you will be permitted to directly solicit your former employer's customers, although you will never be allowed to use confidential information.

The issue of whether you will be held to a higher standard as a fiduciary is an important one, which you need to properly resolve prior to joining a competitor.

4. DISCLOSE YOUR PRIOR OBLIGATIONS TO YOUR NEW EMPLOYER

Be candid and honest with your new employer concerning any restrictions on your right to solicit customers. The best approach is to provide your new employer with a copy of your contract and any documentation, such as a non-competition/non-solicitation agreement. By doing so, it is common for a new employer to pay the costs of litigation should your former employer decide to sue you.

5. NEVER REMOVE CUSTOMER INFORMATION

Customers are generally free to choose who they will deal with but you should not think that because you have a relationship with the customer, the customer's information belongs to you. In most cases, companies will have policies, either in writing or in practice, as to who "owns" the customer, but in every case, any documentation, including customer lists, addresses, phone numbers, customer purchase history, pricing strategy, etc., clearly belongs to the company and not to you. If you take this information to your new employer, you may be in breach of your obligations to your former employer. Return any company information that you were using at your home office.

6. PROTECT CUSTOMER INTERESTS

Avoid any conduct that will adversely affect your customer's interests. Ask yourself whether your action will be in any way harmful to the customer and if so, do not do it. Your reputation and the reputation of your new employer can be severely damaged by self-serving conduct that harms the customer.

7. PLAN YOUR DEPARTURE CAREFULLY

You can search for a job while you are still employed but you cannot let your job search conflict with your obligations to your current employer. Disclosing confidential information to your prospective employer during job interviews is wrong and should be avoided. You should also avoid using your company laptop or BlackBerry® to conduct your job search as all your communications will likely be reviewed after your departure.

It is also inappropriate to advise the customer that you are leaving the company prior to advising your current employer, as it may provide you with an unfair advantage. A court will have no sympathy for any disloyal behaviour that you engage in prior to announcing your departure.

You can and should plan your departure carefully, including when to provide your notice of resignation, which customers you should contact and when, and the type of contact that you are permitted to make. In order to avoid litigation and hard feelings, you should act professionally both prior to and after your departure. If you honour your obligations and compete fairly, you will likely avoid costly litigation.

38

OBLIGATIONS OF DEPARTING EMPLOYEES

The Supreme Court of Canada has released an important decision touching on the duties owed by departing employees to their former employers. *RBC Dominion Securities Inc. v. Merrill Lynch Canada Inc.*, [2008] S.C.J. No. 56 (S.C.C.) was a decision arising from the town of Cranbrook, British Columbia.

In November 2000, a Royal Bank of Canada (RBC) branch manager, without warning, coordinated a move by virtually all of the branch's investment advisors to a competitor, Merrill Lynch, effectively "hollowing out" the branch. Moreover, in the weeks preceding the employees' departure, RBC's confidential client records were secretly transferred to Merrill Lynch. RBC's branch nearly collapsed.

The trial judge found for RBC, holding that the former employees had breached an implied term of their contracts of employment requiring reasonable notice and prohibiting unfair competition with RBC during the reasonable notice period. The trial judge also found that the branch manager had breached his contractual duties by coordinating the departure of the employees to Merrill Lynch and by failing to inform RBC management of his impending departure. However, the trial judge failed to find the branch manager a fiduciary. Merrill Lynch was also found jointly and severally liable for the award, as it induced the employees' breach of their implied duty not to compete unfairly. Significantly, the trial court awarded $1.5 million against the branch manager personally for loss of profits suffered by RBC, based on a five-year period.

The Court of Appeal for British Columbia varied the trial judgment on the quantum of damages ([2007] B.C.J. No. 48).

However, the Supreme Court of Canada granted leave to appeal and reversed the decision. Chief Justice McLachlin wrote the majority judgment ([2004] B.C.J. No. 2337), reinstating the trial judgment, except for the unfair competition award arising out of the investment advisors' conduct during the 2.5 weeks reasonable notice period.

Damages for breach of contract are governed by the principle in the old English case of *Hadley v. Baxendale* (1854), 9 Ex. 341, 156 E.R. 145. They are to be assessed by what was reasonably contemplated by the parties, at the time the contract was formed, of the consequences of such breach. In organizing the mass exodus, the branch manager breached his duty of good faith and the implied term of his contract of employment to retain employees under his supervision. Damages were measured by the loss suffered by RBC, which was reasonably in the contemplation of the parties, as a consequence of the mass exodus. Thus, the award of $1.5 million against the branch manager personally for loss of profits due to the near collapse of the RBC office was upheld.

Nevertheless, the Court made it clear that at common law, damages are not to be awarded on the basis of a duty not to compete during the notice period, absent a restrictive covenant. A former employee is not prevented from competition with his or her former employer during the notice period in the absence of working notice or a restrictive covenant. The employer only gets damages for the failure of an employee to give reasonable notice. The trial judge, therefore, erred in law in awarding damages for a general duty not to compete.

With respect to the conversion of documents, Chief Justice McLachlin said that the trial judge took into account the use of confidential information in determining the loss of profits award against the branch manager. Because of this award, "it would be inappropriate to award additional damages against the investment advisors for loss of profits based on improper use of confidential information" (see para. 21). This would amount to double recovery for RBC.

This decision represents an important development in the duties and obligations of departing employees to their former employers. It will be interesting to see how the lower courts interpret this important precedent. This decision appears to create a halfway house between the obligations of fiduciary employees on the one hand and ordinary employees on the other. Justice Abella, in dissent, cautioned that the imposition of a new category of "quasi-fiduciary" employees will create a "chilling effect" on the mobility of non-fiduciary senior employees in situations where no restrictive covenant exists.

39

INTERLOCUTORY RELIEF: A MODIFIED APPROACH

Employers are often faced with the reality that a negative covenant in one of its employment contracts will be breached by a wayward former employee. Even more worrisome for an employer and its lawyer, however, is the risk that a court will decline to enforce a carefully crafted negative covenant on a motion for an interlocutory injunction. The test to meet for a successful motion for interlocutory relief can be a tough legal battle to win. On top of this, courts do not always look favourably upon an employer's attempt to enforce a term in an employment contract where it seeks to restrict a former employee's ability to be gainfully employed. In *Hargraft Schofield LP v. Schofield*, [2007] O.J. No. 4400 (Ont. S.C.J.) Justice Himel had a chance to review the test to be met when asking the Court for such interlocutory relief.

In 2000, John Schofield ("Schofield"), an experienced insurance broker, sold his business to Hargraft Wood Flemming Limited to create Hargraft Schofield Limited ("Hargraft"). On the closing date, Schofield entered into a three-year employment contract that included a confidentiality and non-disclosure agreement and a non-competition clause. The three-year employment contract was extended twice by the parties. The last extension expired on December 31, 2006.

During Schofield's employment with Hargraft, he became romantically involved with one of its employees, Patti Hull ("Hull"). On June 9, 2006, Hull and Schofield were married. Approximately five months later, Hargraft dismissed Hull. The parties entered into a settlement agreement that prohibited Hull from soliciting Hargraft's clients and restricting her from using any confidential information.

After she left Hargraft, Hull incorporated a company, Edgehill Insurance Brokers Limited ("Edgehill"). Schofield, unable to continue working at Hargraft without his spouse, turned down the chance to extend his contract for a third time and instead joined Hull at Edgehill.

This legal proceeding arose when Hargraft made an application for injunctive relief against Schofield's and Hull's actions. Hargraft requested three types of relief. First, it asked the Court to restrain the defendant Schofield from competing with Hargraft until after December 31, 2009. Second, it asked the Court to restrain Hull and Edgehill from employing Schofield until after December 31, 2009. Hargraft argued that since Schofield's employment contract expired on December 31, 2006, the three-year negative covenant restricted him from competing with the company until December 31, 2009. Finally, Hargraft asked for an order restraining all of the defendants from using Hargraft's confidential information.

Ordinarily, the test for interlocutory relief is fairly straightforward. It includes the following three questions:

1. Is there a serious issue to be tried?
2. Will the applicant suffer irreparable harm if the injunction is not granted?
3. Which party will suffer the greatest harm from granting or refusing the injunction, that is, where does the balance of convenience lie?

What sets the *Schofield* decision apart from other decisions on interlocutory relief is the fact that Justice Himel suggests that a modified version of the test is applicable to the defendant Schofield. Rather than having to prove all three branches of the test, Hargraft only had to satisfy the first question: whether or not there is a serious issue to be tried. According to Himel J., the negative covenant between Hargraft and Schofield formed part of the transaction in which Schofield sold his business interests to Hargraft. Rather than interpreting the relationship as a typical employment relationship, where there is an inequality of bargaining power, Himel J. found Schofield to be a seller and Hargraft to be a buyer. In this context, the parties were on an equal footing. Furthermore, Himel J. noted that each party had independent legal advice when it negotiated the agreement.

Justice Himel found the scope of the negative covenant to be *prima facie* reasonable between the parities; there was no evidence to suggest that it was contrary to the public interest. On this basis, she was satified that there was a strong *prima facie* case that the non-compete clause was enforceable, and thus, a serious issue to be tried.

Despite her finding that Hargraft only had to satisfy the first branch of the test, Himel J. went on to analyze the second and third branches of the test. With regard to irreparable harm, Himel J. notes that this is a case where it may be difficult to assess damages in a way that will provide adequate compensation for the harm suffered. While there was no suggestion that Hargraft would be put out of business if the injunction was refused, according to Himel J., Hargraft could suffer permanent market loss or damage to its reputation. This type of loss is very difficult to quantify. Justice Himel also points out that because Edgehill is a new company, it may not have sufficient assets to cover a damage award if Hargraft were successful at trial. Given the above, Himel J. found clear evidence of irreparable harm.

Justice Himel also found that the balance of convenience favoured Hargraft. The evidence showed that Hargraft had paid a substantial amount of money to acquire Schofield's business interests. There was evidence that the actions of Hull and Schofield were having a detrimental impact on Hargraft's business, including the loss of several clients. In these circumstances, Himel J. found that the public interest favoured granting injunctive relief.

Despite Hargraft's success in obtaining interlocutory relief, it is hard to know exactly what this case will mean for employers. While Himel J. applies a modified test in reaching her conclusion, her reasoning in doing so had to do with the fact that the negative covenant at issue arose out of a transaction for the sale of his business. Justice Himel suggests that the principle behind this approach is the fact that the parties to the contract in these circumstances have equal bargaining power. The Court uses a modified test because all it is doing is enforcing a contractual provision agreed to by the parties. The question for employers and their lawyers then becomes whether or not this principle can be extended to apply to other employee-employer relationships where the parties are, arguably, also on an equal footing.

What about senior executives who get independent legal advice? If Himel J.'s basis for modifying the test is accepted, in cases where an employer can show equality of bargaining power, *Schofield* may serve to be an important precedent for employers in the future.

40

EMPLOYERS BEWARE: ONTARIO PASSES CONTROVERSIAL AMENDMENTS TO THE ONTARIO HUMAN RIGHTS CODE

1. The Human Rights Code Undergoes Major Renovations
2. Individuals Can and Must Apply Directly to the Tribunal
3. Applications May be Made up to One Year Following the Incident
4. Tribunal Practices and Procedures
5. Whether Tribunal can Award Damages for Mental Anguish
6. Civil Courts and Human Rights Complaints
7. Decisions of the Tribunal
8. Prevention is the Key

1. THE HUMAN RIGHTS CODE UNDERGOES MAJOR RENOVATIONS

On December 20, 2006, Bill 107, or the *Human Rights Code Amendment Act, 2006*, S.O. 2006, c. 30, received Royal Assent. When the substantive provisions of the Act were proclaimed into force, it brought about the most significant changes to the Ontario human rights system since its inception in 1962. The primary aim of the amendments was the creation of a more efficient and effective complaints regime. Although it remains unclear whether the amendments have had their anticipated effect, what is clear is that the *Human Rights Code Amendment Act, 2006*, has changed the manner in which human rights complaints are initiated, tried, resolved and appealed in the province. In the employment context, these changes have for the most part benefited complainant employees at the expense of their employers.

2. INDIVIDUALS CAN AND MUST APPLY DIRECTLY TO THE TRIBUNAL

The new amendments require complainants to apply directly to the Human Rights Tribunal of Ontario for relief. The Ontario Human Rights Commission no longer investigates and filters out unworthy applications. Under the new Act, all applications to the Tribunal that are timely and within the Tribunal's jurisdiction will be heard on their merits. There is only one small exception to this general principle. The Tribunal may hold a summary hearing on the question of whether an application should be dismissed on the basis that there is no reasonable prospect it will succeed. This limited exception came into effect July 1, 2010. The fundamental changes are of obvious benefit to complainants. The outlook for employers, on the other hand, is not so favourable. As it will be significantly easier for complainants to have their cases heard by the Tribunal, employers can expect a marked increase in the amount of time and money they are forced to spend on litigating human rights complaints.

3. APPLICATIONS MAY BE MADE UP TO ONE YEAR FOLLOWING THE INCIDENT

The amendments extended the time limit for applications from six months to one year following the incident that gave rise to the complaint.

4. TRIBUNAL PRACTICES AND PROCEDURES

The Tribunal has greater power to determine its own practices and procedures but must afford every complainant the opportunity to make oral submissions and the benefit of written reasons.

Since the Commission no longer plays a role in the resolution of most complaints, the Act provides the Tribunal with the power to collect evidence and determine its own practices and procedures. Although the Tribunal is permitted to adopt alternatives to traditional adjudicative procedures, the amendments require that the Tribunal afford the parties to every complaint the opportunity to make oral submissions, as well as the benefit of written reasons. Requiring the Tribunal to provide the above-mentioned procedural rights ensures that every application receives substantial consideration and, consequently, requires a substantial amount of time.

5. WHETHER TRIBUNAL CAN AWARD DAMAGES FOR MENTAL ANGUISH

It is unclear whether damages for mental anguish can still be awarded by the Tribunal and, if so, in what amount?

The remedial power provided to the Tribunal by the amendments appears to be almost identical to the broad remedial power set out in the old Act. As was the case in the old Act, the amendments place no limit on the award of general damages for losses arising out of the infringement. However, the old Act specifically empowered the Tribunal to award additional compensation, up to $10,000, for "mental anguish" where the infringement was "wilful" or "reckless". The amendments do not specifically provide for mental anguish damages and, accordingly, it remains unclear whether the amendments contemplate awarding such compensation. If the Tribunal adopts an interpretation permitting awards for mental anguish, there is a real risk that the frequency and amount of aggravated damages could rapidly increase. The amendments do not impose a ceiling on the amount of compensation, nor do they specifically require that the relevant infringement was wilful or reckless. Accordingly, the amendments may expose employers to much greater liability through human rights complaints.

6. CIVIL COURTS AND HUMAN RIGHTS COMPLAINTS

Civil courts can consider and determine human rights complaints appended to other civil proceedings.

From an employer's perspective, one of the most concerning developments from the new Act is that the courts are empowered to find that a party to a civil proceeding has infringed a right under Part I of the Ontario *Human Rights Code*, R.S.O. 1990, c. H.19, and remedy such an infringement through monetary compensation or restitution. Although the amendments do not permit a person to commence an action in court based solely on a human rights infringement, the door is open for plaintiffs in wrongful dismissal cases to claim damages for alleged human rights violations.

What is unclear is whether the amendments intend to provide civil courts with the power to reinstate a dismissed employee. The amendments specifically provide that a civil court may award monetary compensation and restitutive remedies, which have traditionally been held to include reinstatement. However, Courts have historically been unwilling to make reinstatement orders because they involve the imposition of a positive obligation.

Employers are certain to face a substantially greater number of human rights allegations in civil court. The inclusion of human rights complaints in wrongful dismissal claims is likely to become standard practice, especially if civil courts embrace reinstatement as an appropriate remedy. Furthermore, the amendments may encourage the recent judicial trend of permitting punitive awards for violations of the *Human Rights Code*. This would not only dramatically increase the risk to employers, but would further encourage complainants to look to the courts, as opposed to the Tribunal, for relief.

7. DECISIONS OF THE TRIBUNAL

Decisions of the Tribunal are not subject to appeal; however, the Tribunal may reconsider its own decisions.

Under the old Act, any party to an application could appeal a decision or order of the Tribunal to the Divisional Court. Under the new Act, decisions of the Tribunal are final and not subject to appeal. The only recourse is to request that the Tribunal reconsider its own decision. It is in the Tribunal's discretion whether or not to grant such a request. The new appeal provisions, which apply to any Tribunal decision on a complaint referred to it on or after December 20, 2006, have increased the finality of Tribunal decisions. No matter the result, employers will generally find the added certainty to be a benefit of the new regime.

8. PREVENTION IS THE KEY

The *Human Rights Code Amendment Act, 2006*, instituted a substantial number of changes to the current human rights regime in Ontario. On the whole, it is unclear whether the amendments have achieved the goals of efficiency and efficacy that sparked their inception. What is clear is that the new procedure has had a significant effect on the way alleged human rights infringements are resolved in Ontario.

For the most part, the changes have resulted in increased risk to employers. Employers must be aware of the potential for much larger awards being granted by the Tribunal or the courts under the new regime. Consequently, employers should take steps to increase their awareness of human rights issues in the workplace, including the development of proactive procedures and policies to prevent harassment and discrimination. Preventing human rights issues from arising is more important than ever because the potential cost of remedying complaints that do arise will become significantly more expensive.

41

UNDUE HARDSHIP AND THE EMPLOYER'S DUTY TO ACCOMMODATE

Finding ways to accommodate employees with disabilities can be one of the most challenging responsibilities faced by employers. This is particularly the case where an employee's disability causes him or her to be away from work for months, or even years. In this situation, employers may be tempted to end the employment relationship. But in doing so, the employer risks facing allegations of discrimination for failing to accommodate the disabled employee. How can an employer know when it has satisfied its duty to accommodate in these circumstances?

The Ontario *Human Rights Code*, R.S.O. 1990, c. H.19 (the "Code") states that an employer must accommodate a disabled employee to the point of "undue hardship". But how do you know when accommodating an employee causes "undue hardship"? The Code offers minimal guidance, saying only that consideration must be given to the cost of, and any health and safety issues arising from, accommodating the employee. Unfortunately, neither the courts nor human rights tribunals have established clear rules on when accommodation causes "undue hardship".

Recognizing the uncertainty in this important area of human rights law, the Supreme Court of Canada has offered guidance on when accommodation causes undue hardship in its recent decision in *Hydro-Québec v. Syndicat d'employées de technique professionnelles et de bureau d'Hydro-Québec, section locale 2000*, [2008] S.C.J. No. 44 (S.C.C.).

In this case, the complainant was an employee with numerous physical and mental ailments that caused her to miss 960 days of work over seven years of employment with Hydro-

Québec. Hydro-Québec took numerous steps to try to accommodate the employee. It provided her with light duties, had placed her on gradual return to work following depressive episodes, and even provided her a new position when her position was eliminated after a restructuring. Despite these attempts at accommodation, the employee's doctors concluded she would not be able to work without continuing to suffer from chronic absenteeism for the foreseeable future. Hydro-Québec therefore terminated the employee.

The employee's union disputed Hydro-Québec's decision, claiming that Hydro-Québec had failed to satisfy its duty to accommodate the employee. The union's expert was of the opinion that if Hydro-Québec completely changed the employee's work environment (*i.e.*, by providing a new supervisor and co-workers), this would remove the "stressors" that made her unable to work and therefore would allow the employee to return to work. The arbitrator rejected the expert's opinion, saying this type of accommodation would cause Hydro-Québec undue hardship. The arbitrator therefore concluded that Hydro-Quebec had satisfied its duty to accommodate.

The arbitrator's decision was upheld by the Quebec Superior Court ([2004] J.Q. No. 11048), but was reversed by the Quebec Court of Appeal ([2006] J.Q. No. 907), which concluded that Hydro-Québec did not satisfy its duty to accommodate because the evidence of the union's expert demonstrated that it was not "impossible" to accommodate the employee.

The Supreme Court of Canada ([2008] S.C.J. No. 44) rejected the Quebec Court of Appeal's conclusion that an employer must show it is "impossible" to accommodate an employee. As stated by the Supreme Court, at para. 14, "The purpose of the duty to accommodate is to ensure that persons who are otherwise fit to work are not unfairly excluded where working conditions can be adjusted without undue hardship." Requiring an employer to fundamentally change an employee's working conditions causes undue hardship. Instead, the Supreme Court said that the duty to accommodate requires an employer to make more reasonable changes, such as adopting a variable work schedule, providing light duties or authorizing a staff transfer. If such changes still do not allow the employee to return to work for the reasonably foreseeable future, the employer has satisfied its duty to accommodate to the point of undue hardship, and the employer can safely end the employment relationship.

The Supreme Court concluded that Hydro-Québec had satisfied its duty to accommodate to the point of undue hardship. The Court noted that Hydro-Québec had taken a number of reasonable steps to try to accommodate the employee (including the unnecessary step of giving the employee a new position), yet despite these efforts it was clear she would continue to suffer from chronic absenteeism for the foreseeable future. According to the Supreme Court, at para. 19, "the employer's duty to accommodate ends where the employee is no longer able to fulfill the basic obligations associated with the employment relationship for the foreseeable future."

The *Hydro-Québec* case is a welcome decision for employers and their legal counsel, who for many years have struggled with assessing the scope of the duty to accommodate employees with serious disabilities.

The key lesson from *Hydro-Québec* is that terminating a seriously disabled employee is not discriminatory so long as the employer has taken reasonable steps to accommodate that employee to the point of undue hardship. If you are considering terminating an employee who has been absent from work because of a physical or mental disability, you should consider the following when assessing whether you have satisfied your duty to accommodate:

1. **Investigate into the employee's prospects of recovery.** A court or tribunal will not likely find it causes undue hardship for an employer to maintain the position of an employee who has a reasonable prospect of fully recovering in the foreseeable future.

2. **Determine whether reasonable modified work is available.** If the employee will remain disabled for the foreseeable future, examine whether reasonable work modifications can be made, such as adopting a variable work schedule or providing light duties, which would allow the disabled employee to continue working. Remember that the *Hydro-Québec* decision says that fundamental changes to the workplace – such as complete reorganizations or creating a new position - are not required.

3. **Assess whether the disabled employee can perform work for the foreseeable future.** If the employee cannot perform regular or modified work for the foreseeable future, the employer will establish "undue hardship" and the duty to accommodate ends. Ending the employment relationship in this circumstance is not discriminatory.

42

ADGA GROUP CONSULTANTS INC. V. LANE – WHAT TO DO WHEN AN EMPLOYEE HIDES A DISABILITY?

Accommodating disabled employees is a constant concern for employers. The duty to accommodate employees with disabilities is paramount. Yet, employees may have disabilities they have kept hidden from employers in fear of being stigmatized and alienated. When those disabilities come to the employer's attention, what obligations does an employer have under the duty to accommodate? In *ADGA Group Consultants Inc. v. Lane*, [2008] O.J. No. 3076, the Divisional Court of Ontario upheld an Ontario Human Rights Tribunal decision ([2007] O.H.R. T.D. No. 34) that found a bipolar employee was terminated without any attempt at accommodation of his disability to the point of undue hardship.

Paul Lane suffered for years from "Bipolar 1 Disorder," which is characterized by a fluctuation in moods, varying between highs of mania and lows of depression, but with periods of stability. Lane told previous employers they should contact his wife when he was exhibiting bipolar symptoms like mania and depression. To recover, Lane would seek medical help and take time off. Despite these safeguards being accepted by previous employers, Lane did not disclose his disability during his interview with ADGA Group Consultants Inc. He even lied about the number of days he had been on sick leave for the last 12 months. Lane said he lied because he was afraid of being stigmatized due to his condition.

Lane told ADGA of his disability five days after commencing work. At the start of the next week, Lane was in an obvious pre-mania phase. At a meeting scheduled later that day, ADGA terminated Lane because he had lied on his job application and they could not afford to have him away for long periods of time. Lane made a complaint under Ontario's *Human Rights Code*, R.S.O. 1990, c. H.19.

The Human Rights Tribunal found ADGA had discriminated against Lane because of his bipolar disorder. ADGA had both a procedural and substantive duty to accommodate Lane's bipolar disorder up to the point of undue hardship. The procedural duty to accommodate was violated because ADGA did not engage in any exploration of what a bipolar disorder is, talk with Lane about his disability, investigate if it could manage Lane's condition or seek legal advice. The substantive duty to accommodate was violated because ADGA did not accommodate Lane to the point of undue hardship.

The Divisional Court upheld the decision of the Tribunal and clarified the requirements of proving discrimination under the Ontario *Human Rights Code*. When a party alleges discrimination in violation of the *Canadian Charter of Rights and Freedoms*, Part I of the *Constitution Act, 1982*, being Schedule B to the *Canada Act 1982* (U.K.), 1982, c. 11 it is required to select a comparator group or a group to which the person is being discriminated against. The Divisional Court stated the selection of a comparator group is not required under the Ontario *Human Rights Code*. Disability cases under the Code bring with them particular and individualized situations and once it is established the employee was terminated because of, or in part of, his or her disability, the employee has established a case of discrimination. Since Lane was dismissed because of his disability and the perceptions of that disability on his workplace performance, he had established discrimination. It was now up to the employer to prove it had accommodated the employee to the point of undue hardship.

It was also upheld that ADGA had violated both the procedural and substantive duty to accommodate. A procedural duty to accommodate includes obtaining all relevant information about the employee's disability, which could include information about a current medical condition, prognosis for recovery, ability to perform job duties and capabilities for alternate work. The Divisional Court wrote, at para. 106, "[a] failure to give any thought or consideration to the issue of accommodation, including what, if any, steps could be taken constitutes a failure to satisfy the 'procedural' duty to accommodate."

ADGA did not meet the substantive duty to accommodate, which requires the employer to show that it could not have accommodated the employee's disability short of undue hardship, because ADGA did not show it was *impossible* to accommodate Lane. The Divisional Court rejected ADGA's arguments that it could not accommodate Lane because the work was safety critical and there was no room for error. Lane could do the essential duties of the job when not at either ends of the bipolar spectrum and ADGA had found ways to deal with other short-term and long-term employee absences. Accordingly, ADGA failed to establish it accommodated Lane to the point of undue hardship.

This reaffirms employers must always make an effort to fulfill the duty to accommodate when dealing with disabled employees. Accommodation includes more than making sure the employee has a job. It involves an education of the employer by gathering information about the disability that is being accommodated. The more informed an employer is about the employee's disability, the more clear it will be to determine whether or not there is undue hardship.

Employers should note the Supreme Court of Canada explicitly rejected that undue hardship is found when an employee's disability is impossible to accommodate in *Hydro-Québec v. Syndicat des employées de techniques professionnelles et de bureau d'Hydro-Québec, section locale 2000*, [2008] S.C.J. 44 (S.C.C.). In that decision, released before the Divisional Court could release the *ADGA Group Consultants Inc. v. Lane* decision, the Supreme Court stated, at para. 16, "The test is not whether it was impossible for the employer to accommodate the employee's characteristics. The employer does not have a duty to change working conditions in a fundamental way, but does have a duty, if it can do so without undue hardship, to arrange the employee's workplace or duties to enable the employee to do his or her work." The common ground is that employers must be responsive and accommodating to employees with disabilities, both known and recently discovered. Employers who rely on rash decisions based on fear will find no solace in a court of law.

43

DISMISSED EMPLOYEES MAY NEED TO RELOCATE TO MITIGATE THEIR DAMAGES

Recessionary global financial markets and rising unemployment have made it increasingly difficult for terminated employees to find alternative work, especially in industries like construction, manufacturing and financial services. Ontario was hit particularly hard in 2009. According to a Statistics Canada survey for 2009, 35,000 Ontario jobs were lost in February, chiefly in construction and finance. The unemployment rate rose 0.7 per cent to 8.7 per cent, the highest level in 12 years. Ontario's unemployment rate rose by 2 per cent from October 2009 to March 2010. In fact, just over half of Canada's 160,000 job losses for this period occurred in Ontario, well beyond the province's 39 per cent share of the total workforce. These numbers are startling.

Not all provinces are suffering. For example, while Ontario was shedding jobs, in 2009, Premier Brad Wall of Saskatchewan sent a delegation to Toronto to promote career opportunities in Saskatchewan and a new provincial refundable tax credit of up to $20,000 for post-secondary graduates who choose to stay there.

This raises a difficult question: in tough economic times, should dismissed Ontario employees be required to relocate to job-rich areas in order to mitigate their damages?

In *Smith v. Aker Kvaerner Canada Inc.*, [2005] B.C.J. No. 150 (B.C.S.C.), a case involving a terminated employee in British Columbia's hard hit pulp and paper industry, the British Columbia Supreme Court said at para. 31 "the plaintiff has a duty to act reasonably and to take such steps as a reasonable person in the plaintiff's position would take in his own interest to maintain his income and his position in his industry, trade or profession. The duty involves a constant and assiduous application for alternative employment, *an exploration of what is available through all means*".

Courts have concluded that an employee is required to relocate to find new employment where doing so is reasonable. The courts look at a number of factors when determining the reasonableness of relocation.

If an employee has a history of frequently relocating across the country, failing to relocate could be considered unreasonable, especially if other opportunities were readily available elsewhere. In a Newfoundland case, *Harris v. Eastern Provincial Airways (1963) Ltd.*, [1981] N.J. No. 118 (Nfld. T.D.), the Court said that a young man who was used to travelling and who had been employed outside the province previously, had no reason for not seeking employment elsewhere in Canada.

Several cases have also found that an employee will have a duty to relocate where this is customary in the industry.

Courts are, however, very hesitant to require workers with families to relocate. For example, in an Ontario case, *Schalkwyk v. Hyundai Auto Canada Inc.*, [1995] O.J. No. 3964 (Ont. Gen. Div.), the Court found that it was unreasonable for an employee with a wife and two children to relocate across the country or to the U.S. in order to mitigate his damages, as this was too disruptive and costly to the employee's family.

When Does an Employee Have NO Duty to Mitigate? The Case of Wronko v. Western Inventory Service Ltd.

It is a general principle of employment law that dismissed employees have an affirmative duty to mitigate their damages by seeking alternative employment, and that any income received through mitigation must be deducted from any damages award obtained. However, the Court of Appeal for Ontario, in a supplement to *Wronko v. Western Inventory Service Ltd.*, [2008] O.J. No. 2396 (Ont. C.A.), has recently held that such duty may be implicitly waived by the language of the contract of employment.

Wronko's contract of employment contained a termination provision that provided for a lump sum severance payment of two years' salary in the event of dismissal. Wronko asserted that his damages award in the amount of $286,000 was not subject to mitigation because it was payable within one pay period, rather than being structured as salary continuance. The Court of Appeal agreed. Clause 2.4 of Wronko's contract stated (see para. 3) that:

> Within one (1) pay period after the end of the month in which the effective date of termination occurs…the accountants of the Company for the time being shall report as to the amount of remuneration payable to the Employee as aforesaid, and the amount shown to be payable (taking into account any prior payments that have been made on account thereof) shall be paid within one (1) pay period of the making of the report…. A pay period is equivalent to two (2) weeks from the date of [the] last previous pay day.

A unanimous Court of Appeal interpreted this provision as effectively waiving the duty to mitigate. The Court said, at para. 4, that "[b]y requiring the [employer] to make a lump sum payment shortly after termination, this term of the contract amounted to a waiver by the [employer] of any obligation on the part of the [employee] to mitigate". Thus, even though Wronko earned more than $200,000 in the two years immediately following his dismissal, he was also entitled to two years of termination pay under his original contract with Western Inventory Services.

45

THE WAIT IS OVER — THE SUPREME COURT OF CANADA CLOSES THE FLOODGATE TO PUNITIVE DAMAGES CLAIMS

After the Ontario Court of Appeal decided the case of *Keays v. Honda Canada Inc.(c.o.b. Honda of Canada MFG)*, [2006] O.J. No. 3891, employers were holding their breaths to see what the Supreme Court of Canada would do with the apparent opening of the floodgates to employees to claim punitive damages in the context of wrongful dismissal claims. The wait is over and employers can rest assured that the Supreme Court set things straight. Punitive damages will only be available in rare cases.

It goes without saying that employers should act in good faith and have a strong basis with which to support a termination for cause. In wrongful dismissal cases, the onus is on the employer to establish just cause for termination. If the employer fails to do so, the Court will award the employee a sum of money that represents the employee's reasonable notice of termination, as well as any other damages and costs that the Court deems appropriate. In the recent case of *Honda Canada Inc. v. Keays*, [2008] S.C.J. No. 40 (*"Honda"*), the Supreme Court of Canada took the opportunity to clarify the proper allocation of damages in wrongful dismissal cases. The Supreme Court of Canada set down several important principles that other courts are likely to follow in the future and, as such, the judgment provides some valuable guidance to employers with regard to appropriate termination practices and procedures, especially when the termination involves disabled employees.

Kevin Keays ("Keays") began working at Honda Canada Inc. ("Honda") in 1986. Although he started work as a production line employee, he joined the Quality Engineering Department after 20 months. Soon after commencing work, Keays began to experience health problems due to chronic fatigue syndrome ("CFS"). His resulting occasional absences caused problems for the lean staffing model used by Honda. Ultimately, Keays went on disability leave in October 1996, and remained on leave until December 1998. Honda's long-term disability insurer then determined that he was able to return to work and terminated his benefits. Keays consequently returned to work under the protests of both himself and his treating physician that he was too ill to do so. He soon began to experience intermittent work absences that resulted in his being "coached" by way of written report, the first step in Honda's progressive discipline plan.

Pursuant to the coaching program, Honda provided some accommodation for Keays's intermittent absences, thus recognizing his CFS disability as a legal and medical excuse for the absences. However, Honda also instituted a requirement that Keays had to get a doctor's note validating each absence before he could return to work. Because employees with "mainstream" illnesses did not face this requirement, Keays retained a lawyer who wrote a letter to Honda outlining Keays' concerns and offering to work toward a resolution of their differences. Honda did not respond to this letter, but instead met with Keays on March 21, 2000 to inform him that he must meet with the company's occupational medicine specialist, Dr. Brennan. Honda also advised Keays that it was cutting off what little accommodation it was providing to Keays for his disability. The day after the meeting, Keays informed Honda that he would not meet with Dr. Brennan until he was provided with clarification of the purpose, methodology and the parameters of the assessment to be done by the doctor. On March 28, 2000, Honda sent Keays a letter stating that Honda did not intend to elaborate further on the purpose of Keays's meeting with Dr. Brennan, and that if Keays did not meet with the doctor, he would be terminated. Keays maintained his position and was terminated after 14 years of service with Honda. After being fired, Keays suffered a three- or four-month period of post-traumatic adjustment disorder and qualified for a total disability pension under the Canada Pension Plan. Keays commenced a wrongful dismissal suit against Honda.

The trial judge held that Keays was entitled to 15 months' notice, but extended the notice period to 24 months based on the "egregious bad faith displayed by Honda in the manner of this termination and the medical consequences flowing therefrom". The trial judge also awarded $500,000 in punitive damages. Honda appealed. The Ontario Court of Appeal upheld the trial judge's ruling regarding the appropriate notice period required under the circumstances. The Court of Appeal went on to find that the award of punitive damages was a rational response on the part of the trial judge. The majority of the Court did, however, reduce the punitive damages award to $100,000. Honda appealed to the Supreme Court.

The first issue addressed by the Supreme Court was what factors should be considered when allocating compensatory damages in lieu of notice for wrongful dismissal. The Court reaffirmed that the factors articulated in *Bardal v. Globe and Mail Ltd.*, [1960] O.J. No. 149, 24 D.L.R. (2d) 140 (Ont. H.C.J.) and *Minott v. O'Shanter Dev. Co.*, [1999] O.J. No. 5, 168 D.L.R. (4th) 270 (Ont. C.A.) are to be considered. These factors include, but are not limited to, the character of the employment, length of service, the age of the employee and the availability of other employment. These factors are considered, having regard to the experience, training and qualifications of the employee. The Court summarized that it was the particular circumstances of the individual employee that are the concern of the courts in determining the appropriate period of reasonable notice. In the circumstances of this case, there was no basis to interfere with the 15-month notice period awarded by the trial judge.

The Supreme Court next addressed the basis for, and the calculation of, damages for conduct in dismissal. Justice Bastarache, in writing for the majority, took the unusual step of finding that the trial judge made a number of significant errors in findings of fact. More specifically, Justice Bastarache found that the trial judge made the following errors:

- Honda's letter to Keays requesting that he meet with Dr. Brennan was not callous and insensitive. It conveyed to Keays that Honda wanted him to meet with their doctor, because their experts had advised them that his condition did not preclude him from working. Honda was entitled to rely on their experts. The context indicated that Honda recognized Keays had a disability that had to be dealt with.

- Dr. Brennan was following the prevalent approach for diagnosing CFS adopted by the Centers for Disease Control in Atlanta. It cannot then be said he took a "hardball" approach. "However, even if... Dr. Brennan [did take a] 'hardball' approach... Honda cannot be faulted for accepting his expert evidence unless a conspiracy exists." Honda was merely listening to expert advice (see para. 45).
- Honda's decision to stop accepting doctors' notes was not reprisal for Keays seeking legal counsel. Honda was simply seeking to confirm Keays's disability.
- It was improper to consider Keays's disability subsequent to termination because there was no evidence that the disability was caused by the manner of termination.

The Supreme Court of Canada found that the overriding and palpable factual errors made by the trial judge formed the foundation that justified the trial judge's award of *Wallace* damages. *Wallace* damages are traditionally awarded for bad faith conduct on the part of an employer in regard to the manner of termination. In light of the errors of the trial judge, the appropriate notice period in this case was reduced from 24 months to 15 months. The Court went on to clarify that damages attributable to conduct in the manner of dismissal are not to be framed as an extension of the notice period. Rather, the amount is to be fixed according to the same principles and in the same way as all other cases dealing with moral damages. In other words, if the employee proves that the manner of dismissal caused mental distress that was in the contemplation of the parties, damages will be awarded through an award that reflects the actual damages, not an extension of the notice period. Examples of conduct that would attract this form of compensable damages include attacking the employee's reputation by making declarations at the time of dismissal misrepresentation regarding the reason for dismissal or dismissal intended to deprive the employee of a pension benefit.

Another significant aspect of the *Honda* judgment was the Supreme Court's discussion of awards of punitive damages in the context of a wrongful dismissal case. The Court distinguished between damages for conduct in the manner of dismissal, which are compensatory in nature, and punitive damages, which are intended to punish. While damages for conduct in the manner of dismissal are available where the manner of dismissal caused mental distress, as outlined above, for punitive damages to be awarded there must be an independent actionable wrong on the part of the defendant. In *Honda* the question of whether the tort of discrimination could constitute an independent actionable wrong was left open for another day. The Court held there was no evidence of discrimination to support Keays's claim, and thus declined to comment on this issue.

After determining whether there is an independent actionable wrong, an award of punitive damages is only warranted where there is harsh, vindictive and malicious conduct on the part of the defendant. In *Honda*, Justice Bastarache again found the trial judge committed overriding and palpable errors in findings of fact. He overturned the trial judge and accepted that Honda's program requiring medical notes to establish that absences were related to the disability was justified. Honda's conduct was not sufficiently egregious or outrageous to warrant a punitive damages award.

In summary, the decision in *Honda* will have a significant impact on employers' future termination practices and procedures. Indeed, it is an important case for establishing that damages for conduct in dismissal will be paid out in accordance with the actual damage sustained, not in the form of an extended notice period. Furthermore, the Court's comments on punitive damages limits the applicability of these awards to rather narrow circumstances. Employers should continue to proceed carefully when terminating employees, especially when the employee has a disability and will thus likely be considered particularly vulnerable in the eyes of a court. If employers continue to act in good faith vis-à-vis their employees and ensure that their actions and reasons for termination are reasonable in the circumstances, employers should be able to avoid the sanctions discussed in this important case.

46

HOW TO AVOID WALLACE DAMAGES

In *Wallace v. United Grain Growers (c.o.b. Public Press)*, [1997] S.C.J. No. 94, [1997] 3 S.C.R. 701, the Supreme Court of Canada established that where an employer engages in bad faith conduct at the time of termination, the employee will be entitled to a longer notice period. Dubbed *"Wallace"* damages, it was originally anticipated that they would only be awarded in exceptional cases. Since their inception, however, claims for *Wallace* damages have crept into almost every wrongful dismissal case in Canada. In fact, with the proliferation of *Wallace* damage claims, employers have reason to wonder if they will ever be able to terminate an employee without being accused of acting in bad faith. Given this context, employers may be relieved to know that the seemingly exponential increase in claims for *Wallace* damages has not gone unnoticed by the courts. In the case of *Mulvihill v. Ottawa (City)*, [2008] O.J. No. 1070, the Ontario Court of Appeal overturned a trial judge's award for *Wallace* damages and clarified the grounds on which a dismissed employee may be entitled to them. This judgment, in addition to that of *Honda Canada Inc. v. Keays*, [2008] S.C.J. No. 40 (S.C.C.) (*"Honda"*), should provide employers with some comfort that there is now appellate authority providing guidance as to the circumstances in which it is, and is not, appropriate to award *Wallace* damages.

In *Mulvihill*, the trial judge awarded *Wallace* damages on two grounds: (1) the City had alleged just cause but had abandoned this allegation prior to trial; and (2) the City had terminated Mulvihill while she was on sick leave. The City appealed to the Court of Appeal.

The main issue on appeal was whether or not the trial judge had erred in awarding *Wallace* damages. In overturning the trial judge's finding, the Court of Appeal reviewed the purpose of

Wallace damages, which is to compensate employees for the manner of dismissal if the employer falls below an acceptable standard of conduct. The Court reiterated that dismissed employees will be entitled to *Wallace* damages only where the employee can establish that the employer engaged in bad faith conduct or unfair dealing in the course of dismissal. Finally, the employee must show that the injuries flow not from dismissal, but from the manner in which the dismissal was carried out.

The Court went on to review the two grounds on which the trial judge had awarded *Wallace* damages. With respect to the first ground, the allegation for just cause, the Court held that the mere fact that cause is alleged, but not ultimately proven, does not automatically entitle a plaintiff to *Wallace* damages. Rather, an employer has a right to dismiss an employee for just cause as long as it has a reasonable basis on which to believe the employee engaged in misconduct that amounts to just cause. Notwithstanding this right, it is entirely reasonable for an employer to back down from this position if it becomes aware that it misunderstood the facts supporting just cause. In fact, employers should be encouraged to take such steps.

In this case, the Court of Appeal found that the employer had a reasonable basis on which to allege insubordination. First, Mulvihill had persistently accused her manager and the city clerk of being biased and incompetent. Second, Mulvihill had refused to return to her job unless the City met her condition of transferring her to another department. Finally, Mulvihill escalated her complaint of harassment to a point where she had the mayor involved. These factors were enough to support the City's reasonable belief of just cause.

Employers can take some comfort in the Court of Appeal's pronouncement on this issue: if an employer has a reasonable basis on which to allege just cause, but turns out to be mistaken or chooses to withdraw the allegation, the Court will not automatically impose a finding of bad faith.

With respect to the trial judge's second ground for *Wallace* damages, dismissing an employee while on sick leave, the Court of Appeal held once again that a "mistake" on the part of an employer is not enough to warrant *Wallace* damages. In this case, the City officials who made the decision to terminate Mulvihill believed that she was at home either because she was attending to her son's needs or because she would not return to work until she was transferred. The trial judge, however, accepted Mulvihill's evidence that she was at home on sick leave due to the stresses she was experiencing at work. While the Court of Appeal did not interfere with the trial judge's finding that Mulvihill was home on sick leave, it did not agree that the employer's misunderstanding amounted to bad faith conduct.

The Court of Appeal's finding with respect to the trial judge's second ground for *Wallace* damages suggests that the courts will need more than just careless behaviour on the part of an employer to warrant a finding of bad faith.

What are some other tips to avoid a finding of bad faith?

- When alleging just cause, be sure that the misconduct you are relying on to form the basis of just cause is well-documented. This will help to support your position that you had a reasonable belief of just cause.

- Prepare for the termination interview. The key is to conduct the interview in a professional, polite and discreet manner.

- If you are terminating without cause, ensure that an appropriate severance package is offered to the employee at the time of termination. Avoid debate or negotiation of the terms of the severance package.

- Allow the employee, with supervision, to return to his or her office to gather personal belongings.

- Consider having a professional outplacement counsellor on hand to meet with the employee immediately following the termination.

- Avoid making any untruthful disparaging comments about the employee.

While the Court of Appeal's decision in *Mulvihill* and the Supreme Court of Canada's decision in *Honda* may limit the circumstances in which an employer will be liable for *Wallace* damages, an employer's best defence is to take steps to avoid conduct that could be construed as bad faith in the first place.

47

ONTARIO COURT OF APPEAL MAKES IT MORE DIFFICULT FOR EMPLOYEES TO WIN WALLACE DAMAGES

Since 1997, employees have been able to claim *"Wallace"* damages as compensation for bad faith conduct by employers during dismissal. In an employer-friendly decision released on December 15, 2008, the Ontario Court of Appeal in *McNevan v. AmeriCredit*, [2008] O.J. No. 5081, has limited the type of conduct that may expose employers to *Wallace* damages.

McNevan, an assistant vice-president, was terminated without cause after only 13 months because upper management determined he was not a "good fit". Surprisingly, the trial judge awarded Wallace damages based on actions commonly taken by many employers in Ontario:

1. Management did not warn the employee about his lack of "fit";
2. No reference letter was provided;
3. No outplacement assistance was offered;
4. There were delays in processing the employee's T4 slip, record of employment, and vacation pay; and
5. The employee's property was accidentally damaged while being shipped to the employee.

The Court of Appeal disagreed with the trial judge's conclusion that this was "bad faith" conduct justifying *Wallace* damages. The Court held that the employer had no duty to "warn" its employee that he was not a "good fit" prior to dismissing him without cause, saying that such a warning would have been a "potentially hurtful charade".

The Court also concluded that employers are under no legal obligation to provide reference letters or outplacement assistance, and that failing to do so will not result in a finding of bad faith. The Court held that the damage to the employee's property was accidental and therefore was not done in bad faith. Finally, the Court held that the delay in processing the employee's vacation pay, T4 slip and record of employment was not so "callous" to justify a finding of bad faith.

The Court of Appeal's decision in *McNevan* is good news for employers as it continues the trend of setting a high bar for employees claiming *Wallace* damages, recently set by the Supreme Court of Canada's recent decision in *Honda Canada Inc. v. Keays*, [2008] S.C.J. No. 40.

However, the *McNevan* decision is not all good news. This decision unfortunately sets a high-water mark for reasonable notice for short-service employees. Despite McNevan's short employment of only 13 months, he was awarded six months' reasonable notice. The Court of Appeal found that this award was within the "acceptable range" given McNevan's management responsibilities and the dearth of comparable job opportunities in his region. Employers should, therefore, be cognizant of the risk of a large reasonable notice award when considering the termination of senior, short-service employees.

PART FOUR

Practical Tips

48

HOW TO BULLET PROOF YOUR JOB

1. Document Your Side of the Story
2. Avoid Insubordination
3. Don't Poison the Workplace
4. Hire a Ghostwriter
5. Know When to Make a Deal

You may think that you have very little job security and that your employer can dismiss you at any time without notice or compensation.

Although it is true that an employer in a non-union workplace can dismiss you at any time, you should know that in the absence of just cause, *i.e.*, the legal grounds to dismiss, you are entitled to receive reasonable notice or pay in lieu of notice. How much you are entitled to will depend on your age, length of service, position and responsibilities and your chances of getting another job. How this usually works is that an employee with long service will be entitled to more compensation. The general rule is that an employee is entitled to two or four weeks notice or pay in lieu, for every year of service.

In some cases, however, an employer facing a hefty severance bill will try to avoid paying severance by trying to build a case for cause. The employer has the onus to prove cause for dismissal. If an employer can prove cause for dismissal then the employee is not entitled to any compensation whatsoever. As an example, there is a case where the employee, who had a flawless work record for almost 29 years, was fired for cause without compensation within six months after a new supervisor was appointed. Suddenly, after 28-and-a-half years, the supervisor started sending the employee written warnings that she would be fired for cause if her performance and attitude did not improve. Confident that she would never lose her job, let alone be fired without compensation, the employee grossly misread the signals and in fact suffered a humiliating dismissal for cause. She is now suing her employer. So how can you avoid misreading the signals that your job is on the line? What should you do if you think your boss wants to fire you? Are there any steps that you can take to ensure that you will at least get fair compensation? Here are a few suggestions:

1. DOCUMENT YOUR SIDE OF THE STORY

Make sure that when you receive a written warning from your employer you read it carefully and respond to each and every allegation of wrongdoing raised in the letter. Usually there is always an explanation that can be offered in reply or at the very least, a simple correction of any misstated facts. Remember, your boss is giving you the warning letter not only to advise you of your shortcomings but with the intention to rely on the letter in the event of your dismissal. You are entitled to know what you have done wrong and what is required to improve your performance. You also have the right to a reasonable amount of time in order to improve your performance. Usually the length of time will depend on length of service, your job duties and the nature of your performance problems.

Remember that if you are dismissed for cause your employer will rely on these written warnings to justify the dismissal without compensation. If you choose not to document your own response, it will be very difficult to convince a trial judge later on that the employer's version of the facts was inaccurate. You should also make sure that your response is timely and polite.

2. AVOID INSUBORDINATION

Like it or not, your boss deserves some level of respect. Insubordination, either by insulting your boss or swearing or refusing to follow company orders, can be grounds for dismissal in the right circumstances. If there is an obvious personality conflict, avoid any conduct or remarks that might constitute insubordination. Sometimes it is better to get a third party involved, such as the human resources manager, to assist in making the working relationship function more smoothly. Always avoid sending impulsive, aggressive emails or memos to your boss. Just one ballistic email response to your boss can trigger your dismissal.

3. DON'T POISON THE WORKPLACE

Many employees facing an impending dismissal attempt to "position" themselves among their co-workers by confiding in them about all the problems they are having on the job. Often, the same employee will criticize the boss for being unfair and hard to work for and will try to encourage other employees to feel the same way. Typically, this is a bad strategy and will cause disruption to the workplace. In some cases, it will give the employer even more motivation to summarily dismiss you. The better approach is to always keep it confidential and well-documented.

4. HIRE A GHOSTWRITER

If you are faced with a letter campaign by your employer, it is probably wise to retain an employment lawyer who will ghostwrite your responses to your employer and will provide you with objective advice and a strategy. It is usually preferable for you to write the letter directly to your employer, with your lawyer's input, rather then to send a threatening legal letter. It may be necessary later on to have your lawyer communicate directly with your employer, but the "soft approach" is probably a better strategy to begin with.

5. KNOW WHEN TO MAKE A DEAL

Remember that your single objective after you start receiving warning letters is to prevent your employer from dismissing you without compensation. In some cases, you may even be able to keep your job, but that decision is clearly within the control of the company. The most you can do in some cases is to make it as difficult as possible for your boss to fire you without compensation. Obviously, improving your performance, if there really is a problem, is constructive but the documentation strategy is critical. So at what point do you move away from the documentation process and move into the negotiation process?

Timing is everything and you may not have much control over it in any event. Depending on the circumstances, your boss may realize early on that the documentation process will take too much time and effort and in light of your documentation efforts, that the best solution would be to dismiss you immediately and to provide a reasonable severance package. Conversely, you may have to approach your boss and cordially admit that the relationship is not working well for both parties and that you would welcome a severance package if one were offered. Your boss might just be relieved by your invitation to leave the company. Make sure, however, that you never resign without first agreeing to a severance package.

Although there is no entitlement to a job, per se, and therefore arguably no job security, if you read the signals properly when your boss starts the discipline process, you can strategically make your job last longer and you may be able to secure a severance package.

49

WHAT TO DO WHEN YOU GET FIRED

1. No Job Security
2. There is a Difference
3. Onus of Proof
4. Grounds for Dismissal
5. Mitigation
6. Get Advice

Being fired is a traumatic experience for most people. Feelings of shock, anger and fear are normal. Most employees do not understand their rights at the time of their dismissal and therefore often make serious mistakes that may adversely affect them financially and may harm their chances of finding another job.

Here are a few things that you should know when you get fired:

1. NO JOB SECURITY

An employer in a non-union workplace can dismiss you at any time provided there is no violation of a statutory right as, for example, under the *Human Rights Code*. Apart from any specific contractual terms or statutory protections that you may have, an employer may fire you at any time for cause or in the absence of cause, by providing you with notice or pay in lieu of notice.

2. THERE IS A DIFFERENCE

Although it has often been said that it feels the same to be fired regardless of whether it is for cause or without cause, there is a significant difference between these two positions. When you are fired for cause you are generally not entitled to any compensation. The allegations of cause are usually serious, emotionally upsetting and potentially harmful to your reputation. In a dismissal without cause, you are entitled to compensation during a reasonable notice period and there are no serious allegations that will be raised by your employer. Usually you will be provided with a reference letter and outplacement counselling to assist you in your job search. There is usually no need for litigation as it is generally easy to calculate what you are entitled to receive at the time of dismissal.

3. ONUS OF PROOF

If your employer is dismissing you for cause, the onus of proof will be on the employer to establish that cause at law exists for your summary dismissal. It is not for you to prove that you were a good employee.

Importantly, the standard of proof is not whether the employer honestly believes that there is just cause, but rather whether a reasonable person would conclude that there is just cause. It is an objective test, not a subjective one. Equally important is that the employer only has to meet a civil standard of proof, not a criminal one. This means that the employer must be able to prove cause on a balance of probabilities, which is translated to mean over a 50 per cent level of certainty, rather, than the criminal standard of beyond a reasonable doubt, which is much higher. To complicate things even further, the civil standard of proof may move closer to the criminal standard of beyond a reasonable doubt where the alleged misconduct is criminal in nature (for example, theft).

4. GROUNDS FOR DISMISSAL

Just about any type of misconduct may be grounds for a dismissal for cause depending on the circumstances. However, some of the more recognized types of misconduct include theft, dishonesty, incompetence, personality conflict, insubordination, misappropriation of funds, damage to property, failure to report to work, conflict of interest and breach of company policy.

Whether cause exists at law will depend on all the circumstances surrounding the misconduct. Until recently, courts would approach cases involving dishonesty by simply determining whether the employee committed an act of dishonesty and if so, the court would conclude that cause existed. However, courts are now prepared to engage in a much broader examination of all the circumstances relating to the employee's employment in all cases of alleged misconduct, not only dishonesty. This "contextual" approach recognizes the importance of employment in one's life and the vulnerability of most employees at the time of dismissal. This means that in most cases there is a lot of uncertainty with respect to whether the employer can actually prove just cause in court. There are very few cases where an employment lawyer will be able to accurately predict the outcome of a just cause case. The contextual approach now followed by the courts has definitely created more uncertainty for employers in deciding whether just cause should be alleged.

5. MITIGATION

If you have been dismissed, you have an obligation to search for another comparable job. If you fail to take reasonable steps to secure another job, the court may conclude that your failure to mitigate your damages should reduce the amount of compensation that your former employer has to pay you. If you do secure alternate work, any income you earn will be offset against the money your employer has to pay you as reasonable notice of termination.

Before you consider commencing litigation against your former employer for wrongful dismissal, evaluate what your chances are of getting another job and how that could affect your claim.

6. GET ADVICE

If you are dismissed for cause, consult an employment lawyer who can provide advice on whether your employer had cause to dismiss you. An experienced lawyer will be able to assess your case and you can make an informed decision whether you should commence a wrongful dismissal action. Litigation is expensive, time-consuming and emotionally draining for most dismissed employees. Litigation often takes on a "life of its own" and the employee focuses on the litigation rather then on trying to secure a new job. Remember that litigation will not get you your job back. The litigation is usually about money and there are a lot of unpredictable risks associated with just cause litigation.

In some cases a better approach may be to try to negotiate terms that will help you move on with your life, and will help you during your transition. Depending on the nature of the misconduct, you may be able to negotiate with your former employer to provide you with a reference letter and outplacement counselling.

50

Considerations During the Holiday Season

1. Dismissals
2. Lateness/Absenteeism
3. Alcohol Consumption
4. Harassment
5. Conflict of Interest

The Yuletide season raises several interesting issues for employers. Following are some suggestions on how to approach them.

1. DISMISSALS

It is never a good idea to dismiss your employee during the holiday season. Clearly, this applies to cases where the employee is being dismissed on a without-cause basis and with compensation. Judges are usually sympathetic to dismissed employees who are asked to leave at this time of year and therefore, there is always the risk that a court could increase the notice period beyond what might otherwise be considered to be normal.

If you are considering the dismissal of one of your employees at this time of year, ask yourself why the dismissal cannot wait until January. If there is no sound business reason for doing it at this time of year, it is probably best to postpone the dismissal.

Although there may be those who disagree, these considerations do not apply when dismissing an employee for cause. Where cause is alleged to exist for the dismissal, it is usually better to proceed with the dismissal soon after you have completed proper due diligence in order to avoid any allegation that you condoned the employee's conduct by not acting sooner. However, even in these circumstances, extra steps should be taken to make sure that the dismissal is handled professionally and with the utmost respect for the employee.

2. LATENESS/ABSENTEEISM

Employees have an obligation to maintain regular attendance at work even during the busy holiday season. However, being late will not be cause for dismissal unless there is a pattern of lateness and specific warnings have been given. Even an absence from work may not be sufficient cause unless the absence has had adverse effects on the company's operations or there has been a previous incident accompanied by a warning to the employee that any further absences would result in dismissal from employment.

3. ALCOHOL CONSUMPTION

Following several Court decisions, employers have been much more cautious about alcohol consumption at company holiday parties. The decision in *Jacobsen v. Nike Canada Ltd.*, [1992] B.C.J. No. 2626 (B.C.S.C.) opened the way for claims by third parties against employers arising from injury sustained in a motor vehicle accident caused by an employee following excessive alcohol consumption at a company party.

The most prudent way for employers to limit their exposure to these types of claims would be to highly publicize that the company expects its employees to avoid driving while under the influence, and to provide taxi chits for employees to discourage them from driving. It is also probably wise to have a cash bar as opposed to an all-evening open bar.

4. HARASSMENT

Believe it or not, there is still a sharp increase in the number of harassment complaints filed this time of year as compared to other months. Often, the conduct complained about involves inappropriate touching, kissing or comments. Usually these acts are precipitated by alcohol consumption and may simply be a case of poor judgment. These cases, at the request of both parties, can usually be easily resolved. Other cases, however, are more serious and involve aggressive inappropriate touching, which will necessitate a full investigation and potentially serious discipline.

Many companies are diligently creating work environments where mutual respect is the norm, and therefore the issue of harassment at holiday parties is not high on the radar screen. For others, it may be wise to include specific mention about alcohol consumption in a memo, that the company expects employees to behave professionally and respectfully to each other during the event. Another good idea is to plan an early redistribution of the workplace harassment policy.

5. CONFLICT OF INTEREST

The holidays are usually the time when customers, suppliers and business contacts are acknowledged and appreciation is expressed for their patronage. Gifts usually flow in both directions. For most companies, small gifts either given or received are not a problem.

However, if an employee inappropriately gives or receives a gift where business relationships are in play, there may be a conflict of interest that could justify summary dismissal. Generally, a conflict of interest occurs in any situation where the employee is doing something for the employee's own benefit, which runs counter to the best interests of the employer's business. Both real and potential conflicts of interest can be grounds for dismissal for cause. For example, in *Durand v. Quaker Oats Co. Canada Ltd.*, [1990] B.C.J. No. 725, 32 C.C.E.L. 63, the British Columbia Court of Appeal upheld a dismissal for cause, where a manager obtained free tickets to Las Vegas, without the employer's knowledge, from an advertiser doing business with the company. The Court found that the manager's conduct breached a clear company policy on conflict of interest and the tickets could compromise the employer's relationship with the advertiser.

The best approach is to have a clearly written conflict of interest policy distributed to all employees outlining what, if any, gifts are acceptable.

"'Tis the season to be jolly..."

51

HOW TO DEAL WITH A WORKPLACE DISABILITY

What do you think will happen to your job if you become disabled because of a serious health problem? Will your boss allow you to continue to work? Will he or she allow you to work modified hours or reduce your job duties to allow you to have more flexibility? Will your boss force you to see an independent doctor for a second opinion about the nature and severity of your medical condition? Will you lose your job?

These are the typical questions that will arise if your disability interferes with your ability to work. The fact that 50 per cent or more of all human rights complaints in Canada are disability related is evidence of the fact that employees and employers are battling over their respective rights once a disability arises.

To put this into perspective for you, a recent case involved an employee with multiple sclerosis (MS). John has been working for the same company for almost 20 years in the same job in middle management, and has suffered from MS for most of that time. He uses a wheelchair, has limited functional use of his hands and has home care. He loves his job and by all accounts he does it well. During his entire career, he has rarely ever had a performance review and has never received any performance-related discipline. His disability may be getting worse but no one really knows for sure.

Recently, John's boss shows up at his office without any notice, and tells John that he has received a few verbal complaints from employees about John's behaviour in the workplace, along with some personal observations of performance issues and that he wants John to immediately take a disability leave and to consent to a medical examination by an independent physician. John is shocked by the news. He does not want to go on disability leave because he wants to continue working. John thinks that he is doing a good job and cannot understand what his boss is doing.

John is suspicious that his boss wants to replace him with a younger and healthier person and feels strongly that if he agrees to go on disability leave and sees a company-referred physician, that his boss will never allow him to return to his job. John refuses to go on disability leave but is now suffering severe stress.

This is a classic case of where John's boss is doing everything wrong. His actions are callous and insensitive to John and without strong legal foundation.

How should John's boss have dealt with this issue? What should John do in order to minimize stress but also protect his job?

It is obvious that John's boss does not understand his legal obligations to a disabled person like John. If he really had performance concerns, he should have met with John and openly discussed the issues with John and allowed John an opportunity to respond. By immediately jumping to the conclusion that John should go on disability leave and see a company-appointed doctor, his assessment of John's ability to perform his job was biased and discriminatory.

John's boss did not have the right to unilaterally remove John from his job and require him to take a disability leave. If the conduct complained about is disability-related, John could not be fired as that would also be discriminatory. The problem for John's boss is that he incorrectly thought that by putting John on disability leave he could avoid any allegation of discrimination because he was not firing John. That is clearly incorrect and now John's boss can virtually do nothing without the risk of engaging in unlawful discriminatory conduct.

The other significant mistake that John's boss made was that he did not recognize that he has an obligation to accommodate John because of his disability. He overlooked the fact that John does not have to perform all of his job duties and that it was his obligation to determine what were the essential duties of his job and what, if any, accommodation efforts could be made to assist John in performing those essential duties. The fact is, as a disabled person, John, has a right to continue working as long as he can perform the essential duties of his job. The obligations on John's boss to accommodate John are extensive and rarely can a company avoid this legal obligation in circumstances where the employee genuinely wants to continue working.

How should John respond? John needs to involve experienced legal counsel. In these circumstances where stress can contribute to John's disability, retaining counsel to deal directly with John's boss is a smart move and one that the company cannot easily sidestep.

John does not have to agree to go on disability leave. He has a right to keep working. However, John must be co-operative with his boss and must respond to reasonable requests. At this point, John does not even have to agree to a medical examination because John's boss has not disclosed any basis for making the request.

If and when John's boss provides the basis for the request to attend a medical examination, John can insist on requiring that his boss provide him with a list of the essential duties of the job. Without this list of the essential duties, any assessment by the doctor will not be helpful in determining whether John can continue in his current job.

Unfortunately, for both John and his boss, this entire situation is unlikely to get resolved quickly or easily. At present, because of the serious mistakes made by his boss, John is in a much stronger position. Unfortunately, John will likely suffer stress because of how poorly this has been handled by his boss and the unknown fact is whether the stress will cause his disability to worsen, which could result in John having to go on disability leave.

This is what should have happened in this case:

1. John and his boss should have had an open discussion about any performance concerns.
2. If there is no evidence that the performance issues are related to John's disability, his boss should have provided John with a warning letter, outlining clearly what the problems were and what is expected of John.
3. If the performance issues were caused by John's

disability, then both John and his boss should have retained experienced legal counsel to assist them in working through the accommodation process.

4. If John's boss wants to confirm whether the performance issues were disability-related, then John should have been allowed to see his own specialist, someone he has seen for many years. Forcing John to see a doctor who he has never seen as a first step is unnecessary and insensitive.

5. If John's boss is still unhappy with the findings of John's doctor, then it may be reasonable for John to see an independent doctor.

6. Both John and his boss need to agree what are the essential duties of John's job. This list needs to be provided to the doctor who will examine John.

7. Depending on the results of the medical examination, John and his boss will have to discuss what steps can be taken by John's boss that will assist John to perform the essential duties of his job.

If John can perform the essential duties of his job with accommodation, then John has a right to continue to work. Any attempt by John's boss to fire John, even with a generous severance package will, in these circumstances, result in serious financial liability for the company.

52

TOP BLOOPERS TO AVOID IF YOU ARE AN EMPLOYER

1. Don't Forget to Use a Contract
2. Forgetting to Sign the Employment Contract Before the Employee Starts Work
3. Calling a Termination a Layoff
4. Unilateral Changes in the Employee's Pay or Work Duties
5. Don't Forget to Pay Overtime Pay
6. Terminating a Disabled Employee
7. Age Doesn't Mean Anything

If you are an employer who has not yet hired a human resources professional but has to deal with all the employee-related issues that arise in your workplace, top seven employment law bloopers you will want to avoid these.

1. DON'T FORGET TO USE A CONTRACT

Hiring a new employee on a handshake is something that you should never do. Even when you do not have a written contract, the law will imply a number of obligations on you as the employer. These obligations can be modified and clarified if you use a written contract. Does an employment contract have to be formal and legalistic to be enforceable? Absolutely not. As long as the agreement is in writing and signed by both parties and the terms are clear, you may even use the company letterhead if you wish to.

Obviously, the shorter the contract the more difficulty you will have in covering all of the essential terms. The important thing to remember is that you should reduce your agreement to writing and make sure that you include at least the basic terms such as the start date, the compensation, the title and the duties, reporting structure and a termination and resignation clause. Remember that a termination clause should be reviewed with your lawyer to make sure that it at least complies with minimum statutory obligations.

2. FORGETTING TO SIGN THE EMPLOYMENT CONTRACT BEFORE THE EMPLOYEE STARTS WORK

If you want your contract to be enforceable, you should be sure to provide the employee with the contract well in advance of the employee's first day on the job. You should make sure that the employee's attention is specifically drawn to the termination clause and ensure that the employee fully understands the terms of the contract.

A contract that is not signed until after the employee starts work is unenforceable because it lacks what is referred to as legal consideration. Another way of looking at this is why should an employee be bound by any contract that is only presented after the employee has already verbally agreed to the terms of his or her job and has already started working? What else is the employee getting for signing the contract? It is important for you as the employer to advise the employee when the offer is verbally communicated that the employee must sign an employment agreement before he or she starts work.

3. CALLING A TERMINATION A LAYOFF

Now here is a big problem. Many employers incorrectly assume that they can simply lay off an employee for shortage of work and that they will not have to pay the employee a severance package. The only time that this can work is when it is a part of the company practice and the layoff is for a definite period of time. Otherwise, in these circumstances, a layoff will be treated as a termination and you will have to provide the employee with a severance package.

4. UNILATERAL CHANGES TO THE EMPLOYEE'S PAY OR WORK DUTIES

Can you reduce an employee's compensation? Sometimes you can but it depends on the amount. More than 10 per cent to 15 per cent is likely going to be a constructive dismissal. Can title, duties and reporting structure be changed? There is definitely more flexibility for this type of change, particularly if the change comes without a reduction in salary. As long as the duties are comparable and the title and reporting change are not embarrassing to the employee, it will be very difficult for the employee to successfully assert that he has been dismissed.

From a practical perspective, you should approach making any significant change to an employee's employment terms by having an honest discussion with the employee in order to explain the reasons for the change and when possible, seek an agreement. Otherwise, think about staging the changes so that they do not occur all at the same time. Usually one single change is not enough to prove a constructive dismissal. Your employee will try to show that all the changes add up to a dismissal.

5. DON'T FORGET TO PAY OVERTIME PAY

There are a few exceptions that you need to be aware of, but not paying overtime pay for excess hours or not keeping proper records is a recipe for disaster. It is your obligation to not allow your employee to work overtime unless you intend to pay the employee. Even if you do not direct your employee to work overtime you will be deemed to have authorized the work if you accept the benefit of having the work done. In some cases, the employee will go back several years and disclose that they have been keeping records of all his or her overtime hours. If you cannot disprove that the employee worked the excess hours, you will have to pay overtime pay. You need to familiarize yourself with the relevant legislation that exists in your province, which provides your employee with minimum statutory protection. It does not matter whether you did not understand the law or that your employee may have consented to a lesser standard than required by the law, you will have to pay. You may even have to pay interest plus a penalty.

6. TERMINATING A DISABLED EMPLOYEE

Although in some very limited circumstances you may be able to dismiss an employee who is unable to come to work because of a disability, you need to be extremely cautious. Employees with disabilities have a special status that needs to be understood. Obviously, disability fraud or unauthorized absence from work can be dealt with. A legitimate disability claim needs to be properly administered to avoid costly and embarrassing litigation.

You need to understand what the employee's restrictions are in performing the essential duties of his or her job. Not all duties are essential and not all duties have to be performed by a person with a disability. You have an obligation to assist or to accommodate the disabled employee. Can you replace the employee if he or she is away from the workplace? Yes, you can get someone else to do the employee's work functions while the employee is away from work, but the disabled employee does have a right to come back to his or her job, if it still exists, once he or she is capable of performing the essential duties of his or her job.

How long do you have to wait before you permanently replace the employee? There is no specific time frame to assist you. It could be as short as three months or as long as three years. It depends on the nature of the illness and the prognosis. Obviously, the longer the employee is away from work, the more likely you will be able to permanently replace the absent employee.

7. AGE DOESN'T MEAN ANYTHING

Mandatory retirement at the age of 65 was abolished in Ontario in December 2006. This means that you cannot force someone to retire at 65. It also means that even if you are prepared to treat it as a termination with a severance package instead of retirement, you still cannot do it. This obviously can have a lot of consequences for your workplace. What has often happened over the years is that employers have been reluctant to either discipline or fire aging workers and would rather just let them ease into retirement. By following this approach, they avoid a wrongful dismissal claim or severance pay obligations and they allow the employee to simply retire without any obligation to provide a severance payment.

Well, how do you get rid of Charlie down the hallway who spends more time reading obituaries at work than actually doing any work? Can you fire poor Charlie at all, or do you just have to accept his lacklustre performance?

The answer is that you need to manage Charlie like you manage any other employee at your workplace. Your work expectations of Charlie have to be reasonable and may have to be modified slightly. You will have to provide Charlie with written warnings outlining his performance deficiencies along with your expectations, with a specific warning that he could lose his job if his performance does not improve. If Charlie has been working for you for 25 years and has never received even the slightest warning, one warning letter is not sufficient.

Although it was recently suggested that an employer could simply provide a person like Charlie two years' working notice when he reaches 63, you should not count on that option either, as any scheme designed to frustrate the law would be quickly attacked by the Human Rights Tribunal as being discriminatory.

53

THE TEN MOST COMMON ERRORS IN HUMAN RESOURCES POLICY MANUALS

1. Not Including an Introduction
2. No Accommodation/Substance Abuse Policy
3. Incorrect or Vague Definition of Workplace Harassment
4. Overtime
5. Zero Tolerance Policies
6. Falling Behind the Legislation
7. Failing to Keep Employees Appraised of Changes
8. Failing to Make it Binding
9. Not Sticking to It
10. Not Having One at All

As employment lawyers, we are often asked to review our clients' human resources policy manuals to ensure they are compliant with all relevant legislation and that they will be an effective tool in governing employee behaviour. No matter what the industry or how sophisticated the client, we see the same errors over and over again. Human resources policy manuals can be an important means of communicating with your employees and managing their workplace activities – if they are written and applied correctly. Ten common missteps that can result in headaches for employers and human resources professionals are set out below:

1. NOT INCLUDING AN INTRODUCTION

The employer's introduction to its human resources policy manual is an important opportunity to inform the employee of the employer's expectations with respect to the manual and its contents. Every introduction should clearly state that it is the employee's responsibility to inform himself or herself about the current contents of the manual and to ensure that his or her behaviour complies with its provisions. The introduction should also make it clear that the employer reserves the absolute right to alter the policy from time to time.

2. NO ACCOMMODATION/SUBSTANCE ABUSE POLICY

Despite the prominence of disability-related issues in today's workplace, many managers and supervisors are still not up to speed on the extent of their obligations to accommodate a person with a disability, including substance abuse. A detailed and up-to-date accommodation policy that explicitly sets out the employer's procedure for dealing with disability is a valuable means of communicating with all levels of employees, including those responsible for dealing with the practical aspects of accommodation.

3. INCORRECT OR VAGUE DEFINITION OF WORKPLACE HARASSMENT

While most human resources policy manuals address the issue of workplace harassment, it is quite common for their definitions of inappropriate behaviour to be vague, unhelpful or even misleading. For example, we recently reviewed a policy manual that defined workplace harassment as demanding sexual favours in exchange for advancement or raises. While this is certainly prohibited behaviour, it is not the only activity captured by the term "workplace harassment". A good manual should refer to all of the prohibited grounds of discrimination and make it clear that harassment is any behaviour that is unwelcome or should reasonably be known to be unwelcome.

4. OVERTIME

In Ontario, employees are entitled to overtime pay for all overtime hours worked, whether those hours were approved or not. Every human resources policy manual should clearly state that employees are not permitted to work overtime without preauthorization from their supervisors. Supervisors should be instructed to strictly enforce this policy.

5. ZERO TOLERANCE POLICIES

A popular way of illustrating an employer's commitment to eradicating harassment in the workplace is to state that it has "zero tolerance" for inappropriate behaviour and that violations of the policy "shall" result in termination. Although zero tolerance policies send a strong message to employees, they are not really appropriate for the Canadian workplace. Canadian case law clearly demonstrates that employers have an obligation to consider the individual circumstances of each employee, even if the employee has engaged in serious misconduct. No policy manual should have the effect of limiting an employer's discretion.

6. FALLING BEHIND THE LEGISLATION

Many employers allow their human resources policy manuals to fall out of step with relevant statutory developments. As a result, employees and supervisors may not be aware of the employer's obligations with respect to such areas as emergency leave, maternity leave and mandatory retirement, which could lead to human rights complaints or complaints under employment standards legislation.

7. FAILING TO KEEP EMPLOYEES APPRISED OF CHANGES

It is very difficult to take the position that an employee is required to abide by a policy when the employee is not updated on its revisions. Any amendments to your human resources policy manual should be brought to the attention of all employees, whether by email, seminars or handouts.

8. FAILING TO MAKE IT BINDING

If you intend to rely on your human resources policy manual to support disciplinary action or termination for cause, it is important to ensure that it is binding on your employees. Employees should be provided with a copy of the manual prior to commencing employment and should sign an acknowledgement stating that they have read and understood its terms. Where the policy manual is new to the workplace or has been significantly revised, employees should receive notice of the changes or some consideration for executing the acknowledgement. If an employee is provided with a manual after he or she has signed the employment agreement and the employee does not receive any payment or other consideration for signing the acknowledgement, a court may hold that the employee is not bound to observe its terms. This reaffirms the importance of always reserving the contractual right to alter company policies without notice.

9. NOT STICKING TO IT

The worst thing that an employer can to do a human resources manual is fail to apply it. Ignoring one's own policy manual has the effect of undermining the policy's ability to govern workplace practices and can even undermine the employer's attempts to discipline employees. For example, if an employer fails to apply its own sexual harassment complaint procedure when terminating an alleged harasser for cause, a court may find that the dismissal was wrongful.

10. NOT HAVING ONE AT ALL

Human resources policy manuals are the employer's best opportunity to communicate its expectations and practices to employees. They can also be a valuable resource for both employees and supervisors. Employers who choose not to make use of a human resources policy manual risk creating confusion about their internal policies and worse, developing inconsistent practices with respect to discipline and employee benefits. Workplaces are not well-served by ambiguity and unpredictability. A clear, concise and current policy manual can be an important means of eliminating these unwanted influences.

When is a Workplace Human Rights Investigation Necessary? Practical Tips for Managers and Human Resources Professionals

Most employers are well aware of their obligation to ensure that all employees are treated fairly and in a good faith fashion, particularly when meting out discipline or conducting a termination. Employers are also very conscious of their duty to provide employees with a safe workplace that is free from harassment. Unfortunately, the issue of human rights complaints in the workplace presents special problems for employers and often gives rise to conflicting obligations. Employers are forced to weigh the duty to be fair to the accused against their obligation to protect the complainant. As an additional complication, supervisors occasionally overreact when they receive a complaint of harassment, seeing it as a personal indictment of their management style or abilities. In these circumstances, a systematic and measured approach to assessing complaints can be an employer's best friend. This article is intended to provide human resources professionals and managers with a practical guide for choosing when to investigate a complaint of workplace harassment and when to employ more informal dispute resolution techniques.

There are several ways in which a human rights issue can come to the attention of the employer. Sometimes the victim will come forward to his or her manager with a complaint, either written or verbal. Managers should be trained to immediately bring such issues forward to human resources or to more senior management. Occasionally, the issue will arise after co-workers witness an inappropriate interaction between employees. Even where there is no formal complaint, managers should be instructed to act on any reports or indications of potential harassment.

The first step every employer should take upon receiving a complaint of workplace harassment is to get it in writing. If the complainant has not already provided a written version of the grievance, the complainant should be asked to do so. If the complainant does not wish to put the complaint in writing or has difficulty articulating the issues, the employer should restate the allegations and ask the complainant to sign an acknowledgement that the document accurately reflects the complaint.

It is essential that the employer have a clear understanding of the complainant's allegations. A complaint cannot be properly assessed or dealt with if there is any doubt about the grounds or the involved parties.

Not every complaint requires a formal investigation. It may be possible to resolve the issue simply by meeting with the employees involved and discussing the matter to the point of a mutually acceptable solution. For example, where the complaint is the result of a personality conflict and not a pattern of harassment, adjusting work schedules or moving workstations can be sufficient to resolve the matter.

Special considerations arise where the complaint involves allegations of criminal conduct in the workplace. The *Criminal Code*, R.S.C. 1985, c. C-46, prohibits criminal harassment, assault, uttering threats and sexual assault. Where there are serious allegations of stalking, unwanted touching or threats of bodily harm, the employer should first notify the complainant that he or she has made allegations of criminal conduct that may lead to a police investigation. The employer should also ask the complainant if he or she intends to notify the proper authorities. In the event that the complainant does not intend to involve the police, the employer must then consider whether or not it should do so.

Employers should be very wary of permitting allegations of criminal conduct in the workplace to go unaddressed. We recommend that the assessment of whether to proceed with an internal investigation should be conducted independently of the decision to refer the matter to the police.

Before deciding how to proceed with a complaint, employers should conduct a preliminary evaluation of the allegations using the following four questions:

1. **Is it prohibited harassment?** Does the harassment described fall within the company's harassment policy (if any) or under the relevant human rights legislation or health and safety legislation? Where the subject matter of the complaint is clearly covered by either the company's own policy and/or legislation, an investigation is more likely to be appropriate.

2. **Is it prohibited harassment in employment?** Where the matter is entirely removed from the workplace, the employer may do more harm than good by investigating. However, since courts, human rights commissions and workers' compensation boards tend to apply a broad definition of the term "workplace", this factor will rarely be determinative.

3. **Is the complaint timely?** Most human rights acts have a limitation period for filing complaints. In Ontario, the limitation period is six months. Where the complaint is older than the relevant limitation period and where passage of time would significantly impair the ability of the accused employee to respond to the allegations, the employer should consider foregoing a formal investigation. However, each allegation of harassment, no matter how stale-dated, must be dealt with in some fashion.

4. **Is the complaint frivolous or vexatious?** Human Rights Commissions may reserve the right to decline to deal with a complaint where it appears to be made in bad faith or with mischievous intent. Employers may also decline to initiate a formal investigation where they have reasonable grounds to believe that the complaint is not well-founded. However, as noted above, it is never advisable to ignore a complaint of harassment, no matter how trivial it may seem when it is received.

Preliminary assessments must be conducted thoroughly and with a full understanding of all aspects of the complaint. Where there is any doubt as to whether or not an investigation is required, it is generally advisable to err on the side of caution and proceed with a formal investigation. It is also recommended that employers seek external advice when considering whether or not to initiate a human rights investigation, particularly where the allegations involve members of senior management or touch upon matters covered by the Criminal Code.

Although internal investigations arise from the most unfortunate of circumstances, if used appropriately, they can also be a valuable tool in demonstrating the employer's commitment to a safe and productive workplace.

55

A Practical Guide for Employers Defending a Wrongful Dismissal Action

1. Review the Claim Carefully
2. Choose the Right Lawyer
3. Pick a "Point" Person
4. Ask for a Legal Opinion
5. Co-operate With Your Counsel
6. Never Allege Cause if None Exists
7. Investigate for Other Improper Conduct
8. Avoid Defamatory Statements
9. Reference Letters
10. Offer to Settle
11. Mediation
12. Document Disclosure and Retention

If you have recently received a statement of claim from a former employee alleging that you have wrongfully terminated his or her employment, consider carefully how to proceed. Wrongful dismissal litigation can be very expensive and time-consuming and, when handled improperly, can even have a negative impact on workplace morale and productivity.

Litigation in this area was traditionally focused on relatively straightforward issues of reasonable notice and/or just cause. However, in recent years, related claims of mental distress, punitive damages, defamation and harassment have become more common in wrongful dismissal litigation. Such claims often involve serious allegations of misconduct on the part of supervisors and/or co-workers and can have a distracting and divisive effect on the workplace. The following are some suggestions for managing a wrongful dismissal lawsuit and for minimizing its potential impact on the work environment.

1. REVIEW THE CLAIM CAREFULLY

Assess whether it is a claim that you need or want to defend. On occasion, a quick and confidential settlement may be the best result for the employer. Where an employee has been named as an individual party to the lawsuit, consider whether it is appropriate for the employee and the employer to share counsel. Often, it will be necessary to investigate the allegations against the individual defendant before making a decision. Where the employer's interests are likely to diverge from those of the individual defendant, separate counsel is advisable.

2. CHOOSE THE RIGHT LAWYER

If you have decided to proceed with filing a defence, find a lawyer who practises in the area of employment law and whose litigation strategy matches your own.

3. PICK A "POINT PERSON"

To prevent confusion and disorganization, designate one person in your office to manage the litigation and provide instructions to counsel. The individual selected should have knowledge of the facts of the case and have sufficient authority to make decisions with respect to the conduct of the lawsuit.

4. ASK FOR A LEGAL OPINION

At an early stage, request that your counsel provide you with a legal opinion about the merits of the case. It is better to learn of potential weaknesses at the outset before significant costs have been incurred.

5. CO-OPERATE WITH YOUR COUNSEL

Knowledge is power. Be sure to provide your counsel with all relevant facts and documentation as soon as possible. Concealing weak points or discarding relevant documentation will only hurt you in the long run.

6. NEVER ALLEGE CAUSE IF NONE EXISTS

Many cases should only be defended on the basis of what constitutes reasonable notice and not whether just cause exists. A just cause defence is typically quite complicated and will result in a lengthier legal proceeding. Where a just cause defence is put forth and abandoned before trial, a court may impose severe costs consequences on the employer.

7. INVESTIGATE FOR OTHER IMPROPER CONDUCT

Where just cause is a part of your defence, it may be appropriate to conduct a thorough investigation following the employee's termination. Where the employer discovers further misconduct after the employee in question has been terminated, it may still be relied upon to justify termination for cause. This is known as "after-acquired cause".

8. AVOID DEFAMATORY STATEMENTS

Making false statements about the terminated employee or the lawsuit may lead to a claim for defamation or result in an increase in the reasonable notice period, or "*Wallace*" damages" (See *Wallace v. United Grain Growers Ltd. (c.o.b. Public Press)*,

[1997] S.C.J. No. 94 (S.C.C.)). This is particularly true where the false statements are made in the relevant business community.

9. REFERENCE LETTERS

Whether you should provide a reference letter will depend upon the facts of your case and the nature of your defence. Where the only issue in the litigation is reasonable notice, it may be desirable to provide a reference in order to encourage re-employment. Consider each case separately and obtain legal advice.

10. OFFER TO SETTLE

Always consider whether or not to serve an offer to settle on the employee. Even if the employee rejects the offer, legal costs may be imposed on the employee if the employee recovers less than the amount of the offer at trial.

11. MEDIATION

Mediation involves referring the dispute to a third party who will assist the parties in reaching a settlement. There are few wrongful dismissal actions that cannot be successfully mediated. While reaching settlement at mediation will inevitably require compromise, parties often prefer it to litigation because it allows them to retain a degree of control over the outcome. Once the matter proceeds to court, the result is out of your hands.

12. DOCUMENT DISCLOSURE AND RETENTION

Employers are obliged to maintain and disclose all relevant documents, including electronic copies, throughout the progress of litigation. All relevant documentation should be provided to your counsel at the earliest opportunity, and he or she will advise which documents may be withheld on the basis of privilege. Regardless of legal obligations to retain documents, it is advisable to keep copies of any legal decisions, minutes of settlement and releases in perpetuity.

There are many different approaches to defending a wrongful dismissal action. Careful consideration should be given to your strategy throughout the litigation process. In the majority of cases, an early settlement is the best result for the employer. The strategy you choose, and the time spent managing the lawsuit, will have a significant impact on the results achieved.

56

E-DISCOVERY IN ONTARIO: WHAT ARE EMPLOYERS' OBLIGATIONS?

In late 2005, the Task Force on the Discovery Process in Ontario published its "Guidelines for the Discovery of Electronic Documents in Ontario" (the "E-Discovery Guidelines"). These guidelines were intended to provide some guidance to parties and their lawyers regarding the extent of parties' obligation to produce electronic documents and information. The Task Force has defined electronic documents as documents that exist in a medium that can only be read through the use of computers, as well as electronic documents that can be printed, such as email, web pages and word processing files.

Since their publication, the E-Discovery Guidelines have been widely discussed within the legal community and have been cited with approval by Ontario courts. Although they do not have the force of law in Ontario, courts may still apply them in deciding what parties to litigation must produce and how this production must be accomplished.

All parties to litigation are required to produce any documents or evidence under their possession or control that are not privileged and that may potentially be relevant to any matter at issue in the case. There are four basic steps to meeting your production obligations:

1. location of potential document sources;
2. preservation of potentially relevant materials;
3. review of documents for relevance, privilege and other issues; and
4. production to other parties for use in court proceedings.

Each of these steps must be engaged regardless of whether electronic or paper documents are being produced. However, because of the special issues raised by electronic documentation, the Task Force has created 13 principles to help parties deal with e-discovery in a fair, thorough and efficient manner. These principles, which are quite detailed, can be found on the Ontario Bar Association website (see www.oba.org/En/pdf_newsletter/E-DiscoveryGuidelines.pdf).

This article is not intended to provide a complete summary of each of the 13 principles. Rather, the E-Discovery Guidelines have been distilled into the following five key points of note that Ontario employers should take into account when faced with litigation:

1. **Wherever possible, reach agreement with the other parties to the litigation regarding the form and extent of electronic production.** No fewer than seven of the 13 principles specifically encourage parties to meet to discuss issues arising from electronic discovery. In particular, parties should agree on the manner in which the information will be produced (electronically or otherwise) and the scope of the searching party's retrieval efforts. Where one party believes that a particular piece of information or type of data may not turn up in an ordinary search, it should immediately notify opposing counsel and ask that this information be preserved and produced. As a human resources manager dealing with wrongful dismissal litigation, it is advisable to meet with the former employee's manager and an information technology professional to discuss what data may be relevant and how it can be best preserved and produced. This information should then be passed along to your lawyer to ensure the lawyer has all of the information necessary to deal with opposing counsel.

2. **The scope of the obligation to retrieve and produce electronic documentation must be "reasonable".** The E-Discovery Guidelines are very clear that electronic discovery should not become an overwhelming burden that causes parties to lose focus on the main issues in the litigation. Rather, the burden it imposes on the parties should be consistent with the scope of the litigation itself. Where the lawsuit is significant and involves many parties or large amounts of money, the parties' obligations

regarding electronic discovery are likely to be more onerous. The Task Force has also indicated that parties should be entitled to avoid searches that will retrieve mostly redundant or irrelevant information, particularly where such a search would be expensive and time-consuming.

3. **Deleted files need not be preserved or searched.** In keeping with the principle that e-discovery should be reasonable, the Task Force has specifically stated that, unless the parties agree or the court orders otherwise, parties need not search for, produce or review documents that are deleted or hidden. However, if you receive notice from opposing counsel that he or she is seeking a particular piece of information that you know to be in deleted or archived files, you should take steps to preserve it just in case you are later required to produce it.

4. **Key word searches and data sampling are permissible.** Where there is a large database or cache of information, parties are allowed to use internal search engines or functions to sift through the documents and retrieve relevant items. They are not obliged to personally examine each document for relevance. It is advisable to keep track of the terms and keywords used in the search, as this information may be sought by opposing counsel or be required by the court.

5. **The producing party bears the cost of production.** Where there are significant costs associated with retrieving and reviewing relevant electronic documentation, the party in possession of the data must absorb the cost of production. The exception to this principle is where the receiving party wishes to have a copy made for its use. In that situation, the receiving party must pay for the items to be copied and made available to it.

Although electronic discovery may seem overwhelming, especially for smaller companies that do not have information technology professionals on staff, it is really just an extension of existing obligations to produce documents relevant to the lawsuit. Where your company has been sued for wrongful dismissal or is facing any employment-related litigation, protect yourself by speaking to your legal counsel about production issues early in the litigation. While the issues are fresh in your mind, sit down and make a list of potential sources for relevant documentation and then immediately take steps to ensure that these sources are not inadvertently deleted or modified.

57

WHAT EMPLOYERS NEED TO KNOW ABOUT SUMMARY JUDGMENT

When reorganizing or downsizing employees, all businesses wish for it to go quickly and smoothly. Disagreements about severance can disrupt a reorganization and threaten to accumulate unforeseen legal bills. Due to a recent Ontario Court of Appeal decision, employers should be aware that these disagreements could be decided by a judge more quickly, and generously, than ever before, due to summary judgments.

Summary judgments, as the title suggests, means judgment is obtained quickly and with no trial. A judge has to be convinced there is no genuine issue for trial. Summary judgments in wrongful dismissal cases were barred by the Ontario Court of Appeal in *Kilpatrick v. Peterborough Civic Hospital*, [1999] O.J. No. 1505. At the time, the determination of a notice period involved a finding of fact based on the circumstances of each case. The Court held that it was inappropriate for a judge to do so without a trial. Therefore, it effectively banned summary judgments in wrongful dismissal cases.

Since that decision, the use of summary judgments in the context of wrongful dismissals has become increasingly popular in the Ontario Superior Court of Justice. In December, the Ontario Court of Appeal, in *Adjemian v. Brook Crompton North America*, [2008] O.J. No. 5230 surprisingly endorsed an Ontario Superior Court of Justice decision allowing summary judgment on the amount of notice to be given in a wrongful dismissal lawsuit, overruling *Kilpatrick*.

In *Adjemian*, the plaintiff was downsized from her position as administrator and paid four months' notice. The plaintiff sued for wrongful dismissal, bringing a motion for summary judgment. Despite the employer stating they disagreed on how much notice should be paid to the plaintiff and the adequacy of the plaintiff's mitigation efforts, the Ontario Superior Court of Justice found summary judgment appropriate, awarding 16 months' notice, an increase of 12 months. The employer appealed, but the Ontario Court of Appeal dismissed it, stating disagreements about the plaintiff's mitigation efforts are fairly assessed without the need to question witnesses.

Therefore, while it is always important to consult a legal professional before taking any action, this decision means employers should take these tips into account:

1. **Get Ready**. Summary judgment, even where there are disagreements about the notice period and mitigation efforts, is now an effective strategy for employees seeking greater notice periods. It is a cost-efficient and quick way for plaintiff's counsel to gain an advantage for their client when the only disagreement is about notice.

2. **Increased Notice Periods**. Notice awarded by the court is more generous than any that could be negotiated. Summary judgments could increase your liability beyond your expectations.

3. **Know the Issues**. Be aware of any disagreements between you and the employee. Disagreements over facts requires investigation, which is not always appropriate for summary judgment. Stating you do not want to pay a certain notice period without any evidence will not bar summary judgment.

58

FAMILY DAY: WHAT EMPLOYERS NEED TO KNOW

1. Background
2. Step 1: Understanding the Employment Standards Act Entitlement
3. Step 2: Evaluate your Employment Contracts or Holiday Policies in Comparison to the Employment Standards Act Standard
4. Conclusion

1. BACKGROUND

In October 2006 the Liberal government in Ontario announced its intention to create a new public holiday: Family Day. Family Day now falls on the third Monday in February and is the ninth paid public holiday under the *Employment Standards Act, 2000*, S.O. 2000, c. 41 (the "ESA"). Since the government's announcement of a new public holiday, there has been some controversy among employers as to whether or not they are obligated to give their employees Family Day. Under the ESA, the addition of a new statutory holiday does not automatically entitle employees to an extra day of holiday with holiday pay. Rather, the ESA sets out a floor of rights that must, at a minimum, be observed by employers. If an employment contract provides for a greater right or benefit with respect to paid holidays, the terms of the employment agreement will apply and minimum standard will not. Accordingly, an employee's entitlement to the Family Day holiday is dependent on the terms of his or her employment contract.

There are two important questions for employers to ask when deciding whether or not their employees are entitled to Family Day. First, what constitutes a greater right or benefit; and second, is a greater right or benefit provided for under their employment contracts or their policies on paid holidays? Unfortunately, because of the nature of the benefit under the ESA, the answers to these questions are not as simple as they may seem. The first step for employers is to understand the nature of the benefit provided for under the ESA. The second step for employers is to evaluate their employment contracts and holiday policies to see how they compare to the ESA standard.

2. STEP 1: UNDERSTANDING THE EMPLOYMENT STANDARDS ACT ENTITLEMENT

The public holidays provided for under the ESA have five main components.

1. **The number of holidays:** The ESA provides for nine public holidays: New Year's Day, Good Friday, Victoria Day, Canada Day, Labour Day, Thanksgiving Day, Christmas Day, Boxing Day and Family Day.

2. **The qualifier:** The ESA provides a condition for employees to meet in order to be entitled to holiday pay:

    - An employee has to work his or her entire regularly scheduled day of work before and after the holiday.

    - However, if the employee misses either of those days for "reasonable cause," he or she may still be entitled to holiday pay.

    - "Reasonable cause" generally refers to something beyond the control of the employee.

3. **The alternate day off designation:** If the holiday falls on a day that the employee would not normally work, or on a vacation day, the employee is to be given an alternate day off with holiday pay. Unless the employer and employee agree otherwise, the alternate day off must be within three months of the public holiday. In either case, the alternate day off must be within 12 months of

the public holiday.

4. **The holiday work requirement:** An employee can agree to work on a public holiday. The agreement must be in *writing*. If an employee works on a public holiday, he or she may get an alternate day off with holiday pay or be paid holiday pay plus premium pay for each hour of work on the holiday.

5. **The premium:** The premium is at least one-and-one-half times the employee's regular rate.

3. STEP 2: EVALUATE YOUR EMPLOYMENT CONTRACTS OR HOLIDAY POLICIES IN COMPARISON TO THE EMPLOYMENT STANDARDS ACT STANDARD

While the number of paid holidays is not definitive in determining whether or not an employment contract provides for a greater right or benefit, it will be an important consideration. If you provide for less than the nine paid holidays mandated under the ESA, you will likely be legally obligated to give your employees the Family Day holiday. If you provide a number of paid holidays that is equal to the number under the ESA, you may not be legally obligated to provide an additional day of holiday; whether or not you can switch one of your existing holidays with Family Day will depend on the language of your employment contracts and holiday policies. If you provide for ten or more paid holidays, you may not be legally obligated to give your employees the Family Day holiday. This latter circumstance will also depend on the language of your employment contracts and holiday policies and whether or not the conditions for the holiday entitlements are more onerous than those found in the ESA. If you are thinking about not giving your employees Family Day, it is advisable that you have legal counsel review your employment contracts and holiday policies to ensure that you will not be in violation of the ESA.

4. CONCLUSION

Since the Ontario government declared a new public holiday, Family Day has garnered a lot of attention from the media. The attention is focused primarily on the debate about whether an employer has to give its employees the holiday. Employers, on the one hand, may feel less inclined to provide Family Day when they already provide for nine or more paid holidays. The general perception of the public, on the other hand, is that workers are entitled to Family Day regardless of their current holiday entitlements. In terms of good human resources policy, employers should take a critical look at their holiday entitlements and their bottom line before they decide not to provide their employees with a holiday that is geared toward giving employees time with their families. The amount an employer has to spend on one extra day of holiday will most likely be recouped by the boost in employee morale brought about by a new day off in the middle of a long winter.

59

H1N1 IN THE WORKPLACE

In late October 2009, Health Canada reported an increase in Influenza A virus subtype H1N1 ("H1N1") cases across the country. The media reported daily on the spread of H1N1, the rollout of the H1N1 vaccine and the potential for vaccine shortages. Deaths of otherwise healthy children from H1N1 prompted heightened awareness and fear of the disease. As a result of increased instances of H1N1, more employers dealt with H1N1 and fear of H1N1 amongst employees. In order to be prepared, employers were made aware of their legal obligations in managing H1N1 in the workplace.

Before reviewing the legal landscape, a few basic facts about H1N1 and the associated risks may be of assistance. H1N1 is a respiratory disease that originated with swine influenza, a disease affecting pigs. In rare occasions swine influenza can infect humans. The current strand of swine influenza, H1N1, is of particular concern because it has mutated to allow for human-to-human transmission. In most individuals, symptoms of H1N1 are similar to those of the seasonal flu. Health Canada reported that the majority of individuals affected with the illness experience regular flu symptoms and recover in about one week; however, in rare cases H1N1 can have more serious consequences, including death.

A vaccine against H1N1 became available to Ontarians at the end of October 2009, but higher than anticipated demand for the vaccine caused shortages. Ontario planned to administer the vaccine only to those in the following high-risk groups: children over six months but under five years of age, health-care workers, caregivers for those who were vulnerable and unable to get the vaccine, people under 65 with pre-existing health conditions, and those who lived in remote or isolated communities. The vaccine shortage was expected to be temporary.

Employers should be up-to-date about their legal obligations in the event of another outbreak of H1N1 or similar virus in the workplace. Under Ontario's *Occupational Health and Safety Act*, R.S.O. 1990, c. O.1 ("OHSA"), employers have the obligation to maintain a safe and healthy workplace for employees and must take every reasonable precaution to protect employees. Accordingly, employers are required to take all reasonable steps to protect employees from H1N1, and similar potentially fatal viruses, in the workplace. Employers may wish to consider the following measures to prevent or control the spread of H1N1 and similar viruses in the workplace:

- Remind employees to wash their hands frequently. Consider distributing hand sanitizer and posting handwashing instructions in the workplace.

- Encourage employees to voluntarily be vaccinated against influenza. While employers cannot require employees to get the vaccine, they can advise employees of the availability and benefits of the vaccine and allow employees to take time off work to get the vaccine.

- Consider suitable creative measures to prevent the spread of the disease, such as allowing employees to work from home, holding conference calls instead of meetings and allowing employees to work flexible hours in order to avoid public transportation during peak times.

- Advise employees to remain away from the workplace if they are exhibiting flu-like symptoms.

- Communicate with employees regarding H1N1 and similar viruses. Provide up-to-date information to employees about the disease and relevant workplace policies such as sick leave and working from home. Consider appointing one person or a team of people to coordinate communication.

Despite an employer taking all reasonable measures to prevent H1N1 from entering the workplace, outbreaks may occur and result in employees being absent from work. The Ontario *Employment Standards Act, 2000*, S.O. 2000, c. 41 ("ESA") accords employees, whose employer regularly employs 50 or more employees, the right to 10 unpaid days of personal emergency leave per calendar year. Personal emergency leave may be used in the event of personal illness or the illness of certain family members. An employer may require that an employee provide evidence of the situation necessitating the leave. However, in many cases an employer's policy on sick leave and benefits exceeds the minimum requirement under the ESA. In those cases the greater benefit offered by the employer replaces the legislative minimum.

In preparation for potential employee absences due to H1N1 and other illnesses, employers should review and communicate to employees all relevant policies regarding the availability of sick leave and benefits. Employers may wish to encourage employees who become ill to remain at home by implementing pandemic specific, non-punitive sick leave policies such as offering paid leave that does not reduce an employee's regular entitlements. Where sick leave benefits are unavailable or have been exhausted, employees who experience reduced weekly earnings of at least 40 per cent as a result of an absence from work due to illness or quarantine are eligible for employment insurance benefits providing they have accumulated sufficient insurable hours.

While rarely available, employers should be aware of the existence of declared emergency leave. In order for declared emergency leave to apply, H1N1 or similar virus must be declared an emergency under the *Emergency Management and Civil Protection Act*, R.S.O. 1990, c. E.9, by either the head of a municipal council or by the premier. In the event that H1N1 had been declared an emergency in October 2009, employees unable to perform their duties due to H1N1 (including a case where an employee must be absent to care for a family member) would have been entitled to take a leave of absence without pay. In order to take such a leave of absence, the employee would have to advise the employer of his or her intention to take emergency leave and provide reasonable evidence of the circumstances requiring the employee to take the leave.

Employers should require an employee infected with H1N1 or similar virus to remain out of the workplace. However, there are some privacy and human rights pitfalls that employers managing employees with H1N1 or similar viruses must be careful to avoid. Federal and provincial human rights legislation prohibits discrimination on the basis of disability or handicap, which can include diseases. Employers should be aware that human rights protections could extend to persons who have or who are perceived to have H1N1, for example. Employers should also be careful to respect an employee's privacy. Employees generally cannot be required to disclose information regarding the nature of their illness. Even if an employee is exhibiting the symptoms of H1N1, for example, employers should avoid asking the employee specific questions about the nature of his or her illness. However, employers can request that the employee obtain medical information indicating that the employee is fit to work.

Employers should also recognize that under the OHSA employees have the right to refuse work if a condition in their workplace is likely to endanger their health and safety. Employees who are exposed to H1N1 or similar potentially fatal viruses in the workplace may wish to exercise their right to refuse work. In the event that an employee refuses work, the OHSA requires that a specific procedure be followed. Employers may not discipline an employee exercising his or her right to refuse unsafe work. Rather, employers should immediately investigate any work refusal. If the employer fails to resolve the situation directly with the employee a Ministry of Labour inspector should be notified.

Employers who are covered by Workplace Safety and Insurance should be aware of the possibility that H1N1 or similar viruses could result in increased Workplace Safety and Insurance Board ("WSIB") claims. The *Workplace Safety and Insurance Act, 1997*, S.O. 1997, c. 16, Sched. A, section 13, provides compensation for "personal injury or illness arising out of and in the course of employment". A worker infected with H1N1 in the course of employment may be eligible for benefits. For example, WSIB claims were made by health-care workers during the Severe Acute Respiratory Syndrome (SARS) crisis in 2003.

Finally, it is recommended that employers monitor the spread of H1N1 or similar viruses in the future and the availability of vaccine. Further information is available from the Public Health Agency of Canada at http://www.phac-aspc.gc.ca/alert-alerte/h1n1/index-eng.php.

60

TIPS FOR MANAGING YOUR WORKPLACE IN TIMES OF ECONOMIC CRISIS

1. How to Structure Severance Packages
2. Forget About the Non-Compete Clause
3. Payment Without Release
4. Avoid Constructive Dismissal Claims
5. Deal with Disability Cases

Many companies are facing serious economic crisis. Human resources professionals are dealing with plant closures, downsizing, increased stress claims and a surge in employment litigation.

These tips will help guide you through rough economic waters.

1. HOW TO STRUCTURE SEVERANCE PACKAGES

Employees being dismissed from their jobs these days are suffering even more anxiety and stress caused by the uncertainty of when they will become re-employed. Employers should be more inclined to use the modified bridge formula (salary continuation with a 50 per cent lump sum payment on re-employment) rather than the lump sum payment method or the salary continuation method. The modified bridge formula allows the employer to provide a lengthier notice period while at the same time provides the employee with the incentive to become re-employed as soon as possible. The employer's obligations will be reduced by the employee's early re-employment.

A longer notice period also means that the employee will be entitled to the continuation of health-care benefits for a longer time period, which has become a growing concern for many dismissed employees.

2. FORGET ABOUT THE NON-COMPETE CLAUSE

For the most part, a non-competition clause is not enforceable, although a properly drafted non-solicitation clause may be enforceable. Trying to introduce even a non-solicitation clause at the end of the employment relationship is not a good strategy and generally leads to a breakdown in negotiating an amicable severance package. The better approach at the time of dismissal is to reinforce the employee's obligations of confidentiality and the obligation to return all company documents.

3. PAYMENT WITHOUT A RELEASE

Some employers refuse to make any payments to the dismissed employee unless the employee has signed a release. At the very least, the employer should make the statutory payment owing under the *Employment Standards Act, 2000*, S.O. 2000, c. 41 ("ESA"). Playing economic hardball with your former employee in these difficult economic times is insensitive and high-handed. As an employer, if you have made a severance offer to the employee, even in the absence of a signed release, you should make the payment. If the employee commences litigation seeking a greater amount of compensation, the employer will get a credit for what has already been paid and the court is likely to view your actions toward the employee more sympathetically than if you chose to withhold the payments pending the execution of a release.

4. AVOID CONSTRUCTIVE DISMISSAL CLAIMS

Challenging economic times usually results in an increase in constructive dismissal claims because employers are forced to change organizational structures, which often requires changes to an employee's employment terms. Remember that a unilateral change to a fundamental term of a contract requires you to provide the employee with reasonable notice. Courts have recently re-enforced their view that a dismissed employee may have an obligation to mitigate their damages by accepting alternative employment with the employer while they seek employment elsewhere. This is an effective strategy for employers, but remember that the relationship with your employee cannot be acrimonious and the new working terms and conditions cannot be humiliating or demeaning to the employee.

5. DEAL WITH DISABILITY CASES

Many human resources professionals incorrectly assume that employees who are on disability cannot be terminated even in the context of a corporate downsizing. A *bona fide* corporate reorganization or downsizing does not have to exclude employees on disability leave. If, as a result of the reorganization the employee's job is declared redundant, the employee on disability leave has no greater rights than the employee who is not disabled. The obligation to accommodate an employee with a disability does not extend to the employee a life-time immunity from job loss caused by a corporate reorganizing or downsizing.

Although there may be valid considerations that would convince you to not terminate an employee who is on disability leave, for instance, the loss of health-care benefits and the inability to look for employment, you are not in law obligated to skip over the employee on disability leave just because the employee is inactive at the time of the reorganization or downsizing.

61

NEW RULES CHANGE EMPLOYMENT LITIGATION LANDSCAPE

1. Increased Cap for Small Claims Court Actions
2. Increased Cap and Discovery for Simplified Procedure Actions
3. Evidence on Summary Judgment Motions
4. Other Changes to Civil Actions over $100,000

As all human resources professionals know, the employment law landscape is always changing. Among the most recent changes that have an impact on employment law are the significant amendments to the Rules of Civil Procedure, which govern practice and procedure in the Ontario courts. This article provides an overview of the changes to the Rules of Civil Procedure (R.R.O. 1990, c. 194) that came into effect on January 1, 2010 and discusses the impact of such changes on human resource professionals.

The Rules of Civil Procedure, known in the legal community as simply "the Rules", govern the conduct of the parties in a civil action, such as a claim for wrongful dismissal. The Rules provide the procedural framework by which the court will handle the dispute. More particularly, the Rules require the parties to take certain steps at particular points in time and provide procedural safeguards throughout the process.

The new Rules are designed to make the civil justice system more accessible and affordable for the public. The Attorney General's press release boasts that the reforms will make it less expensive to access justice and easier to use the courts to quickly resolve disputes. Justice Coulter Osborne, whose recommendations formed the basis for the reforms, had the following to say about the new Rules:

> The reforms reflect the need for proportionality in our civil justice system, which means that straightforward, lower value cases should not take as long or cost as much as large, complex cases. (December 11, 2008)

While accessibility and affordability are noble objectives, the changes to the Rules are not all good news for employers. Many of the Rules may actually end up costing employers more money and cause disputes to take longer to resolve. The balance of this chapter will discuss the specific changes that will have an impact on employers and human resources professionals navigating the civil justice system in Ontario.

1. INCREASED CAP FOR SMALL CLAIMS COURT ACTIONS

The previous cap was $10,000. Under the new Rules, the cap is raised to $25,000. This means that more wrongful dismissal claims will fall within the jurisdiction of the small claims court. Accordingly, you can expect to see that more employees will file wrongful dismissal claims in small claims court. Furthermore, such claimants will often not be represented by legal counsel. This will undoubtedly present difficulty to employers as they attempt to negotiate reasonable settlements with the claimants. Without the benefit of independent legal advice, the claimants will likely have an inflated view of their legal entitlements making settlement of the dispute at an early stage more difficult.

2. INCREASED CAP AND DISCOVERY FOR SIMPLIFIED PROCEDURE ACTIONS

The previous cap was $50,000. Under the new Rules, the cap is raised to $100,000. This means that many more wrongful dismissal claims will fall within the jurisdiction of the simplified procedure.

Under the new Rules, however, the simplified procedure is less streamlined than it was previously. The parties to a simplified procedure action will now be permitted to engage in limited examinations for discovery (up to a maximum of two hours). Limiting the time does limit the cost of the discovery itself but a discovery does not consist only of the few hours in an official examiner's office. Other costs associated with the discovery process include discussions with the client, scheduling the examinations, travel time, advising the client afterwards, purchasing and analyzing the transcripts, and answering undertakings. These costs to the client for even a limited discovery are substantial. In the result, simplified procedure claims will cost employers more than they did in the past and will likely take longer to resolve under the new Rules than before.

On the other hand, justice may be better served by allowing a limited discovery. In some cases, for example where there is an allegation of constructive dismissal on the basis of harassment by a supervisor, it is preferable to have the opportunity to proceed to discovery to learn further particulars of the employee's case before proceeding to trial. A limited discovery would ensure the employer is not taken by surprise by the particulars raised by the employee and would better enable the employer to assess the merits of the employee's position. These factors set up the parties to be better able to settle their disputes without the necessity of proceeding to trial. In summary, the usefulness of limited discovery depends on the circumstances of each case.

3. EVIDENCE ON SUMMARY JUDGMENT MOTIONS

Recently, there has been an increase in the number of employees who are bringing motions to have their action disposed of by the court without a full trial where there is "no genuine issue for trial". Under the new Rules, judges will be able to weigh evidence, evaluate credibility, draw reasonable inferences and order oral evidence to be presented on such motions. Previously, these powers were prohibited. The result will be to allow a mini-trial of sorts and widen the scope of matters that can be determined by way of summary judgment.

These changes will almost certainly result in more wrongful dismissal claims being decided by way of summary judgment.

Employers should therefore be aware of this possibility, particularly as a judgment may occur before the notice period is over and, therefore, before mitigation can be fully evaluated. It remains to be seen how the courts will resolve situations where the employee mitigates during the notice period, but after summary judgment has been rendered.

4. OTHER CHANGES TO CIVIL ACTIONS OVER $100,000

One of the most significant changes to civil actions over $100,000 is the "one day Rule", which limits the length of examinations for discovery. Pursuant to this new Rule, a party can examine the opposing party or parties for a maximum of seven hours. The time limit applies regardless of the number of parties to be examined. It can, however, be varied by consent with permission from the court.

In addition, the scope of discovery has been refined by the new Rules. Previously, every document *"relating"* to any matter in issue was required to be disclosed. Under the new Rules, every document *"relevant"* to any matter in issue is required to be disclosed. This is more than a change in semantics. The new language serves to narrow the scope of production obligations. The effect of the change is to remove the broader semblance of relevance test and replace it with a simple relevance test. This is a positive change for employers as it will (a) minimize the ability of employees to engage in a fishing expedition by demanding voluminous productions, and (b) limit the expense associated with far reaching production obligations.

In summary, the new Rules attempt to introduce a principle of proportionality such that the time and expense devoted to the proceeding reflects what is actually at stake. While the new Rules attempt to ensure that cases that are straightforward and of lower value do not take as long or cost as much as large complex cases, the new Rules may actually end up costing litigants, particularly employers, more money in some circumstances.

It remains to be seen whether the new Rules have caught up with today's times and have struck the appropriate balance between procedural safeguards on the one hand and timeliness and efficiency on the other.

62

VIOLENCE AND HARASSMENT IN THE WORKPLACE

1. What are Workplace Harassment and Workplace Violence?
2. What are the New Requirements for Employers?
   a. Risk Assessment
   b. Written Policies and Implementation Programs
   c. Extension of Existing Occupational Health & Safety Obligations to Workplace Violence
   d. Domestic Violence in the Workplace
   e. Disclose Risks of Violence to Employees
3. What Should Employers Do to Comply With the New Requirements?

In recent years, concerns regarding workplace violence and harassment have escalated. A high proportion of violent incidents in Ontario occur in the workplace. In fact, a 2004 Statistics Canada survey found that 17 per cent of violent incidents occur at the workplace (Statistics Canada (2004), *Criminal Victimization in the Workplace.*) Extreme incidents such as the 2005 workplace murder of nurse Lori Dupont by her ex-boyfriend Dr. Marc Daniel at the Hôtel-Dieu Grace Hospital in Windsor, Ontario, have raised public awareness of workplace violence. Not only in Ontario, but across Canada, the issue of workplace violence and harassment is attracting a high profile.

On December 15, 2009, the Ontario government approved Bill 168, the *Occupational Health and Safety Amendment Act (Violence and Harassment in the Workplace), 2009* (the "Act"). The amendments came into force on June 15, 2010, making Ontario the most recent Canadian province to update its occupational health and safety legislation to address workplace violence and harassment. The amendments both added new provisions to the current *Occupational Health and Safety Act*, R.S.O. 1990, c. O.1 ("OHSA") and extended existing OHSA duties to cover situations of workplace violence and harassment. Importantly, these amendments imposed complex new obligations on employers to address issues of workplace violence and harassment.

1. WHAT ARE WORKPLACE HARASSMENT AND WORKPLACE VIOLENCE?

As a result of the Act, workplace harassment and workplace violence are now specifically defined in section 1 of the OHSA as follows:

- "workplace harassment" involves engaging in a course of vexatious comment or conduct against a worker in a workplace that is known or ought reasonably to be known to be unwelcome.

- "workplace violence" means (a) the exercise of physical force by a person against a worker in the workplace that causes or could cause physical injury to the worker; (b) an attempt to exercise physical force against a worker in a workplace that could cause physical injury to the worker; or (c) a statement or behaviour that is reasonable for a worker to interpret as a threat to exercise physical force against the worker, in a workplace, that could cause physical injury to the worker.

2. WHAT ARE THE NEW REQUIREMENTS FOR EMPLOYERS?

With the amendments outlined in the Act, the OHSA now requires employers to take positive steps to prevent violence and harassment in the workplace. The following is an overview of the most significant new requirements.

(a) Risk Assessment

Under the new legislation employers are required to conduct a risk assessment to determine the risks of workplace violence that may arise from the nature of the workplace, the type of work or the conditions of work. The results of the assessment will be reported to the Occupational Health and Safety Committee where one exists and otherwise to the workers. The employer is required to reassess the risks in the workplace as often as necessary to ensure that workers are protected from workplace violence.

(b) Written Policies and Implementation Programs

The amendments to the OHSA require employers to develop policies and programs with respect to both "workplace violence" and "workplace harassment". First, written policies must be developed and posted. Second, employers must design programs to implement those policies.

With respect to "workplace violence", once the risks inherent to a particular workplace are identified, and where there are more than five employees in the workplace, the Act requires employers to develop and post a workplace violence policy and to develop a program to implement that policy. The program to implement the workplace violence policy must include the following elements:

- Measures and procedures to control the risks identified in the required assessment;
- Measures and procedures to summon immediate assistance where workplace violence occurs or is likely to occur;
- Measures and procedures to allow workers to report incidents or threats of workplace violence to the employer; and
- The procedure the employer will follow to investigate and deal with incidents of workplace violence.

With respect to "workplace harassment", workplaces with more than five employees will be required to develop and post a policy regarding workplace harassment and to develop a program to implement that policy. The program to implement the workplace harassment policy must include measures and procedures for employees to report incidents of workplace harassment and must set out the way in which employers are to investigate incidents of workplace harassment.

(c) Extension of Existing OH&S Obligations to Workplace Violence

The amendments extend the obligations contained in section 25 of the OHSA, which requires employers to provide information and training, and section 27 of the OHSA, which imposes on a supervisor the duty to advise workers of any potential hazard, to apply in situations of workplace violence.

Additionally, the right to refuse work has been extended. Currently, under section 43 of the OHSA, an employee has the right to refuse unsafe work. The modifications contained in the Act extend the right to refuse unsafe work to an employee who has reason to believe that workplace violence is likely to endanger him or her. It should be noted that the right to refuse work has not been extended to cover a situation of workplace harassment.

Under section 52 of the OHSA, the employer must now notify the Ministry of Labour if a worker is disabled from his or her regular duties, or requires medical attention, as a result of workplace violence.

(d) Domestic Violence in the Workplace

Ontario is the first Canadian jurisdiction to specifically address domestic violence in the workplace. As a result of the amendments to the OHSA, if an employer is aware or ought to be aware that domestic violence likely to expose a worker to physical injury may occur in the workplace, the employer must take every reasonable precaution to protect the worker from such violence. This new requirement may be seen in part as a response to Lori Dupont's murder by her co-worker and ex-boyfriend and the subsequent recommendations made following the coroner's inquest into her death.

(e) Disclose Risks of Violence to Employees

The new amendments require employers to provide information, including personal information, related to a risk of workplace violence from a person with a history of violent behaviour if the worker can be expected to encounter that person in the course of his or her work and the risk of workplace violence is likely to expose the worker to physical injury. However, employers are limited to disclosing only personal information that is reasonably necessary to protect the worker from injury.

3. WHAT SHOULD EMPLOYERS DO TO COMPLY WITH THE NEW REQUIREMENTS?

Employers must be aware of their new obligations that came into force on June 15, 2010. Employers must develop and implement programs that will comply with the amendments to the OHSA. Many employers already have workplace discrimination and harassment policies that need to be evaluated and adapted to meet the new requirements of the OHSA. Employers must now also address workplace violence. This process begins with an assessment of the risks inherent to the individual workplace. Employers must then develop a workplace violence program that includes policies, procedures and implementation.

63

AMENDMENTS TO THE OCCUPATIONAL HEALTH AND SAFETY ACT HAVE AN IMPACT ON DIRECTORS AND OFFICERS OF A CORPORATION

The amendments to the *Occupational Health and Safety Act*, R.S.O. 1990, c. O.1 ("OHSA") and the general obligations of employers are set out in the previous article of this book. It should be noted that the amendments also bring considerations for directors and officers of a corporation. The impact of the amendments on directors and officers is detailed below.

Pursuant to section 32 of the OHSA, every director and officer of a corporation is required to take all reasonable steps to ensure that the corporation complies with the OHSA and the regulations. This obligation must be read in conjunction with the amendments to the OHSA, which came into force on June 15, 2010 (S.O. 2009, c. 23, s. 3). In other words, every director of a corporation is required to take all *reasonable steps* to ensure that the corporation complies with the updated legislation, including the following (see sections 32.0.1 to 32.0.7):

1. The employer shall prepare a policy with respect to workplace violence;
2. The employer shall prepare a policy with respect to workplace harassment;
3. The employer shall review the workplace violence and harassment policies as often as is necessary, but at least annually;
4. The employer shall develop and maintain a program with

respect to workplace violence;

5. The employer shall assess the risks of workplace violence that may arise from the nature of the workplace, the type of work or the conditions of work. The employer shall reassess the risks of workplace violence as often as is necessary;

   a. The employer shall advise the committee or health and safety representative, if any, of the results of the assessment, and if the assessment is in writing, provide a copy of the assessment; or

   b. If there is no committee or health and safety representative, the employer shall advise the workers of the results of the assessment, and if the assessment is in writing, provide copies on request or advise the workers how to obtain copies;

6. If an employer becomes aware, or ought reasonably to be aware, that domestic violence that would likely expose a worker to physical injury may occur in the workplace, the employer shall take every precaution reasonable in the circumstances for the protection of the worker;

7. The employer shall provide the worker with information and instruction that is appropriate for the worker on the contents of the policy and program with respect to workplace violence;

8. The employer shall develop and maintain a program with respect to workplace harassment; and,

9. The employer shall provide the worker with information and instruction that is appropriate for the worker on the contents of the policy and program with respect to workplace harassment.

Failure by a director or officer of a corporation to take all *reasonable steps* to ensure that the corporation complies with the OHSA (including the amendments) may result in personal liability for the director or officer. What is reasonable will, of course, depend on the circumstances of the case. Simply stating that the business has been in operation for a considerable number of years without having had a workplace accident will not be sufficient to establish that all reasonable steps had been taken. The Workplace Safety and Insurance Board ("WSIB") is likely to find that such evidence demonstrates merely good fortune, rather than good management. Some steps that a Board of Directors may take to satisfy their obligations under the OHSA are as follows:

1. Give specific directions to the human resources department to take immediate steps to comply with the OHSA obligations;
2. Request that the human resources department provide a copy of the written assessment and a report on what has been done;
3. Follow up on any issues raised in the written assessment to ensure they are being addressed;
4. Take accurate minutes at the Board meetings to ensure they reflect what the Board has directed the human resources department to do; and,
5. Review the issue of workplace violence and harassment at least annually. The annual reviews should be accurately documented in the minutes of the Board meetings and should include directions to the human resources department to take any necessary steps.

Going forward it is prudent for a director or officer to concentrate his or her mind on the likely risks in a workplace, including violence and harassment. It is also prudent for a director or officer to ensure that a proper system is established to prevent those risks from arising and to provide adequate supervision to ensure that the system is properly carried out. The onus is on a director or officer to establish that they took all reasonable steps. If a director or officer is not successful in showing that all reasonable steps were taken, he or she may be convicted under the OHSA. Upon conviction of an offence, a director or officer may be personally liable for a fine of up to $25,000 and/or imprisonment for a term of 12 months or less.

With that in mind, keep doing what you are doing to meet the obligations of OHSA. It is in the best interests of both the corporation and the directors and officers, personally.

INDEX

ABSENTEEISM, 216

ACCOMMODATION. *See* **DUTY TO ACCOMMODATE**

ADGA GROUP CONSULTANTS INC. V. LANE, 185–187

ADJEMIAN V. BROOK CROMPTON NORTH AMERICA, 249–250

AFTER-ACQUIRED CAUSE, 119, 129–134

AGING WORKERS, 226–227

ALCOHOL CONSUMPTION, 216

ALTERNATE DAY OFF DESIGNATION, 252–253

APPLICATION FORMS, 146

ASSELSTINE V. MANUFACTURERS LIFE INS. CO., 157–158

ATKINS V. WINDSOR STAR, 121–122

BAD FAITH CONDUCT. *See* **"WALLACE" DAMAGES**

BALANCE OF CONVENIENCE, 173, 212

BANNISTER V. GENERAL MOTORS OF CANADA LTD., 127

BARDAL V. GLOBE AND MAIL LTD., 195

BINDING CONTRACTS, 39–40

BIOMETRIC SCANNING TECHNOLOGIES, 106, 108

BLUE PENCIL SEVERANCE, 16

***BONA FIDE* OCCUPATIONAL REQUIREMENT (BFOR),** 4

BRAIDEN V. LA-Z-BOY CANADA LTD., 23–27, 37–39

BURDEN OF PROOF
constructive dismissal, 135–137, 139
just cause, 207, 212

CANADA COUNCIL FOR THE ARTS V. PUBLIC SERVICE ALLIANCE OF CANADA, 49–50

CANADIAN CHARTER OF RIGHTS AND FREEDOMS, 186

CAVALIERE V. CORVEX, 125–127

CHAPMAN V. BANK OF NOVA SCOTIA, 135–136, 139–140

CHILD PORNOGRAPHY, 118–120

CIARDULLO V. PREMETALCO, 69

CIVIL ACTIONS. *See* **RULES OF CIVIL PROCEDURE (ONT.)**

CIVIL ACTIONS OVER $100,000, 266

CLARKE V. INSIGHT COMPONENTS, 41–43

COLWELL V. CORNERSTONE PROPERTIES INC., 153–155

COMMON LAW REASONABLE NOTICE. *See* **REASONABLE NOTICE**

COMMUNICATION TO EMPLOYEES
appropriate workplace behaviour, 48, 54

COMMUNICATION TO EMPLOYEES — *cont'd*
changes in human resources policy manual, 231–232
disabled employees, 103
as documentation, 77
employer's expectations, 54
with job offer, 3–7
performance standards, 48, 54
risk of violence, disclosure of, 271
termination clause, 43

COMPANY HOLIDAY PARTIES, 216

COMPANY RETREATS, 89–91

COMPENSATION
company retreats, 89–90
discretionary basis, 137
fluctuations in income, 136, 137, 142
minor changes to, 140–141
overtime pay, 93–95, 225–226, 231
salary reviews, 50, 141–142
stock options, 137, 142

CONFIDENTIAL INFORMATION
breaches of client confidentiality, 115
confidentiality provisions, 11
disclosure during job interviews, 166
removal, and departing employees, 165
and workplace harassment investigation, 64
written guarantee of non-disclosure, 6

CONFLICT OF INTEREST
employee tips, 122–123
employer tips, 123
generally, 121–122
during holiday season, 217–218

CONSIDERATION
changes in terms of contract, 40, 42, 150
common forms of, 12
forbearance from firing insufficient consideration, 39
forgetting to sign contract before start of work, 224
insufficient consideration, 39
for non-solicitation/non-competition agreements, 12
for restrictive covenants, 12

CONSTRUCTIVE DISMISSAL CLAIMS
advance notice of change, 149–151
avoidance of risks of claims, 83, 142–143, 260–261
challenges for plaintiff, 135–137
employee's heavy burden of proof, 135–137, 139
failure of claims, 139–143
reduction of risk of claims, 136–137
video surveillance, 153–155
when successful, 139

CONTEXTUAL APPROACH, 213

CONTRACT OF EMPLOYMENT. *See* **EMPLOYMENT CONTRACT**

CONTROL TEST, 30

CORPORATE POLICIES. *See* **WORKPLACE POLICIES**

CRIMINAL CONDUCT
allegations of, 236–237
off-duty criminal conduct, 117–120
periodic criminal record checks, 109–110

CRIMINAL RECORD CHECKS, 109–110

CRISIS MANAGEMENT, 87

DAMAGES
breach of contract, 168
conduct in dismissal, 195–196
duty not to compete, 168
extension of notice period, 196, 197
intentional infliction of mental distress, 160–161, 177
in lieu of notice for wrongful dismissal, 195
mitigation
• duty to mitigate, 213
• offer of altered position, 147
• relocation, 189–190
• waiver of duty to mitigate, 191–192
punitive damages, 160–161, 193, 196–197
"Wallace" damages
• avoidance of, 199–201

DAMAGES — *cont'd*
- award of, 160, 161, 196
- generally, 133
- high bar on claims for, 203–204

DANGEROUS WORK CONDITIONS, 81, 258

DATA SAMPLING, 247

DECLARED EMERGENCY LEAVE, 257

DEFAMATORY STATEMENTS, 241–242

DELETED FILES, 247

DEPARTING EMPLOYEES
harsh treatment of, 82
obligations, 164, 167–169
tips for
- careful planning, 166
- disclosure of non-competition/non-solicitation clauses, 165
- fiduciary employees, 164–165
- generally, 163
- notice of resignation, 164
- protection of customer interests, 166
- removal of customer information, 165
- review of employment contract, 164

DEPENDENT CONTRACTORS, 33–36

DIGITAL VIDEO SURVEILLANCE. *See* **VIDEO SURVEILLANCE**

DIRECTORS, 273–275

DISABILITY
absenteeism due to, 101–102
communication, 103
dealing with your disability, 219–222
disability fraud, 101–104
downsizing, 261
duty to accommodate
- accommodation policy, 82
- employee's prospects of recovery, 183
- hidden disabilities, 185–187
- mentally ill employees, 87
- performance of work in foreseeable future, 184
- policy, 230
- procedural duty to accommodate, 186–187
- reasonable modified work, availability of, 183
- satisfaction of duty, 183–184
- scope of, 183
- substantive duty to accommodate, 187
- undue hardship, 181–184

essential duties of job, 226
legal advice, 102
long-term disability benefits, continuation of, 157–162
proper investigation, 102
review company policies, 102–103
short-term disability benefits, 162
surveillance, use of, 103–104
termination for just cause, 104
"without prejudice" payment, 104

DISCIPLINE
discretion to discipline, 5, 49
no employee acknowledgment, 50–51
performance management program, 47
progressive approach, 60
and zero tolerance, 60

DISCOVERY, 245–248, 264–265, 266

DISEASES, 255–258

DISHONEST PERFORMANCE REVIEWS, 49–50

DISHONESTY, 213

DISLOYALTY. *See* **CONFLICT OF INTEREST**

DOCUMENTATION
by employees, 207
harassment by management, 72
hostile employees, 77
performance management program, 50, 54
poor or non-existent documentation, 50

DOCUMENTS
costs of production, 247
disclosure and retention, 242
e-discovery, 245–248

DOMESTIC VIOLENCE, 270

DOWNSIZING, 41, 43, 249. *See also* **ECONOMIC CRISIS**

DURAND V. QUAKER OATS CO. CANADA LTD., 217–218

DUTY TO ACCOMMODATE
accommodation policy, 82
employee's prospects of recovery, 183
hidden disabilities, 185–187
impossible to accommodate, 182, 187
mentally ill employees, 87
performance of work in foreseeable future, 184
policy, 230
procedural duty to accommodate, 186–187
reasonable modified work, availability of, 183
satisfaction of duty, 183–184
scope of, 183
substantive duty to accommodate, 187
undue hardship, 82, 181–184

E-DISCOVERY, 245–248

ECONOMIC CRISIS
constructive dismissal claims, avoidance of, 260–261
disability cases, 261
non-competition clauses, 260
payment without release, 260
severance packages, 259–260

ELECTRONIC DISCOVERY, 245–248

ELECTRONIC PASS CARDS, 95

EMERGENCY MANAGEMENT AND CIVIL PROTECTION ACT, 257

EMPLOYEE ASSISTANCE PROGRAMS, 65, 87–88

EMPLOYEES
conflict of interest, 122–123
departing employees
- harsh treatment of, 82

- obligations, 164, 167–169
- tips for
  - careful planning, 166
  - disclosure of non-competition/non-solicitation clauses, 165
  - fiduciary employees, 164–165
  - generally, 163
  - notice of resignation, 164
  - protection of customer interests, 166
  - removal of customer information, 165
  - review of employment contract, 164

vs. dependent contractors, 33–36
dismissal for cause
- *vs.* dismissal without cause, 212
- grounds for dismissal, 212–213
- legal advice, 213–214
- onus of proof, 212
- tips for avoiding
  - documentation, 207
  - insubordination, avoiding, 209
  - lawyer, retaining a, 209
  - poisoning the workplace, 209
  - when to make a deal, 209–210

dismissal without cause
- *vs.* dismissal for cause, 212
- mitigation, 213
- no job security, 211

falsification or exaggeration on résumés, 4
fiduciary employees, 164–165
hostile employees
- documentation, 77
- early termination, 78
- extenuating circumstances for behaviour, 78
- generally, 75–76
- look beyond technical skills, 76
- multiple interviews before hiring, 76
- probation term, 77
- reference checks, 76–77
- witness presence at meetings, 77

key employees, 20–21, 165
medical information, requests for, 97–99
mere employees, 165
off-duty criminal conduct, 117–120
opportunity to respond, 133
ordinary employees, 20–21
periodic criminal record checks, 109–110
quasi-fiduciary employees, 169
short-term employees, 81, 204

EMPLOYEES — *cont'd*
suicidal or unstable employees
- assistance, provision of, 87–88
- generally, 85–86
- reinstatement agreement, 87
- removal of individual from workplace, 86
- secure the workplace, 87
- seriousness of issue, 86

EMPLOYEES WITH DISABILITIES. *See* **DISABILITY**

EMPLOYERS
conflict of interest, 123
expectations of employees, 54
harsh treatment of departing employees, 82
mistakes to avoid
- age, and retirement, 226–227
- employees with disabilities, 226
- forgetting to sign contract before start of work, 224
- overtime pay, forgetting, 225–226
- termination not a layoff, 223–224
- unilateral changes to pay or work duties, 225
- written contract, forgetting, 223–224

onus of proof of just cause, 207
wrongful dismissal claim, defence of
- allegation of cause if none exists, 241
- careful review of claim, 240
- choosing the right lawyer, 240
- cooperation with counsel, 241
- defamatory statements, 241–242
- document disclosure and retention, 242
- generally, 239–240
- investigation for other improper conduct, 241
- legal opinion, 241
- mediation, 242
- offer to settle, 242
- "point person," 240
- reference letters, 242

EMPLOYMENT CONTRACT. *See also* **NON-COMPETITION AGREEMENT; NON-SOLICITATION AGREEMENT; RESTRICTIVE COVENANTS**
application form, effect of, 146

binding, 39–40
changes to terms
- consideration, 40, 42, 150
- constructive dismissal claims
  - advance notice of change, 149–151
  - avoidance of risks of claims, 83, 142–143
  - challenges for plaintiff, 135–137
  - employee's heavy burden of proof, 135–137, 139
  - failure of claims, 139–143
  - reduction of risk of claims, 136–137
  - video surveillance, 153–155
  - when successful, 139
- contract for possibility of changes, 142
- unilateral changes, 225

implied terms
- good faith and fairness, 154
- layoff, right to, 146
- reasonable notice of resignation, 167

layoffs, 146
need for, 223–224
termination clause, 41–43
written contract, 7

EMPLOYMENT RELATIONSHIP
context
- determination of status of relationship, 30
- and restrictive covenants, 21

facts indicative of, 24–25
hiring questions, 3–7
independent contractor relationship
- contract stating status, 37–40
- *vs.* dependent contractors, 33–36
- difficulties of establishing, 23–27
- guidelines, 31–32
- reclassification of former employee as, 26, 27, 37
- tests to determine, 29–32
- tips for creating proper relationship, 29–32

performance management program, 47–51
substance *vs.* form, 23–27
tests to determine, 29–32

EMPLOYMENT STANDARDS ACT (ONT.)
Family Day, 251–254
overtime, 93–95
payment without release, 260

EMPLOYMENT STANDARDS ACT (ONT.) — *cont'd*
personal emergency leave, 256–257
probationary period, 4
reasonable notice, 41

EMPLOYMENT STANDARDS LEGISLATION. *See also* **EMPLOYMENT STANDARDS ACT (ONT.)**
probationary period, 4
public holidays, 251–254

EQUALITY OF BARGAINING POWER, 173–174

FAILURE TO COMPLY WITH STATUTORY OBLIGATIONS, 80–81

FAMILY DAY, 251–254

FIDUCIARY EMPLOYEES, 164–165

407 ETR CONCESSION CO. V. C.A.W. CANADA, LOCAL 414, 108

FOURFOLD TEST, 30

FRAUD, DISABILITY, 101–104

FRIVOLOUS COMPLAINTS, 237

HADLEY V. BAXENDALE, 168

HARASSMENT. *See* **WORKPLACE HARASSMENT; WORKPLACE HARASSMENT INVESTIGATION**

HARGRAFT SCHOFIELD LP V. SCHOFIELD, 171–174

HARRIS V. EASTERN PROVINCIAL AIRWAYS, 190

HEALTH CANADA, 255

HIRING
checklist, 7
just cause termination, behaviours justifying, 5
knowledge of applicant, 4
letter of hire, 7
look beyond technical skills, 76
multiple interviews, 76
non-solicitation agreement, 6
performance expectations, 7
poor hiring practices, 81
pre-employment representations, 5
probationary period, 4, 77
promises made, 4–5
questions to ask, 3–7
reference checks, 76–77
rights on termination, 6
trade secrets, inventions or confidential information, 7
written contract, 7

H.L. STAEBLER CO. V. ALLAN, 19–21

H1N1, 255–258

HOLIDAY POLICIES, 253

HOLIDAY SEASON
alcohol consumption, 216
conflict of interest, 217–218
dismissals, 215–216
harassment, 217
lateness or absenteeism, 216

HOLIDAY WORK REQUIREMENT, 253

HONDA CANADA INC. V. KEAYS, 101–102, 158–159, 161, 193–197, 199

HOSPITALITY REWARDS, 89–91

HOSTILE EMPLOYEES
documentation, 77
early termination, 78
extenuating circumstances for behaviour, 78
generally, 75–76
look beyond technical skills, 76
multiple interviews before hiring, 76
probation term, 77
reference checks, 76–77
witness presence at meetings, 77

HUMAN DIGNITY, 154

Index

HUMAN RESOURCES POLICY MANUALS
accommodation policy, 230
communication of changes to employees, 231–232
failure to apply, 232
generally, 229–230
introduction, 230
lack of policy manual, 232–233
legislative changes, knowledge of, 231
making policy binding, 232
overtime, 231
substance abuse policy, 230
workplace harassment definition, 230–231
zero tolerance policies, 231

HUMAN RIGHTS INVESTIGATION, 235–238. *See also* **WORKPLACE HARASSMENT INVESTIGATION**

HUMAN RIGHTS LEGISLATION
bona fide occupational requirement (BFOR), 4
civil courts and human rights complaints, 178
harassment by supervisor or manager, 72–73
Human Rights Code Amendment Act (Ont.)
• damages for mental anguish, 177
• decisions of Tribunal, 178–179
• direct application to Tribunal, 176
• prevention, 179
• proclamation, 175–176
• time limit for applications, 176
• Tribunal practices and procedures, 176–177
Human Rights Code (Ont.)
• civil actions, 178
• discrimination, proving, 186
• duty to accommodate, 181
job application forms, 4

HUMAN RIGHTS TRIBUNAL OF ONTARIO, 176–177, 178–179

HYDRO-QUÉBEC V. SYNDICAT D'EMPLOYÉES DE TECHNIQUE PROFESSIONNELLES ET DE BUREAU D'HYDRO-QUÉBEC, SECTION LOCALE 2000, 181–183, 187

INCOME. *See* **COMPENSATION**

INDEPENDENT CONTRACTOR RELATIONSHIP
contract stating status, 37–40
vs. dependent contractors, 33–36
difficulties of establishing, 23–27
guidelines, 31–32
reclassification of former employee as, 26, 27, 37
tests to determine, 29–32
tips for creating proper relationship, 29–32

INDEPENDENT LEGAL ADVICE
restrictive covenants, 13–14
termination clause, 43

INDEPENDENT MEDICAL EXAMINATION, 162

INSUBORDINATION, 209

INSUFFICIENT GUIDANCE OR INSTRUCTION, 50

INTENTION TO RECALL, 146–147, 148

INTENTIONAL INFLICTION OF MENTAL DISTRESS, 160–161, 177

INTER-OFFICE RELATIONSHIPS, 125–128

INTERLOCUTORY RELIEF, 171–174

INTERNAL SEARCH ENGINES, 247

INTERVIEW TECHNIQUES, 5

INVENTIONS, 6. *See also* **CONFIDENTIAL INFORMATION**

INVESTIGATORS, 58

IRREGULAR PERFORMANCE REVIEWS, 49

IRREPARABLE HARM, 173

IT/NET INC. V. CAMERON, 9–10

JACOBSEN V. NIKE CANADA LTD., 216

JOB OFFER, 3–7

JOB SECURITY, 211

JUST CAUSE
after-acquired cause, 119, 129–134
allegations, where none exists, 241
alleged but not proven, 200
communication of examples of actions justifying, 5
vs. dismissal without cause, 212
employee tips for avoiding dismissal for cause
- documentation, 207
- insubordination, avoiding, 209
- lawyer, retaining a, 209
- poisoning the workplace, 209
- when to make a deal, 209–210
employees with disabilities, 104
grounds for dismissal, 212–213
holiday season, dismissal during, 216
legal advice for employees, 213–214
new meaning for "just cause," 113–115
onus of proof, 207, 212

KELLY V. LINAMAR CORP., 118–120

KEY EMPLOYEES, 20–21, 165

KEY WORD SEARCHES, 247

KILPATRICK V. PETERBOROUGH CIVIC HOSPITAL, 249

LATENESS, 216

LAWYERS
independent legal advice
- restrictive covenants, 13–14
- termination clause, 43

responses to misconduct allegations, 209
and workplace harassment investigations, 58–59, 64
wrongful dismissal claims
- advice to employees, 213–214
- advice to employers, 241
- defence of, 240

LAYOFFS, 145–148, 223–224

LETTER OF HIRE, 7

LIMITATION PERIOD, 73

LONG-TERM DISABILITY BENEFITS, 157–162

LOYALTY. *See* **CONFLICT OF INTEREST**

MANAGEMENT
bullying behaviour by supervisor or manager
- civil action, 73
- communication with manager, 72
- documentation of behaviour, 72
- external complaint, filing, 72–73
- generally, 71
- internal complaint, filing, 72
- resignation, 73
overtime and, 94
performance reviews, training for, 54–55
sexual relationships with subordinates, 125–128

MANDATORY RETIREMENT, 226

MCKEE V. REID'S HERITAGE HOMES LIMITED, 33–36

MCKINLEY V. BC TEL, 131

MCNEVAN V. AMERICREDIT, 203–204

MEDIATION, 242

MEDICAL INFORMATION
employer's entitlement to, 162
independent medical examination, 162
psychiatric or psychological examinations, 98–99

MEDICAL INFORMATION — *cont'd*
requests for
- disability claims, 103
- and privacy, 97–99

MENTAL DIAGNOSES, 98–99

MENTAL DISTRESS. *See* **INTENTIONAL INFLICTION OF MENTAL DISTRESS**

MENTAL ILLNESS, 85–86, 87, 104, 185–187. *See also* **SUICIDAL OR UNSTABLE EMPLOYEES**

MERE EMPLOYEES, 165

MINOTT V. O'SHANTER DEV. CO., 195

MISCONDUCT. *See also* **JUST CAUSE**
allegations of
- documentation of response to, 207
- lawyer, retaining a, 209
- opportunity to respond, 133
types of, 213

MISLEADING PERFORMANCE REVIEWS, 49–50

MITIGATION
duty to mitigate, 213
offer of altered position, 147
relocation, 189–190
waiver of duty to mitigate, 191–192

MODIFIED CONTRACTS
consideration, 40, 42, 150
constructive dismissal claims
- advance notice of change, 149–151
- avoidance of risks of claims, 83, 142–143
- challenges for plaintiff, 135–137
- employee's heavy burden of proof, 135–137, 139
- failure of claims, 139–143
- reduction of risk of claims, 136–137
- video surveillance, 153–155
- when successful, 139
contract for possibility of changes, 142

unilateral changes, 225

MORAL TURPITUDE, 117–120

MULVIHILL V. OTTAWA (CITY), 199

MUNICIPAL FREEDOM OF INFORMATION AND PROTECTION OF PRIVACY ACT, 109

NON-COMPETITION AGREEMENT. *See also* **RESTRICTIVE COVENANTS**
consideration, 12
described, 19
difficulty of enforcement, 15–17
disclosure to new employer, 165
effect of, 6
enforceability of, 260
exceptional circumstances, requirement of, 20
failure of, 9–10
geographic scope, 13
guidelines, 10
independent legal advice, 13–14
interlocutory relief, 171–174
vs. non-solicitation agreement, 21
reasonableness of, 13
as restrictive covenant, 11
scope of, 13
sparing use of, 12
time restriction, 13
too broad, effect of, 9–10
trade connections, protection of, 19–21
in writing, 12

NON-SOLICITATION AGREEMENT. *See also* **RESTRICTIVE COVENANTS**
consideration, 12
described, 19
difficulty of enforcement, 15–17
disclosure to new employer, 165
effect of, 6
enforceability of, 260
failure of, 9–10
geographic scope, 13
guidelines, 10
independent legal advice, 13–14
vs. non-competition agreement, 21

NON-SOLICITATION AGREEMENT — cont'd
reasonableness of, 13
as restrictive covenant, 11
scope of, 13
sparing use of, 12
time restriction, 13
too broad, effect of, 9–10
trade connections, protection of, 19–21
in writing, 12

NOTICE
extension of notice period, 196, 197
reasonable notice
- avoidance of, 148
- change of term of employment, 149–151
- common law amounts, 41
- minimum standards, 41
- short-term employees, 204
- *vs.* statutory minimum, 6
- summary judgment and, 250

of resignation, 164, 167
short-term employees, 81
working notice, 150–151

NOTIONAL SEVERANCE, 16

OBJECTIVE TEST, 212

OCCUPATIONAL HEALTH AND SAFETY ACT (ONT.), 256, 258, 268–271, 273–275

OCCUPATIONAL HEALTH AND SAFETY AMENDMENT ACT (VIOLENCE AND HARASSMENT IN THE WORKPLACE), 2009 (ONT.), 268–271, 273–275

OCCUPATIONAL HEALTH AND SAFETY LEGISLATION, 73

OFF-DUTY CRIMINAL CONDUCT, 117–120

OFFER OF EMPLOYMENT, 4, 5

OFFER TO SETTLE, 242

OFFICERS, 273–275

ONE DAY RULE, 266

ONGOING BACKGROUND CHECKS, 109–110

ONTARIO HUMAN RIGHTS COMMISSION, 176, 177

ONTARIO NURSES' ASSN. V. ST. JOSEPH'S HEALTH CENTRE, 97–99

OPPORTUNITY TO RESPOND, 133

ORDINARY EMPLOYEES, 20–21

ORGANIZATION TEST, 31

OTTO V. HAMILTON & OLSEN SURVEYS LTD., 139, 140–141

OUTPLACEMENT ASSISTANCE, 204, 212

OVERTIME PAY, 93–95, 225–226, 231

PAYMENT WITHOUT RELEASE, 260

PERFORMANCE EXPECTATIONS, 7

PERFORMANCE MANAGEMENT PROGRAM
applying your policy, 48–51
common missteps, 55–56
disciplinary interventions, 47
discretion, exercise of, 49
dishonest or misleading reviews, 49–50
dos and don'ts of, 53–56
effective systems, 48
insufficient guidance or instruction, 50
irregular or tardy reviews, 49
necessity of, 47, 53
no employee acknowledgment, 50–51
poor or non-existent documentation, 50
protection of employer's interests, 48
as risk-management tool, 53–54
salary review, conducted with, 50
scheduled assessments, 47

PERFORMANCE REVIEWS. *See also* **PERFORMANCE MANAGEMENT PROGRAM**
dishonest or misleading reviews, 49–50
irregular or tardy reviews, 49
management training, 54–55
necessity of, 47
no employee acknowledgment, 50–51
salary review, conducted with, 50

PERFORMANCE STANDARDS, 48, 54

PERIODIC CRIMINAL RECORD CHECKS, 109–110

PERMANENCY TEST, 30

PERSONAL EMERGENCY LEAVE, 256–257

PERSONAL INFORMATION PROTECTION AND ELECTRONIC DOCUMENTS ACT, 106

PERSONALITY CONFLICT, 209, 236

PIRESFERREIRA V. AYOTTE, 67–68

POLICIES. *See* **WORKPLACE POLICIES**

PRE-EMPLOYMENT REPRESENTATIONS, 5

PRINZO V. BAYCREST CENTRE FOR GERIATRIC CARE, 158, 160–161

PRIVACY ISSUES
biometric scanning technologies, 106, 108
medical information, requests for, 97–99
periodic criminal record checks, 109–110
privacy legislation, 106
video surveillance
- appropriateness of, 154–155
- as constructive dismissal, 153–155

- covert use, 107, 155
- generally, 105–106
- legitimate objective, 107
- limit on use of surveillance records, 107
- limit retention and access, 108
- notice, 107
- religious beliefs, accommodation of, 108
- restrictions on scope, 107

PROBATIONARY PERIOD, 4, 77

PROCEDURAL DUTY TO ACCOMMODATE, 186–187

PROPORTIONALITY TEST, 131

PSYCHIATRIC OR PSYCHOLOGICAL EXAMINATIONS, 98–99

PUBLIC HEALTH AGENCY OF CANADA, 258

PUBLIC HOLIDAYS, 251–254

PUNITIVE DAMAGES, 160–161, 193, 196–197

QUASI-FIDUCIARY EMPLOYEES, 169

RASANEN V. LISLE-METRIX LTD., 139, 141–142

RBC DOMINION SECURITIES INC. V. MERRILL LYNCH CANADA INC., 167–168

RE-EMPLOYMENT OFFER, 150–151

RE STELCO INC., 158, 159

READING DOWN, 16

REASONABLE DOUBT, 212

REASONABLE NOTICE. *See also* **NOTICE**
avoidance of, 148

REASONABLE NOTICE — cont'd
change of term of employment, 149–151
common law amounts, 41
minimum standards, 41
short-term employees, 204
vs. statutory minimum, 6
summary judgment and, 250

REFERENCE CHECKS, 76–77, 212

REFERENCE LETTERS, 204, 242

REFUSAL TO WORK, 258

REINSTATEMENT AGREEMENT, 87

REINSTATEMENT ORDERS, 178

RELEASE, 104, 260

RELIGIOUS BELIEFS, 108

RELOCATION, 189–190

REMUNERATION. *See* **COMPENSATION**

REORGANIZATION, 249, 261. *See also* **ECONOMIC CRISIS**

RESIGNATION
bullying by manager, 73
notice of resignation, 164, 167
policy for dealing with, 82

RESTRAINT OF TRADE, 12

RESTRICTIVE COVENANTS. *See also* **NON-COMPETITION AGREEMENT; NON-SOLICITATION AGREEMENT**
blanket prohibitions, 20
broadly drafted, effect of, 19–21
clear and unambiguous, 16
consideration, 12
context of employment relationship, 21
defined, 11
difficulty of enforcement, 15–17
in employment context, 11
generally, 11–12
guidelines for drafting, 17

independent legal advice, 13–14
interlocutory relief, 171–174
principles, 15–16, 21
reasonableness of, 13, 16
scope of, 13, 21
trade connections, protection of, 19–21
types of, 11
in writing, 12

RETENTION PROBLEMS
constructive dismissal, 83
duty to accommodate, 82
failure to comply with statutory obligations, 80–81
generally, 79–80
harsh treatment of departing employees, 82
poor hiring practices, 81
workplace harassment, 80

RETIREMENT, 226–227

RETREATS, 89–91

RISK ASSESSMENT, 269

RODGER V. FALCON MACHINERY, 145–148

RODRIGUES V. POWELL, 129–131, 133–134

ROMANTIC RELATIONSHIPS, 125–128

RULES OF CIVIL PROCEDURE (ONT.)
changes in, 264
civil actions over $100,000, 266
discovery, 264–265, 266
generally, 263
one day Rule, 266
proportionality principle, 266
simplified procedure actions, 264–265
small claims court actions, 264
summary judgment motions, evidence on, 265–266

SALARY REVIEWS, 50, 141–142

SARS CRISIS, 258

SCHALKWYK V. HYUNDAI AUTO CANADA INC., 190

SCHEDULED ASSESSMENTS, 47

SETTLEMENT OFFER, 242

SEVERANCE PACKAGES, 259–260

SEXUAL HARASSMENT POLICY, 127–128

SEXUAL RELATIONSHIPS, 125–128

SHAFRON V. KRG INS. BROKERS, 15–17

SHORT-TERM DISABILITY BENEFITS, 162

SHORT-TERM EMPLOYEES, 81, 204

SICK LEAVE, 257

SIMPLIFIED PROCEDURE ACTIONS, 264–265

SIMPSON V. CONSUMERS' ASSN. OF CANADA, 127

SMALL CLAIMS COURT ACTIONS, 264

SMITH V. AKER KVAERNER CANADA INC., 189–190

STANDARD OF PROOF, 212

STATUTORY OBLIGATIONS. *See also* **EMPLOYMENT STANDARDS ACT (ONT.)**
failure to comply with, 80–81
legislative changes, knowledge of, 231
minimum notice, 6
overtime, 93

STOCK OPTIONS, 137, 142

STONE V. SDS KERR BEAVERS DENTAL, 63

SUBSTANCE ABUSE POLICY, 230

SUBSTANTIVE DUTY TO ACCOMMODATE, 187

SUICIDAL OR UNSTABLE EMPLOYEES
assistance, provision of, 87–88
generally, 85–86
reinstatement agreement, 87
removal of individual from workplace, 86
secure the workplace, 87
seriousness of issue, 86

SUMMARY JUDGMENT
breaches of client confidentiality, 115
evidence, 265–266
generally, 249–250
increased notice periods, 250

SUPERVISORS. *See* **MANAGEMENT**

SURVEILLANCE
use of, 103–104
video surveillance
• appropriateness of, 154–155
• as constructive dismissal, 153–155
• overt use, 107, 155
• generally, 105–106
• legitimate objective, 107
• limit on use of surveillance records, 107
• limit retention and access, 108
• notice, 107
• religious beliefs, accommodation of, 108
• restrictions on scope, 107

SWINE FLU, 255–258

TARDY PERFORMANCE REVIEWS, 49

TEMPORARY LAYOFFS, 145–148

TERMINATION BY EMPLOYER
conflict of interest
• employee tips, 122–123
• employer tips, 123
• generally, 121–122

TERMINATION BY EMPLOYER — *cont'd*
constructive dismissal
- avoidance of risks of claims, 83, 142–143
- challenges for plaintiff, 135–137
- employee's heavy burden of proof, 135–137, 139
- failure of claims, 139–143
- reduction of risk of claims, 136–137
- when successful, 139

constructive dismissal claims
- advance notice of change, 149–151
- video surveillance, 153–155

employees with disabilities, 104
during holiday season, 215–216
hostile employees, 78
just cause
- after-acquired cause, 119, 129–134
- alleged but not proven, 200
- communication of examples of actions justifying, 5
- *vs.* dismissal without cause, 212
- employees with disabilities, 104
- employer's onus, 207
- new meaning for "just cause," 113–115

layoffs, 145–148, 223–224
long-term disability benefits, continuation of, 157–162
off-duty criminal conduct, 117–120
rights on termination, 6
romantic relationships, 125–128
termination clause, 41–43
termination interview, 201
"without prejudice" payment, 104

TERMINATION CLAUSE, 41–43

THIRD PARTY BENEFIT PROVIDERS, 157–158

TRADE SECRETS, 6. *See also* **CONFIDENTIAL INFORMATION**

TURNOVER. *See* **RETENTION PROBLEMS**

UNDUE HARDSHIP, 82, 181–184

UNSTABLE EMPLOYEES. *See* **SUICIDAL OR UNSTABLE EMPLOYEES**

VEXATIOUS COMPLAINTS, 237

VIDEO SURVEILLANCE
appropriateness of, 154–155
as constructive dismissal, 153–155
covert use, 107, 155
generally, 105–106
legitimate objective, 107
limit on use of surveillance records, 107
limit retention and access, 108
notice, 107
religious beliefs, accommodation of, 108
restrictions on scope, 107

VIOLENCE. *See* **WORKPLACE VIOLENCE**

VIRUSES, 255–258

WAIVER OF DUTY TO MITIGATE, 191–192

"WALLACE" DAMAGES
avoidance of, 199–201
award of, 160, 161, 196
defamatory statements, 241–242
difficulty of winning, 203–204
generally, 133

WALLACE V. UNITED GRAIN GROWERS LTD. (C.O.B. PUBLIC PRESS), 133, 199, 241–242

WHITEHOUSE V. RBC DOMINION SECURITIES INC., 113–115

"WITHOUT PREJUDICE" PAYMENT, 104

WORK-RELATED TRIPS, 89–91

WORKERS' COMPENSATION LEGISLATION, 73

WORKING NOTICE, 150–151

WORKPLACE BEHAVIOUR, APPROPRIATE, 48, 54

WORKPLACE DISPUTES
constructive dismissal, 83
duty to accommodate, 82

WORKPLACE DISPUTES — *cont'd*
effect of, 79–80
failure to comply with statutory obligations, 80–81
harsh treatment of departing employees, 82
poor hiring practices, 81
workplace harassment, 80

WORKPLACE HARASSMENT. *See also* **WORKPLACE HARASSMENT INVESTIGATION**
bullying behaviour by supervisor or manager
- civil action, 73
- communication with manager, 72
- documentation of behaviour, 72
- external complaint, filing, 72–73
- generally, 71
- internal complaint, filing, 72
- resignation, 73

compliance with new requirements, 271
defined, 268
directors and officers, obligations of, 273–275
effect of, 80
holiday season, complaints during, 217
incorrect or vague definition of, 230–231
new requirements, 268–271
policy
- continuous distribution of, 65
- coverage of, 72
- necessity of, 80
- and personal harassment, 72

policy implementation programs, 269–270
written policies, 269–270

WORKPLACE HARASSMENT INVESTIGATION
checklist for investigation, 64–65
criminal conduct, allegations of, 236–237
delay
- effect of, 65
- prompt investigation, need for, 67–69

failure of
- generally, 57–58
- investigators, 58
- lack of flexibility, 60
- lawyers, use of, 58–59
- not protecting participants, 59
- remedial action, 60
- removal of participants, 59
- scope of investigation, 59
- zero tolerance, 60

frivolous complaints, 237
full disclosure, 64
future litigation, possibility of, 69
human rights investigations, 235–238
inadequate investigations, consequences of, 67–68
investigators
- experience of, 63, 64
- and failure of investigations, 58
- independent investigators, 68
- lawyer as, 58–59
- report, 68

legal representation, 64
practical tips, 235–238
preliminary evaluation, 237
proper investigation, 68–69
remedial action, 60, 69
scope of investigation, 64
vexatious complaints, 237
when investigation necessary, 235–238
zero tolerance, 60, 65

WORKPLACE POLICIES
accommodation policy, 82
company retreats, 90–91
disability claims, 102–103
holiday policies, 253
human resources policy manuals
- accommodation policy, 230
- communication of changes to employees, 231–232
- failure to apply, 232
- generally, 229–230
- introduction, 230
- lack of policy manual, 232–233
- legislative changes, knowledge of, 231
- making policy binding, 232
- overtime, 231
- substance abuse policy, 230
- workplace harassment definition, 230–231
- zero tolerance policies, 231

resignation, dealing with, 82
sexual harassment policy, 127–128
sick leave, 257
termination interview, 82
well-drafted policies, use of, 83

WORKPLACE POLICIES — *cont'd*
workplace harassment, 269–270
- continuous distribution of, 65
- coverage of, 72
- necessity of, 80
- and personal harassment, 72

workplace violence, 269

WORKPLACE ROMANCES, 125–128

WORKPLACE SAFETY, AND H1N1, 255–258

WORKPLACE SAFETY AND INSURANCE ACT, 1997, 258

WORKPLACE SAFETY AND INSURANCE BOARD, 274–275

WORKPLACE VIOLENCE
compliance with new requirements, 271
defined, 268
directors and officers, obligations of, 273–275
disclosure of risk of violence to employees, 271
domestic violence in the workplace, 270
extension of existing health and safety obligations, 270
new requirements, 268–271
policy implementation programs, 269
risk assessment, 269
statistics, 267
threats of violence, dealing with, 86

written policies, 269

WRITTEN CONTRACT, 7

WRONGFUL DISMISSAL. *See also* **DAMAGES**
defence
- allegation of cause if none exists, 241
- careful review of claim, 240
- choosing the right lawyer, 240
- cooperation with counsel, 241
- defamatory statements, 241–242
- document disclosure and retention, 242
- generally, 239–240
- investigation for other improper conduct, 241
- legal opinion, 241
- mediation, 242
- offer to settle, 242
- "point person," 240
- reference letters, 242

human rights violations, allegations of, 178
legal advice for employees, 213–214
overtime claims, 93

WRONKO V. WESTERN INVENTORY SERVICE LTD., 191–192

ZERO TOLERANCE, 60, 65, 231

ZORN-SMITH V. BANK OF MONTREAL, 158, 159–160